W9-CPZ-224

EX
LIBRIS
ALE
XAN
DRY

THE CONTRACT:
A LIFE FOR A LIFE

by
Joseph S. Kutrzeba

iUniverse, Inc.
New York   Bloomington

The Contract
A Life for a Life

Copyright © 2009 by Joseph S. Kutrzeba

All rights reserved. No part of this book may be used or reproduced by any means, graphic, electronic, or mechanical, including photocopying, recording, taping or by any information storage retrieval system without the written permission of the publisher except in the case of brief quotations embodied in critical articles and reviews.

iUniverse books may be ordered through booksellers or by contacting:

iUniverse
1663 Liberty Drive
Bloomington, IN 47403
www.iuniverse.com
1-800-Authors (1-800-288-4677)

Because of the dynamic nature of the Internet, any Web addresses or links contained in this book may have changed since publication and may no longer be valid. The views expressed in this work are solely those of the author and do not necessarily refl ect the views of the publisher, and the publisher hereby disclaims any responsibility for them.

ISBN: 978-0-595-45789-2 (pbk)
ISBN: 978-0-595-70075-2 (cloth)
ISBN: 978-0-595-90091-6 (ebk)

Printed in the United States of America

iUniverse Rev. date 10/29/08

This book is dedicated to all those who, in growing up, have been torn asunder by conflicting forces, confusing their identity and conscience, with scars lasting painfully. May this story serve as a catharsis to alleviate their lonely struggle, as it seems to have alleviated mine.

Contents

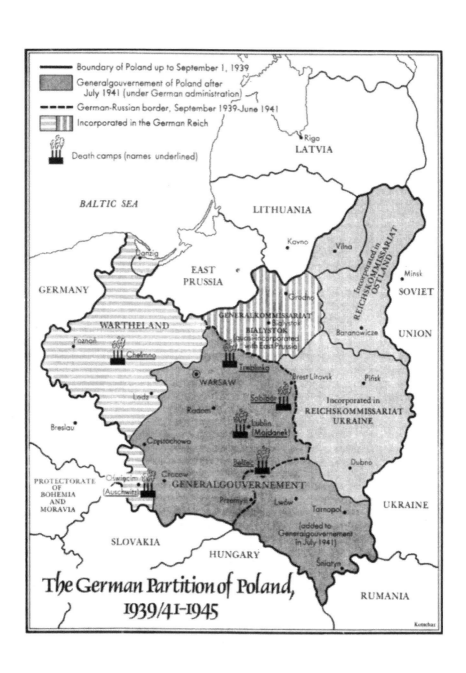

The German Partition of Poland, 1939/41-1945

Boundary of Poland up to September 1, 1939

Generalgouvernement of Poland after July 1941 (under German administration)

German-Russian border, September 1939-June 1941

Incorporated in the German Reich

Death camps (names underlined)

Preface

The past for me has been a conduit for both living nightmares and the joys of freedom.

I wish to share their lows and highs with my fellow humans, for in my view, redemption—if it can be achieved—lies in overcoming both the lows and the highs to draw much wisdom and perhaps solace from one's own and others' journeys through life.

I am grateful to Ms. Sylvia Daneel who first persuaded me to commence writing and to Mr. Bennett Cerf, the erstwhile chairman of Random House who encouraged me to continue my story at the MacDowell Colony, to whom I am also grateful.

Chapter One
In the Trap

IT LOOKED LIKE AN abandoned house on Gęsia Street. I climbed two flights and knocked. There was no sign of life. I knocked again, adding a few words in the established code of the Organization.

Suddenly the door opened. It was Ruth, her dark braids pinned in a crown, her mouth a narrow determined line. Although short and heavyset at seventeen, she towered over me.

"Yes? Oh, it's you."

"I ... er ... ran into a couple of boys from our platoon; they told me you'd be here."

"Well, obviously I am. Where've you been all this time?"

"I was in the hospital, Ruth ... my heart muscles were weak ... it was malnutrition, they said."

I never liked her. She was the opposite of my gentle, quiet-mannered mother.

She was still fat, I noticed. With my buddies in the Organization I had supposed her family was rich, she always looked so healthy. She was the assistant company commander, and the girlfriend of David who commanded the *gdud*.

"In the hospital? How long?" Her lisp was getting more pronounced.

"Almost two weeks." My clean-shaven head bore witness to the mandatory delousing.

"So." She appraised me forbiddingly. "Where've you been since?"

"Ruth, I lost my mother ... to Treblinka."

"That's no excuse. Everybody lost somebody."

The afternoon summer heat was stifling on the unventilated stairway. Perspiration dripped down my shirt.

"But, Ruth ..."

"The orders *were*: 'leave your families and stick together.' One year's training ..."

"I did, Ruth, as soon as I could. My father ... we've been out in the street for three days now. He was watching me like a hawk, I couldn't leave him. First chance I get ..."

She eyed me steadily. My breeding always rubbed her the wrong way. That, and my blond Polish looks.

"'Couldn't leave him ... '" Her narrow mouth smiled sarcastically. "The professor's son. One year in the organization."

"Ruth, please ... I have lived only for the Organization. *Hashomer* is everything to me." I was desperate now.

"You haven't followed orders."

"But, Ruth ... I want to fight ... please let me."

The door was closing.

"Can I talk to David?" He and the other leaders had the compassion that Ruth lacked. They would listen to me.

"No one else is here now. I can't help you. Get your feet out of the doorway."

"Please, Ruth, isn't there anything I can do?" Tears were choking me. "After one year ... I've done my share ... through all the dangers ... haven't I proved myself to the Cause?"

"We don't have enough arms. Our first duty is to take care of the leaders ... smuggle them out of Warsaw into the forests ... We'll fight there. To the death."

"But how do I get there?"

"Let them put you on the train, and jump. If you get there ... get to the Lublin forests. Till then, you have to fend for yourself."

She shut the door.

✠ ✠ ✠

Over one hundred people were packed in the cattle car, as many as the car could hold, their bodies twisted painfully and cramped; they were unable to change the positions they'd taken as they were shoved and beaten into the car. They were hardly conscious of their pain. Speechless, frozen with terror, they waited.

Squeezed against the back wall of the car, I could see out a tiny barbed-wire window above me. The September sky was peaceful, cloudless. The door of the car stood ajar, but there was no breeze. In the stifling heat I listened to the sounds of other cars being loaded: heavy boots on the stones, boots of the police—German, Polish, Ukrainian, Jewish—the thud of whips against flesh; curses; a few shots; the ferocious growling of the dogs and the screams of those they ripped apart; then the scuffling hurried steps of the next crowd herded on board.

Gradually the noise receded, then broke out anew right outside the car.

"Throw these four in! You fucking bastards, get in! You want to get us all shot? *Dawaj go, dalej!* [Get a move on, let's go!]"A Jewish policeman, cursing in Polish. Jews never curse, I thought. Somehow it was out of keeping with our view of the world. I felt a flash of pity for the Jewish policeman—for who could be more terrified of the Germans, I thought, than a Jew executing their orders?

Outside there was more commotion, shoving, a voice moaning. A flat sound as a rifle butt met a body. Inside, the mass squeezed themselves together even closer, and four were added to the car.

Protruding bodies were beaten into the car with rifle butts. Then, in a shower of German curses, the door slid shut.

Bodies were so close there was scarcely any air in the car. In a few moments breathing became an effort. People began to gasp. Someone whispered, "My God, we will suffocate."

An elderly man with a beard recited "*Shma Israel*" (Hear, oh Israel) in a choked whisper.

A small child squirmed, trapped and unbelieving: "Mama, are you there?"

Before an answer could be given, pandemonium broke loose and everybody was standing on their toes looking and yelling for friends and relatives.

"Mama! Mama! I am here!"

"Thank God! Is Daddy with you?"

"No, I thought he was with you!"

People were shouting over one another, some weeping, unable to locate their dear ones, still others begging: "Water, water!"

Many shoved and pushed those near them in a vain effort to free their bodies. Above the din a fat man with a red neck shouted loudest of all: "Shut up, shut up, you bunch of pigs! Cut it out or they will open the door and kill everybody!" Then he added a torrent of Russian obscenities and kept it up until only a few voices still lamented.

These are definitely different kinds of Jews, I thought, for they use foul words.

"Anybody who can't stand it, go ahead and die or faint, damn it! The others want to live!" The fat man puffed more ominously once he was being listened to.

"Live for what? *Oy*, what's going to happen to us?" a woman's voice cried.

"Quiet!" boomed the fat man, "or you won't live long enough to find out!"

The noise subsided. A metal can of the type used in the Warsaw Ghetto to ration out pickled beet marmalade began to make the rounds. Men and women were using it to relieve themselves. This was possible only when some squatted down and others squeezed up even tighter. The stench of human excrement filled the available air. In moments, it seemed, all breathing would stop.

I could breathe, for a trickle of air was entering through the tiny window above me. Every now and then the human mass, by tramping on one another, would float overhead or force through the body of a child, woman, or someone elderly who had fainted to get them near the window. But I clung stubbornly to the wall, for I knew the air meant survival.

Hours passed. Outside it got dark, and cooler air entered the car through the two barbed-wire windows. Still, many lost strength or fainted, sliding downward, to be kept partially upright by other bodies. Eventually, heads, elbows, legs, and shoulders intertwined. The cessation of breathing by some loosened up the mass in spots so that a few were able to lie down, one on top of the other. Every quarter hour or so, people rolled over to change positions to avoid being crushed, crippled, or suffocated. Those who fainted remained on the bottom.

Next to me stood a slim boy, who, it turned out, was sixteen—two years older. His name was Nathan, a bony boy with frightened large brown eyes and a pimpled face. He too had been a student in one of the high school courses given secretly in the Warsaw Ghetto. I discovered we knew some of the same boys.

Nathan had lost everybody, too. He related it to me calmly, without much visible emotion except that, as he talked, his Adam's apple kept riding up and down.

Darkness had long set in when suddenly everything yanked and jolted, and the train moved.

Inside, the human mass swayed; it was too closely knit to bump heads or bodies. Those who remained conscious stirred, praying in weak voices, moaning:

"What's going to happen? Where are they taking us?"

✠ ✠ ✠

They did not know, I thought, because they were afraid to know. And I loathed their blindness, their weakness, their disorganization— these people who in the Ghetto had stood for hours hoping for watery soup, who cowered and ran before the SS and the Gestapo. Rather than degrade myself in the soup line, I would go home without soup. When panic-stricken crowds ran from the police, I would freeze to my spot and calmly nod to the Germans when they rushed past.

During my two years in the Ghetto, I had witnessed countless beatings and degradations meted out to Jews by the SS, Gestapo, and, later, by the Ukrainian auxiliaries. Terrorized by the police, the crowd in the streets, as it panicked and ran, resembled the gyrations of spermatozoa I had once seen under a magnifying glass. I never followed the crowd. Perhaps that was why I had survived until now.

A notorious and favorite daily game of the German Gestapo was to drive down Karmelicka, a street of medieval narrowness packed during daylight hours with native Jews and those resettled and crammed into the Ghetto from every corner of Poland and beyond: Vienna, Prague, Germany.

A Gestapo truck would appear among the crowds, rolling listlessly along, its engine shut off. At the sight of the dark truck painted overripe green and covered with a gray or black canvas top, people would scatter in every direction, flattening themselves against the walls of the houses or, if there was time, ducking into gateways, alleyways, and courtyards to escape. Then the uniformed Gestapo men, members of its Security Branch (*Sicherheitsdienst* or *SD*) pursued, pinning people to the walls with the truck, leaving the victims' torn bodies splattered over the building walls or tearing out chunks of their flesh.

This was a game of precision, very orderly, like clock making. It required great skill in driving. Occasionally, a child impaled on the iron brace supporting the canvas on a fender or bumper would be dragged through the streets or flutter in the air like a flag.

Sometimes the Germans followed a pedestrian until, alerted by the silence about him or the flight of others ahead of him, he would glance back. The truck would then either run him down, to the loud amusement of the Germans, or the SD men, halting the truck, would leap out, thick leather whips in their hands. If the prospective victim stopped, bowed to the henchmen and didn't panic, no harm would generally occur. But the beasts went with a fury after those who ran. They would catch up with their hapless victims in the street, or follow them into the gateway of a house.

I never ran. If I saw crowds running, I'd either turn in the opposite direction, or slowly enter a building, fly upstairs and await the passage of the wave. A number of times the Germans were upon me before I had time to think. Still I refused to acknowledge their superiority by fleeing.

I'd calmly freeze to my spot, inhaling the body smells of the Germans sprinting past, their wool uniforms moist with sweat. And often I looked at my own people with disgust.

"You stupid Jews, must you *provoke* the Germans by showing them your fear of them? They hate you for being Jewish; must you remind them of it by your cowardice, your appearance with *kapotas* [long coats], sidelocks, and *yarmulkes* [scull caps]? You deny yourselves human dignity by running away, long before the German deprives you of it. Is it any wonder that they hate and beat you?"

My mother, even under the worst conditions in the Ghetto, would always inspect my clothes before I left the house. I did not feel part of the hunted, lice-infested multitude.

I was not alone in my attitude. I often heard it expressed by my peers in the Organization and, with a particular vehemence, by my older sister.

I accepted the terror of the German uniform as one accepts the existence of volcanoes and floods, rats, famine, or other eruptions of nature. One could not hate nature's eruptions for they were as inevitable as nature itself, as parents, school, my father's anger, or snow in winter, I thought. But one should be enraged at human failure to act with dignity and self-respect in the face of such cataclysms.

During the Gestapo forays along Karmelicka Street, the Jewish policemen, if there were any present, always sidestepped the onrushing Germans, saluting smartly: forefinger and middle finger joined together in the prewar Polish salute, touching the visor. They were dressed in mufti with the exception of visored caps wrapped in blue, arm brassards reading Jewish Order Service, belted jerkins, and, among the more affluent, knee-high boots.

These policemen, though many had been lured into the service by the torment of having to provide for their starving families, carried with them an irreversible social stigma among the Jews of Warsaw; this despite the oft-heard argument that were it not for the Jewish police—including the dreaded green-capped "Gestapo," the "Thirteen" (as derived from 13 Leszno Street, their headquarters)— the Ghetto would be far worse off, with the German police enforcing order, whereas Jewish policeman sometimes overlooked or else could be bribed to forego enforcement. The fact was, however, that it was the *Ordnungsdienst* (the Jewish police) which largely enforced the German rules and regulations. Moreover, when deportations began, the Jewish police, having been "assured" of immunity from "resettlement" by the Germans, rounded up thousands of fellow Jews daily, dragging them helpless into the streets, often separating them from their families and marching them into the waiting columns of those selected by the

Germans for deportation. Thus they willingly interposed themselves as a dubious buffer between the Nazis and their own folk.

Often during the forays of the Gestapo trucks, Jewish policemen who happened by were ordered to clear away the maimed bodies. At times, when a victim had stubbornly absorbed the blows of their clubs and whips and appeared fit for another work over, the Jewish police or some passersby were commandeered to throw the victim onto the vehicle.

Afterward, at Pawiak, the notorious prewar maximum security prison, there was seldom any return to life. The Gestapo's daily trips to and from Pawiak led them through Karmelicka Street.

I remember the four corners near Pawiak as a favorite hangout for Jewish prostitutes who lurked near the arching doorways of the apartment houses. They would boldly accost the Polish uniformed police and even an occasional German with whom they would disappear inside. (The Germans, forbidden to mix with other races, probably felt "safe" from denunciation in the Ghetto.)

Once, when I was thirteen, I was returning home to Nowolipki Street, one block from Pawiak. I had studied for my Latin exam with a classmate. It was winter and a smelly darkness had set in long before the curfew at nine. On Pawia Street, just as I was passing a familiar house, I heard a voice:

"Come on, little one, I'll make you feel good."

I recognized a familiar face of sharp and brazen features, a woman of provocative figure whose short winter coat was partially open in a deliberate neglect, revealing strong, muscular thighs that evoked an aching sweetness within me.

"How much?" I managed. It was the only thing I could think of, while I also felt a sense of pride in acting the part of a grown-up who would bargain for a price. Yet I was also petrified to stop; I kept walking with the woman following; no one else was in sight.

"Twenty-five," said the woman. "Come, little one." I kept walking, scared to stop, muttering something about the price being too high. After that night and for as long as I remained on Nowolipki, I passed that house with the tremors of longing and fear joined unmistakably together.

✛ ✛ ✛

The cattle car with its human cargo was still now. The pitiful mass had ceased its bewildered, agonizing ululations. It had temporarily paused in its exhausted stupor, duping itself into believing, half-consciously, that the present lull would last.

The train had been stopped for a while. Presently it yanked again, chugged, pulled, and reversed as it seemed to change tracks.

I was awake. Those near me—the boy Nathan, the bearded man and the fat man—were awake, too, breathing in the fresh air from outside.

I couldn't take my eyes off the small barbed-wire window. In my mind I was unraveling the wire, wondering if I could squeeze my body through the tiny cutout. I'd had my escape figured out before I'd even entered the car, but now I wondered if I'd succeed. I wanted to feel Nathan out.

"How would you like to jump?"

"I don't know ... You?"

I swallowed hard. I couldn't do it alone.

"It's either this or get to where we're going."

"Where is that?" Nathan said after a pause.

"You don't know?" I leaned closer to him for fear of being overheard and having my plans frustrated by the opposition of others. "We're going to Treblinka, you don't know that?"

Nathan's eyes waited.

"That's in the East, a few hours' train ride. Gas for everybody."

"How do you know?"

"I know from my Organization, *Hashomer Hatzair.* Our leaders told us. The Polish railroad men brought the word."

"That's not a Bible for me."

"I tell you I know. Two of our comrades, with good Polish looks, had made the trip. Look, where d'you think we're going? All the shooting and slugging, and the dogs, and 'any Jew found outside the Ghetto will be shot.' What's that for? Anyway, wherever we're going, I don't want to get there to find out if I'm right."

Nathan did not answer. He took out a piece of bread from his coat pocket, broke it in half, and offered it to me. I hadn't eaten since noon the day before. I tried to make it last and last.

☩ ☩ ☩

Outside the train, a shot rang out. Then a burst of machine-gun fire. The train, which had been chugging along, lurched and slowed. Its wheels squeaked and groaned through a series of irregular thuds and concussions. We were halted.

A few people awakened. Someone moaned. The fat man said, "Hey, kid, see what you can see."

I was hoisted on the fat man's shoulders. Through the barbed-wire opening I could see dark fields, trees, and a telephone post. I tried the wire. It was stiff and rusted. I tried to turn the ends. Hard and sharp. My fingers bled but the wire gave in. I unraveled some of it.

"C'mon now, what do you see?" repeated the fat one.

"Can't see a thing," I reported, sliding down with the help of the bearded man. Heavy booted steps passed outside. There were shouts in German and hollers from afar. Minutes passed. The train stood still.

I was aware of the passage of time. I figured Treblinka was about one hundred kilometers east of Warsaw. At the rate we were going, including the stops, we would be approaching the halfway point soon—given, as I estimated, the train moving at approximately sixty kilometers an hour. Once we got underway again, it would be another two hours, at the most, until we reached Treblinka. If I were going to make a break for life, it had to be in the next hour. I pulled the bearded man's sleeve.

"Sir, will you help me jump?" We were so jammed together, it was impossible for those nearby not to overhear.

"Are you crazy? You want to get killed?" The fat man's jaw was quivering.

"Son," said the bearded man. "How could you do that?"

"Not now," I said, "when the train gets rolling. In motion."

"You will kill yourself, *hulile* [God forbid], fall under the wheels," the bearded one scolded, but not forbiddingly.

"No, sir, I know how. I used to jump out of streetcars."

"Your father would let you do such things? *Oy, Goteniu!* Such a nice boy."

"My father never knew, else I'd get a whipping. I used to do it with other boys, for sport."

"But why?"

It was no use telling him about the gas.

"Stay with the rest of us. They can't kill us all. Whatever happens to the rest of us ..."

This was said with a certainty with which the whole world wanted to agree. But I had heard this before.

☩ ☩ ☩

"Let us go to Warsaw," my father was saying. "Whatever happens to a half million Jews, will happen to us ... they can't kill us all," he decreed, following our aborted escape in the winter of 1940 across the frozen Bug River, which divided the German and the Soviet zones of occupation of Poland after she was wiped off the map in 1939.

"Hitler or no Hitler," reasoned my father, "we are still dealing with the civilized German nation which gave us much of the world's cultural heritage."

For a serious musical conductor whose entire world, besides Jewish folk music, revolved around the romantic tradition of Beethoven, Brahms, Schubert, and the classicism of Handel and Haydn, as well as Kant and Schopenhauer, coupled with tomes of Goethe and Schiller which he proudly displayed to all behind the living room's glassed-in *gablotka* in their German originals, it was unthinkable to believe otherwise. But my inculcated trust in the "civilized German nation" faded away rapidly with my exposure to countless German bestial cruelties and terror over the passing months. Whatever was happening to the Jews aboard the trains headed for Treblinka, I did not want to be part of it. Some Jews in the Warsaw Ghetto had heard rumors about the destination of the deportations, but they refused to believe them or outright denied them. Adding to the chaos was the confusion deliberately instigated by the invidious German scheme of causing some Jews to receive postcards, seemingly in their relatives' handwriting, extolling their living conditions in the "Eastern Labor Camps."

Only once, since the mass deportations had begun, did my mother bring up the subject, when she stroked my hair especially tenderly and said, "Jozieczku," using my Polish diminutive, "if it ever came to pass that you were to be deported, with or without us, or if you ever found yourself alone on the train—jump!" She made me promise her as she looked at me with love and warmth in her quiet blue eyes that showed much suffering.

Somehow, I never worried about survival. With my blue eyes and flaxen hair—after my mother—I had heard, ever since I could remember, that I "didn't look Jewish." "Your son looks like a real *sheigetz*—a regular Gentile. Are you sure …?" people would often ask while sometimes coveting my looks.

Sometimes, when I was alone in our cramped room, I would look in the mirror studying my face, nose, hair, and eyes. The others were right: I could easily pass for a *goy*. In fact, I thought, you never know … If it ever came to pass, I could.

Chapter Two
The Resistance

THE EVENTS LEADING UP to me jumping off the train began with a chance meeting in the summer of 1941. The Jewish police came for the baker who lived in the next house; he had been baking more bread than he was officially permitted to. Some in the street said that he had not met his quota of bribes to the police. A crowd had gathered outside. Rysiek was among them with Nahum—both looked my age, about thirteen.

"We would never have approached you, were it not for the banter in the street," they told me later. "You just looked like a goy."

Rysiek was shorter, an extrovert, always babbling, always involved in minutiae. Nahum, taller, moved with caution as if his lean joints had not been put together well. He was the more serious one. Both seemed committed, both cared, both managed a rare sense of dry humor. As different as they were in temperament, they shared one common feature: prominent chins.

Rysiek and Nahum told me about Hashomer Hatzair: a quasi-boy-scout organization of socialist leanings. They had regular meetings; their platoon met weekly and the *gdud*—the Hebrew word for a paramilitary company—met once a month: boys and girls. Except for their leaders, who were in their early twenties, all of them were aged twelve to sixteen.

I was not a joiner and I stalled. On the other hand, Rysiek and Nahum, while attempting to enlist me, were probing me about my family background; this was a conspiracy, a resistance group, they explained, and there were many spies in the Ghetto.

"We are Socialists and Zionists," explained Nahum. "No, no, nobody talks Yiddish. We all speak Polish, sometimes sing in Hebrew. But the main thing is, you see what's going on daily: killings, brutality, terror, I don't have to tell you. Thousands are dying daily—starvation, disease. But we're not dying fast enough for the Germans. So—if it should come to pass that the Germans try to exterminate us by force— we are going to fight, and die, to preserve Jewish honor for centuries to come. That's the whole thing."

Like Masada, I thought, a song composed by my father, of the same name, which had become famous.

I went to a few meetings, met Zev, the platoon leader, and was accepted.

Zev, seventeen years of age, was our idol. Of humble origin, he worked for the Ghetto's social "welfare" agency during the day. Gauntness and starvation were etched into his face, along with, as their logical offspring, a taciturnity and strength that commanded respect among his subordinates. Those coming mainly from upper-middle-class families stood in awe of poverty when it seemed to go in tandem with a superior, self-made intellect. Mostly self-taught in history, Hebrew, and Marxism, Zev spoke with cautious deliberation. His sequences were usually preceded by a visible chewing process, so that often, when his turn came, moments elapsed in reverent silence before Zev would speak up. He meticulously avoided taking sides in the frequent heated arguments, whether on personal or ideological subjects.

Zev's steel-gray eyes were deeply set, topped by a long and smooth forehead which arched backward at an almost abnormal diagonal. He had large ears that moved when he spoke, while he drew figures in the air with his hands; these moved in an affected manner, as if seeking to convince his listeners of his acquired intellect.

I was fascinated by his constant bland facial expression held back by prodigious cheek movement as if he were chewing on his saliva. In particular, this happened prior to each expected emotional outburst which never came. For weeks on end I tried to train myself in imitating Zev's outward control; it reminded me of two British Army colonial officers (or were they Scots?) I had seen in a prewar motion picture at the Capitol Theatre in Łódź when I was ten. The Englishmen addressed each other laconically, crouching behind a sand dune in the Sahara desert as, pistols drawn, they faced wild hordes of fanatical, charging Bedouins. The officers also contorted their cheek muscles, which I was sure helped them retain their impassioned, calm faces. As I recalled, one of them turned to the other saying laconically: "What do you say, old chum, shall we take them on?" Ever since, especially after seeing the film *Anthony Adverse,* Englishmen had become for me the epitome of courage, composure, and resourcefulness under duress.

Zev had his girl, Aviva. Like him, she was a leader of a girls' platoon, part of my gdud. Aviva was stunning in her freckled beauty, fair-complexioned and framed by red hair. A white blouse, which she wore most of the time, protected her overripe breasts. She had a typical Aryan appearance and was intensely loyal to Zev. I felt that their outward demeanor had to be supported by private intimacies— such were their deliberately suppressed exchanges of looks and words in public.

From time to time, the leadership of the Organization used Aviva as a liaison with the outside world and, it was rumored, with the Polish resistance. She would make these trips at great risk to herself, although it was unthinkable to take Aviva for anything but a Polish Gentile.

Once a month, the entire gdud would meet in a large hall at Nalewki, Smocza, or Grzybowska Streets. These meetings, numbering about one hundred youths, began with the singing of the Jewish anthem, *Hatikva* (Hope). On special occasions the Polish anthem was intoned, as well. Next, reports were made by the platoon leaders to the commander's deputy, David. David was small of build and stocky, usually dressed in light beige breeches and riding boots, as was Mordechai. Like everyone else, David was his assumed name in this paramilitary organization where few of the *shomrim*, except for close friends, knew each other's real names—in the event of denunciation. Not even all of the platoon leaders knew David's real name. The deputy, it was whispered, had been a chemical engineering student before the war. But David also knew languages, economics, the history of human evolution and philosophy, in addition to being an avowed socialist.

The name of the Organization's commander, Mordechai,* was spoken with special reverence. There was a rare charisma about him and a quiet, strong radiance. I remember my first encounter with him, his profile sharp as an eagle's, supported by a jutting chin, prominent but absolutely straight nose and a proportionately smooth forehead to match, as if chiseled in rock.

Twice, when my gdud joined up with another for a special occasion (it was considered dangerous to hold a meeting of over one hundred "scouts"), Mordechai presided, as always wearing a white shirt, open at the collar in Byronesque fashion, as were the platoon leaders: Zev, Aviva, and Ruth.

Ruth was a stubby, short girl who wore long braids pinned in a crown. She was nominally in charge of the company reporting directly to David. Ruth seemed to know everything, all the answers, all the time. She had a typically Slavic round face framed in broad cheekbones, yet spoiled by a narrow, determined line of mouth that emitted assertive statements with a degree of finality, however marred by a slight lisp. When she gesticulated, which occurred only during an ideological discourse, the air about her was filled with short, tight patterns woven by her stubby fingers. I had never seen her smile, and she looked particularly forbidding if conversation turned to personal subjects.

I knew nothing of her family background except that amidst all the deprivations and starvation, Ruth always looked well fed and even obese. She worshipped David; but in addressing her subordinates, she assumed the air of cold, matter-of-fact authority of one in whom orders were vested to be given out at will.

Rysiek and Nahum always exchanged amused glances whenever Ruth lapsed into her abrasive tone in addressing the gdud. But we

---

*Only years after the war I learned Mordechai's real name: he was Mordechai Anielewicz, the commander of the Warsaw Ghetto Uprising.

had to be careful: this was an underground conspiracy, an honor to belong to, for few were chosen and those few thought of themselves as intellectual and ideological elite. Ruth's repeated displeasure would not augur well for anybody.

My other superiors—Zev, David and Mordechai—all possessed one dominant quality, besides their fanatical dedication, which made them deserving of the idolatry in which they were held: they all seemed driven by great compassion for their fellow man. Ruth, by contrast, was a rigid and impersonal executor of an ideology. Years later, when I heard a character in an Edna St. Vincent Millay play—or was it one of Jean-Paul Sartre's in "The Red Gloves" on Broadway—say, "I am a socialist; I love humanity but I hate people," I thought of Ruth.

At our monthly meetings, following a quasi-military formation, everybody ended up sitting on the floor (no chairs), legs crossed. Guards were posted outside to watch for any suspicious persons.

At first, early in 1941, mainly Hebrew songs were sung. Occasionally, if the guards outside had reported an all-clear, *choras* were danced in a circle and with great abandon. I remember pale faces coming to life with blushing cheeks, starved bodies of young teenagers reaching out for bits of joy, rapturously grasping for the rhythm of the living. Arms outstretched, interlaced with others, aching, starving innards forgotten. Young hopes, doused with man's cruelty, sprang up in renunciation of the imminent; eyes burned with a fierce, defiant glow which found dance in triumph over daily misery; a defiance in survival, in being part of a Cause; an unvanquished reaffirmation of oneself, of the family of man—a life rising over destruction.

Without, the sticky, gulping darkness of an approaching curfew crouched low to devour the young; most old ones had long been broken. Nights brought shrieks of the tormented or the parting or disappearance of the beloved, and the silent pain of hunger that kept one awake. But here, within, was one uniting common purpose, one shared aim, the solace of total dedication and a shelter for the hunted amidst the compassion of one's peers.

A one-time attempt of a few shomrim to intone Yiddish songs was quashed by the majority; after all, for the restless and defiant majority, Yiddish was the symbol of the ghettos—a life of acquiescence, acceptance, and subservience.

One of the choras which was often sung and danced was "Masada," by my father, Professor Izrael Fajwiszys, which he had composed before the war. Its words invoked the glorious defiance and death in mass suicide by the defenders of Masada in Roman times. Everyone knew the "Masada" and that made me stand out somewhat: "Arie's father wrote this." Arie was my conspiratorial nom de plume—from my original middle name.

But after the Nazi attack on Russia in the summer of 1941, when the Red Army troops, despite their initial stunning defeat, became the rallying focus of resistance and virtually the only hope for the Germans' ultimate defeat and for our survival (America being asleep beyond seven seas), Russian songs were introduced into our musical repertoire and sung with great fervor.

One hot summer afternoon in 1941, the two gduds were brought together in an airless hall on Grzybowska Street. Following the customary reports, David spoke. He explained the outlines of the Darwin theory aiming at the poignant point of the survival of the fittest. He wanted every *shomer* to depend on himself.

David toppled one idol after another including the Biblical God. There were no gods; there were only reality and natural selection—intellectually and physically. There were also, to be sure, high ethical principles—many evidenced in the Bible itself—which, however, should be seen merely as the history of the Jewish people with their noble tradition as the People of the Book; indeed, as erstwhile People of the Sword as well, whenever the need arose to defend themselves. There was also their future homeland—to be restored—as defined by Herzl, for which young Jews had to strive, and the brotherhood of men—all men—as the highest postulates.

David was worshipped and his words were unquestioned. He was our prophet-in-residence. When he finished, there was silence interrupted only by the whispered admiration and the adoring looks of the girl members. No one applauded. That was forbidden for fear of attracting outside attention.

Then Mordechai got up. At age twenty-four, he was held in an awe which others reserve for their saints or rare national leaders elevated above other mortals. Mordechai, young and handsome, radiated an inner peace that seemed to emanate from a messianic focus on a remote

Elysium transcending all human potential. Mordechai's deportment appeared oblivious to the trivia of life, as if he had already made a sizable down payment on Immortality Row.

Mordechai spoke of the golden chapters in the history of the Jewish people, of the two thousand years of Diaspora. He invoked the glorious moments in the lives of God's Chosen People while citing a few of the devilish Hamans in their history—Satans obsessed with extermination. The Hamans expired but the people survived.

Mordechai traced the Jew across continents and ages, in strange lands, always in the minority. He survived by accommodating himself instead of offering physical or armed resistance. For, Inquisition and pogroms notwithstanding, ultimately some Jews survived and with them Judaism, humanity's values and conscience. The Gentile, be he Spaniard or German, had periodically sought a scapegoat to blame for political or economic ills and to divert the discontent of the oppressed classes. Jealousy, fear of competition, inferiority syndromes, or rage at the people who had given them the Ten Commandments—and with them conscience—would at times break out into uncontrollable fury, leaving in its wake murder and destruction.

"We have survived," Mordechai was saying, "as many would maintain, by accommodating ourselves to circumstances. We were not able to fight the stronger. 'They cannot kill us all'—so went the reasoning. Also, as you know, bloodshed and violence have been regarded by the Jews as odious transgressions of our ethical tenets. Thus, centuries of Diaspora have lived by that banner, reinforced as of late by the Hassidic tradition teaching passive submission to the Gentile violence. That revulsion to the violence has been a grave by-product of the conviction that through opposition one might 'bring the wolf out of the forest,' as they say in Polish. Thus, by provoking further repression through offering resistance, a Jew would bring on plagues of vengeance upon his brethren, tantamount to treason and murder against his own people, for many more Jews would perish in opposition to the Gentiles, numerically superior and possessors of far greater instruments of violence.

"Centuries passed. Under the visionary leadership of Herzl and Weitzman, Jews began striving for recovery of their national home, to cast off shackles of persecution and become free people.

"Hashomer Hatzair has been in the forefront of the *Halutzim* movement, a pioneering group of idealistic young people such as yourselves."

Mordechai's eyes burned as he traced the heroic epics of the *Hashomer Halutzim*, young dedicated people, many of well-to-do families, who renounced comforts at times secured by generations and cast their lot with others, drying up mosquito-infested swamps and marshes in British-held Palestine, reclaiming their Promised Land foot by foot. Many died of malaria. They toiled by day with ploughs, rifles slung over their backs to defend against Arab terrorists, and by night shared bunks with their *chaverim*—their comrades—to build a future land, free of oppression, free of the humiliating activities of the *Luftmensch*, the percentage man, a money lender born for survival; a land made strong by their labor and courage; men whose sweat and song made them free to inhale deeply and unafraid.

Mordechai paused. Sitting cross-legged at his feet, I was riveted to his finely chiseled face that absorbed the soft dark shadows elongated by the flickering pulses of candles placed on the barren floor. (The windows had to be totally blacked out to conform to rigidly enforced air-raid regulations.)

As he resumed, Mordechai's voice took on a hard edge.

"I said before that the Jew has had to suffer under persecution and violence that begot blows to his dignity and self-respect. But ... he has survived. Even under the Spanish Inquisition the Jew had a chance to flee to other lands or to convert.

"But we are confronting slow genocide—you and I—unprecedented in the history of our nation and of the world. Every day we see the kind of indignities, terror, and bestiality which are aimed to hasten our obliteration but pose a central dilemma: on what terms survival, as long as that is still possible?

"A systematic campaign goes on aimed at starving out an entire people. We are walled in, most unable to earn a livelihood. Our weekly 'food rations' are barely sufficient to keep a person alive for one day. Every day we see emaciated children of Israel dying of starvation in the streets; we see swollen, bloody faces returning home from work commands; we see and hear shootings in the streets; we see young German punks in uniform amusing themselves by subjecting orthodox

Jews dressed in kapotas and yarmulkes, beards and sidelocks, to public indignities: sweeping the ground in front of the *Herrenvolk* with their beards, having their hair and sidelocks cut off in public, being beaten and shot. We see children executed for the 'crime' of attempting to scale the Ghetto wall to fetch some food for their families.

"Do we bear these bestialities in silence? How to 'survive' allowing this to happen? Do we go on living day after day, doomed to gradual extermination without a shred of human dignity left?

"I know that you will say: *No!* We shall fight! But how? The Germans have employed a policy of bloody retribution and vengeance in all Eastern occupied territories. For every German killed, scores of civilians are executed. Do we then have the moral mandate from the people for armed resistance?

"You and I are of a new generation, and I know that many of us would choose to die with dignity rather than go on living in slavery and gradual extermination. We all remember the Maccabaes—we remember Masada and her defenders who chose to die by their own hand rather than go into slavery, with our women dishonored.

"We haven't advocated armed resistance until now, mindful of our responsibility to our brethren and to history. Now, however, there are partially confirmed rumors that the Germans have formed *Vernichtungskommandos*—some call them *Ausrottungskommandos*—special units within the SS with orders to exterminate through mass executions the Jewish population in Poland and perhaps beyond."

Mordechai paused again. All eyes were riveted on him. It was possible to hear the youngsters breathe—those who dared.

"Should this come to pass, should an attempt be made to deport us from the Warsaw Ghetto to a destination unknown, the Hashomer will stand up and fight. We will not go down in history as sheep led to slaughter. We will fight for the honor of the Jewish people forever!

"To this end we are forming an armed partisan unit in the forests. In the days to come we will try to get some of our leaders out of the Ghetto, with the help of our Polish resistance friends.

"I know that some of you are impatient and want to fight *now*. I say to you: *Do not* ... at this time, for the German retribution for even isolated acts of resistance would take many Jewish lives, lives for which you would be responsible.

"I promise you: *we will fight*, and die, if necessary, if survival becomes incompatible with our dignity and honor. We will smite Haman, no matter how hopelessly."

The silence was unbearable. Years later I learned that Mordechai must have known more than he was willing to admit to us kids. I exchanged looks with Rysiek and Nahum. The three of us had discussed the possibility of armed resistance on several occasions, but the subject never took on the imminence of reality: it never went beyond polemics. Nahum, the tall, studious one, was always surprisingly militant. Rysiek, the jovial Rysiek, would ridicule armed resistance, ascribing it to hotheaded utopians. "Where are we going to get the weapons to engage the German Army? Nonsense!" But suddenly it was upon us; Mordechai had spoken the words and they were terrifying.

"Effective immediately," Mordechai continued, "each platoon leader will give first priority to the training of every one of you in armed resistance, in basic familiarity with weapons—which we hope to get—be they sticks or knives, and other guerilla and survival tactics. The hour is upon us, and if we have to perish, we'll each take one or two of the murderous beasts down with us. You are still kids, but you'll grow up fast to write a new chapter in history. And remember, on your sacred honor, your membership in the Organization is not to be disclosed to *anyone*, including your families."**Only years after the war, when I met Antek Cukierman, the last Commander of the Warsaw Ghetto Uprising, did I find out that my father had been on the Uprising Committee; and so, father had not told the son, and the son had not shared his membership in the Resistance with his father.

✠ ✠ ✠

Mordechai dismissed both gduds just before eight-thirty—a half hour before the mandatory curfew. It was late, no time to talk and ruminate. German gendarmes patrolling the streets shot stragglers one minute before nine o'clock. I rushed home, half running, with Nahum and Rysiek. We agreed to discuss the significance of Mordechai's speech before our scheduled meeting three days later.

It was five minutes before nine when I reached Nowolipki 34. Nahum and Rysiek sped ahead. The janitor stood at the heavy iron gate, ready with the house keys. All houses were to be locked at nine. There were tips for the janitor when a late straggler pounded at the gate.

Father stood next to the janitor overflowing with anxiety for my safety. I had been "studying" with friends.

Mother had saved me some watery soup and a slice of dark bread. I had never mentioned my membership in the Organization to anyone in my family. But that night I was still agitated; somehow I broached the subject in general terms.

"What do you think about the possibility of armed resistance, Daddy? I mean, if this goes on?

Father looked at me with one of his paralyzing expressions. "Where did you hear this?"

"Just around," I said evasively. "I mean, I heard people talk about deportations; what if it ever came to that?"

"Yes, every now and then there is an idiot, people who don't know history, have no idea how the Jews have survived. They are provocateurs, most likely Nazi agents in the Ghetto, who want to create a pretext for arrests and executions. They foment unrest, playing right into Nazi hands. Pfui," Father exclaimed, "*paskudstwo*, hooligans! Don't let me catch you having anything to do with them!" Then he appraised me piercingly. "Have you, by any chance, got anything to do with one of those militant groups? Tell me, right now!"

"No, Daddy, I told you, I just heard it said around ... in the street."

"Don't let me ever ..." He lapsed into his professorial mien: "A Jew doesn't stoop to the level of a goy. The Jew who causes bloodshed and physical resistance only brings the worst upon his people."

"But, Daddy," I attempted, "don't you think there are times when one must resist—when everything else is gone, I mean—for self-respect, for honor, and for future generations?"

"Nonsense," shot back the professor. "You are still young, but you remember the Revisionists before the war? They wanted to wage armed struggle against the British in Palestine. What has been accomplished? Nothing. And by contrast, the *Karen Kayemet*, the fund to purchase land in Palestine—look how much it has done: settlements, *halutzim*, a beachhead for a future nation. Only money, patience, and a dedicated sustained effort can get us anywhere. Fight, and what will it get you? There are more Gentiles in this world than Jews, especially now when we are surrounded by Jew-haters and they have the guns."

"But, Daddy, why do they hate us so much?"

"Son, this is an old story: the Christian Church has been behind it ever since St. Paul, as they call him, a Jewish convert, proclaimed to the Greeks and others that it was the Jews who crucified their God."

"Did they?"

"This is the biggest lie in human history. It was the Romans who crucified him. And the Christians have created a myth which satisfied their perfidious need to hate somebody, in order to unify them. Such has been the sorry state of humanity. Hitler, to unify Germany, gave its people some object to hate—the Jews. But the origin of the hatred has been embedded in Christianity. The perfidy of it all has been their adulation of the Apostles and the Virgin Mary—all Jews like Christ."

"But, Daddy, why don't the Gentiles respect us, after their God and the founders of their religion originated with the Jews?"

"Religion, nonsense," retorted my father. "Christ and his Apostles never renounced their Jewishness, never claimed to form a new religion. They merely, if you believe the Scriptures, wanted to reform the practices of the day and widen the commandments to embrace all of humanity. Christ taught the love of God and the neighbor— something long ago proclaimed in the Bible. Instead, the converted pagans spread hatred against Christ's own people. And what we call the universal Christian Church today has promulgated hatred of the Jew throughout the Italian Ghettos, the Inquisition, and the pogroms. Now, Hitler."

I stayed awake for a long time that night. I absorbed my father's diatribe in part, but I had many doubts about his ideas about the resistance. Mordechai spoke so convincingly, and it was unthinkable to distrust him.

✠ ✠ ✠

I missed the next meeting of my platoon. I had forgotten all about my father's concert. It was to be his last one, for permission from the authorities was to be terminated after this concert.

Several hundred of the Ghetto's cultural elite turned out that evening at the Tlomackie Auditorium for a concert featuring excerpts from Mendelssohn's oratoria. After the intermission, the second part consisted of Jewish folk songs orchestrated and elevated to the concert stage. Permission had been granted for the concert, but only if works by Jewish composers were to be played. Father, on the podium, looked like the ghost of a man. His prewar suit hung on him as on a scarecrow. People cried. Everyone feared worse times were lying ahead. Mother sat in our special loge with Rela and me. She was the epitome of elegance and modesty. She'd taught us never to applaud our father. "It is bad manners," she'd say.

Afterward, the concert people came to congratulate us, including several cultural luminaries and members of the Ghetto Council. The mother of one of my classmates—a staunchly assimilated woman who, my mother told me, deeply resented her forced association with Jews in the Ghetto, approached my mother:

"You know, Madame Professor, I never knew Jewish folk songs could be so beautiful."

At home, after curfew that night, sharing the one room all four of us occupied, there was nothing to eat …

✛ ✛ ✛

I did make it to the next meeting of the platoon, which was held in Nahum's home. When I arrived, Rysiek was already involved in a heated argument with Nahum. Zev was chewing his saliva, saying very little.

"I think he's crazy," Rysiek was fuming. "You're all crazy. Fighting the Germans! If there were the tiniest chance of success, I'd say, all right, let's go when the time comes. But we are surrounded by the SS and the German Army which have defeated Poland, half of Russia, France, Belgium, Holland, Norway, Czechoslovakia … you want me to go down the list? And here are two hundred shomrim under Mordechai waging a battle without weapons against the rulers of Europe with some hostile Polish population around us, *and* many fellow Jews condemning it. You must be crazy!"

Rysiek hissed as he finished the argument. He was agitated and red in the face.

"You mean we are crazy if we pledge to defend the honor of the Jewish people? Were the Maccabaes crazy?" Quiet Nahum was raising his voice.

"Of course they were. But they were surely facing mass murder."

"Mordechai said it is imminent," retorted Nahum.

"Imminent, my foot," Rysiek shot back. "So far, no one is killing the entire population of the Ghetto, yet."

"Yet!" exclaimed Nahum. "Only the blind can't see the signals. What're we waiting for? Official notification by the Germans? When that happens, you want to go to your death like sheep to slaughter? What will future generations say?"

"I don't give a shit what they'll say! Sure, the German Army is going to be deterred by a bunch of thirteen- or fourteen-year-old kids … Ha! You are dreamers! Wait and see: we'll survive!"

"Mordechai must know what he's saying." Nahum was trying to level his voice. "Besides, if you don't want to listen to our leaders, how come you're still with us?"

"I am with you, stupid, because I believe in our goals, our comradeship, and everything else. Only so far no one is handing out a half dozen weapons, saying, 'Kill the first German.' When that happens—big *if*—I am not going to be the one to bring vengeance upon half a million Jews in the Ghetto, if a few of your hotheads start something. Until then, I am with you and, don't worry, I won't squeal. By the way, I won't have to; you don't think for one minute they don't have spies everywhere—possibly even among us?"

"So how is it," Zev, who had been listening consummately, asked finally, "that they haven't arrested all of us before now?"

"Because," the recalcitrant Rysiek fired back, "they don't take us seriously, that's why. They figure, 'Let them play their games.' At least this way they know everything that's going on."

"But still," queried the adamant Zev, "what if Mordechai is right?" Somehow I felt that he knew more than he was saying.

"Right about what?" Rysiek was still bellicose.

"Well, if someday they'll want to kill us all?"

"How, I ask you, how?" Rysiek was undeterred. "Kill a half million Jews in the Warsaw Ghetto? Bring back the German Army from the Russian front and aim hundreds of their cannons at us? Sure, they'll starve us and kill some of us; no doubt, more will die. But all of us ... impossible!"

The curfew hour was approaching. As we parted, there were no winners. But Mordechai's words hung over us.

✛ ✛ ✛

At home, my sister Rela complained of a strong headache. The next day she showed a high fever and was barely conscious. The family suspected the worst: typhoid. This dreaded disease had spared barely a single family in the Ghetto. When it struck, most victims succumbed to it instantly. Few survived, as starvation had reaped a grim toll in people's ability to resist. Soap and sanitary facilities were obtainable on the black market only and at a high premium, and otherwise clean people found themselves afflicted with lice—the carriers of typhoid—which crawled everywhere.

It was crucial to keep the existence of this dreaded disease secret within the family, for if discovered, it brought no help or medicine; instead, the entire apartment house would be quarantined and the house interiors sprayed with disinfectants which ruined all possessions unless sanitary crews were heavily bribed.

Doctors were scarce and many ran themselves to exhaustion, assuming they hadn't fallen prey to the epidemic themselves.

Thus it was a steaming summer afternoon when Father said to me: "Joziu, go and look for Dr. Taubenschlag and *don't* come back without him." Doctors made house calls in those days.

I ran over to the doctor's office, then followed directions to a number of addresses where the doctor was due. Some four hours later I ran into Dr. Taubenschlag on Karmelicka Street.

"Follow me," said the tall young physician. "I have a number of calls to make. If you stick with me, I'll get to your sister eventually. Otherwise, somebody may grab me in the street."

As he was saying it, strangers would come up to him, having recognized him by the black satchel he was carrying, begging him to visit a sick member of their families. The doctor would jot down the names and addresses; others he simply refused to promise anything, as by then his entire schedule had been booked in advance.

Toward sunset we finally got to our apartment—four floors up. "It's typhoid, all right," said Dr. Taubenschlag. "Get her all the best food you can. If you have to sell the rest of your possessions, buy her butter and oranges. The only medicine we can get hold of, that is, if you know an apothecary, is a mixture of 0.9 normal saline and 5 percent glucose. There is no other cure available. The rest is up to her system, which alone can overcome typhoid."

The next day I ran all over the Ghetto seeing the few apothecaries still in existence—in vain. Father then left to seek the vital liquid. Somehow, he brought it with him. It was injected into Rela's thigh, causing it to swell to double its size. I couldn't watch.

☩ ☩ ☩

Two weeks went by. Rela was fighting for her life. Every day, hordes of Ukrainian mercenaries in canary yellow uniforms would seal off a number of apartment houses and, under orders from the SS, which came along with the Jewish police trailing, selected the old, the infirm, the sick, and the children for transports.

No one knew the destination of the transports. However, within a few days, news spread that several families in the Ghetto had received postcards from their deported relatives. The notes were brief, praising the new "labor camps" and good food. There were some who doubted the authenticity of these cards.

Another week passed. Rela survived the crisis and seemed to recover miraculously. At my weekly platoon meeting I was told that Aviva, Zev's girlfriend, used previously as liaison with the "Aryan side" of Warsaw, had been sent in the direction of Malkinia and Treblinka—the reputed destination of the transports—to get all possible information firsthand.

One day, late in July, Rela had recovered sufficiently to go out for a walk. A heavy weight had been lifted from our family. For weeks we lived in fear of the Ukrainians searching the apartments to discover Rela ill. During the random selections preceded by the shrieks of

"*Juden 'raus!*"—Jews out!—the residents inside were either shot on the spot or deported instantly.

I stayed at home with my mother. Both of us were weak from hunger as, in addition to the meager food rations, all the "best" food had been provided for Rela to sustain her recuperation.

Suddenly a cascade of shrill whistles pierced the air, shots rang out, and cries of "*Juden 'raus!*" broke out, followed by shouts in Polish from the Jewish policemen: "Everybody down immediately! Anyone found inside five minutes from now will be shot! Quickly, quickly!"

By the time I came downstairs with my limping mother, most residents of this huge apartment complex were already assembled in two groups near the main gate. Mother had taken some time going down. Crossing the River Bug that fateful night two years earlier, with biting frost approaching minus forty Celsius, as the family attempted to escape Hitler's grip, we had been turned back by Soviet border guards. Mother had suffered first-degree frostbite; four of her toes had been amputated. Even ordinary walking caused her pain in spite of having to wear an oversize house shoe.

While the Ukrainian guards were conducting a floor-to-floor search for stragglers, with a shot ringing out now and then, the SS men performed the selection: left and right.

Mother was ordered right and I—left. I looked about me: my group was composed of old and sick people, a number of children, and mothers with children in their arms. There was little doubt that this group was slated for deportation.

Meanwhile, the courtyard having been cleared of everyone, with only SS men and the Ukrainians roaming about, both groups stood near the main entrance gate, only steps from each other, a couple of Jewish policemen guarding them.

I sought out and caught my mother's look. My immaculately bred mother was winking one eye at me—something I had never seen her do—with a slight head movement beckoning me to join her. There was no mistaking it: she, too, understood that my group was to be deported. I nodded my head and I waited. It looked hopeless for a while. The SS men were firing in the air, amusing themselves, sowing terror and fear. If I attempted to cross over to my mother's group, they'd spot me.

But then my chance came. The Ukrainians were emerging from one of the entrances to the hallways dragging with them an obviously sick man dressed in his pajamas. The SS men turned in the other direction. Mother signaled with her eyes: *Now!*

I took three leaps, then ducked under several legs and to the rear of Mother's group. Mother promptly pulled me toward her, forcing my head down. I was safe.

In a few minutes my former group was herded out, molded into a formation and marched toward the Umschlagplatz—the central embarkation point upon a railway siding where all the deportees were loaded on freight trains.

✠ ✠ ✠

Later, when Father and Rela came home, we were still too shaken to talk.

Chapter Three
Deportations: To Where?!

THEN CAME JULY 22, 1942. A stifling, hot day. Posters went up everywhere ordering mass deportations "to the East"—several thousand a day. Exempted were the members of the Jewish Council, the police, hospital personnel, and employees of German firms located in the Ghetto. These included the brushmakers and sewing workshops turning out uniforms for the Wehrmacht. No details were given about the destination.

I remember reading such a poster at the corner of Leszno and Karmelicka Streets. The evacuation decree was taking effect at once. If the daily quota—reporting to the Umschlagplatz—was not filled, roundups would take place at random. One loaf of bread and a can of marmalade would be given to the "volunteers." All violators would be shot summarily.

Crowds gathered in front of the poster. The horrified silence was interrupted only here and there by a gasp from those who did not find themselves listed in the coveted exempt categories; others left in mounting panic to seek out a loved one, gather family, or huddle over the destination of the transports.

I roamed the streets for hours until I ran into Rysiek. When he came near, he started crying. "Nathan was shot dead ... by Gendarms"

"But why?!"

"It was a few minutes after nine o'clock curfew. I was with him," he spouted out between sobs, "and we tried to hide in a door niche. But they spotted us and said, 'Du verfluchte Jüdische Shweine' [You damn Jewish pigs] and Nathan shot back: 'Du verfluchte Deutsche Schweine!' They shot him in the face."

As I stood there frozen in mortification, he uttered breathlessly, "Word was passed: we are to resist deportation. The evacuation from the Ghetto is a trap. Meeting in two days. See you there." And he ran, sobbing.

Nobody said much at home that evening. Father tried to find out more during the day but came back empty-handed.

The next day it was learned that Adam Czerniakow, the president of the German-appointed Jewish Council, had committed suicide. People suspected the worst ("he must have known").

After a great deal of running, buttonholing, seeking, and invoking every contact he had, Father somehow managed to secure "life passes" for his family of four. We were hired by the Toebbens Corporation on Leszno, near the Żelazna entrance to the Ghetto. This was one of the German *Kriegsbetriebe*—war industries whose owners made a fortune on cheap Jewish labor. It became, for the fortunate ones, a way to forestall deportations. Overnight, brushmakers, tailors and seamstresses became the most prized occupations. Some of the Ghetto's artists, scholars, and intellectuals, along with the leaders of the various resistance organizations, vied for the precious few openings in the German shops.

Those with money bribed their way in. As a well-known conductor and a revered musician, Father managed to obtain four spots at Toebbens' without a bribe, which he would not be able to afford.

Starting early in August, the family spent its days there. Father, along with others, moved bales of clothes to and fro; mother pored over her sewing machine, taking great pains to hide her crippled foot. Rela sewed by hand, and I roamed the shop hiding behind heaps of finished uniforms whenever the German foreman performed inspections— having been forewarned by an elaborate set of signals relayed by the employees—or whenever the SS spot-checked, digging their bayonets deep into bales of clothing to make sure no one was hiding there.

Somehow, through sheer chance, their bayonets hadn't reached me, although a few times I could literally feel them probing around me.

A German shop became the safest place to spend one's days, as roving bands of SS men and their Ukrainian auxiliaries went from house to house blowing shrill whistles, firing in the air, and training their dogs on anyone too slow to assemble in the courtyards. Anyone found indoors was shot on the spot.

After one week at Toebbens, we lost our one-room quarters at Nowolipki as the entire block was swept clean by the Germans. For two days, Father ran himself ragged looking for new quarters for us, in the two hours remaining before the nine o'clock curfew, while people were shot in the streets without warning, even those with special passes.

Finally, Father did locate a deserted tiny room with two beds on Karmelicka Street. Evenings, exhausted, we ate whatever had been saved from the meager food rations at the shop, and collapsed, two to a bed, to rise at six in the morning. Hunger was no longer felt. No longer did I stay up nights, my empty stomach causing me inner cramps. Weakness was setting in, and apathy.

Still, I worried about my inability to contact my comrades in the Organization. I racked my brains to find a way to reach them. But during the day, I had to follow my family into the shop. Evenings, in the hours remaining, my father would stop me physically from leaving.

Terror reigned in the streets. A few times I begged to go out for an hour, but Father would not let me out of his sight. I was desperate.

After two weeks at Toebbens, I felt sharp pains in the vicinity of my heart—like needles stabbing me. So, at the end of the working day, my father took me to our doctor who, somehow, still managed to keep an office.

"Weakening of the heart muscle" was his verdict. "Better take him to the hospital where he can relax and get a little food." Luckily, the hospital was also located on Leszno, near Toebbens; another hospital, I learned, was located at the Umschlagplatz.

The next morning, on the way to work, at the corner where Karmelicka met Leszno, I bid my family goodbye. I was to turn toward Tlomackie—to the office of the doctor, who was to escort me to the hospital later; the rest of them proceeded to work.

It was a slow parting. Mother stalled. Only Father's stern urging effected the separation. In one last gesture, Mother took off her brown jacket and forced it upon me. "Please, take it, Jozieczku," despite my refusals, "you might catch a cold; do it for me." She then took off the bread pouch used to carry food and hung it around my neck.

Each time I turned around, my mother was looking at me over her shoulder. I never forgot her loving, aching look which did not fade with distance. I was never to see her again.

☩ ☩ ☩

In the hospital, they rushed me through the *Entlausung*—the dreaded delousing and disinfecting procedure. My hair was shaven clean. Later, I was bedded down with some forty children in a huge room on the second floor. Food was meager—twice a day a bowl of watery soup and a slice of bread—but it was a feast compared with the family's diet lately.

Every other day, father would come to visit me right after work. Mother and Rela would proceed home to warm up the shop cabbage or turnip soup. I learned that Mother was taking the family's laundry to wash clandestinely, in the shop's toilet. One day Father brought me an orange; and I insisted on sharing some candy, which had been given me at the hospital, with the family.

All children in my ward had to stay in their beds all day. One day we were shaken up by staccato shooting that seemed to come from the first floor. All the kids were terrified. Some had hidden under their beds; others had drawn sheets over their heads hoping no one would discover their small bodies in bed. Meanwhile, we had learned from the nurses that the SS had forayed onto the first floor, shooting children in their beds.

Somehow, they never got to our floor. But the terror remained thereafter.

Meanwhile, my heart pains were receding, and I beseeched my father to take me out. At the hospital, there was no one to talk to; most kids appeared starved and apathetic. Many had lost entire families, and no one would visit them—they would just lie all day staring ahead in a blind stupor.

Father promised to take me out of the hospital soon, after several unsuccessful attempts to convince me that it was safer for me to remain there. I yearned for a word from the Organization at a time I thought Hashomer might need me.

On the fourth day, Father came to fetch me. It was late afternoon: as we walked away from the hospital, Father seemed unusually reticent. At the same time, I suspected something; it was unlike my father to be so solicitous toward me—especially lately when his nerves were constantly on edge, sparks flying all the time, and he reprimanded me for just about anything.

"Jòziu," he said finally, "you are old enough to understand."

"What is it, Daddy?"

"Mother is no longer … with us."

"How? When?"

"Two days ago. They came into Toebbens. A selection. Took out old people, children, the infirm. They saw Mother's foot bandaged up with her house shoe on. They took her away … Had you been there, you would have likely … too … they took the children away."

We walked toward Karmelicka in silence the rest of the way.

No one talked at suppertime. We gulped the lukewarm liquid which Rela warmed up. Mother was missed at mealtime.

✠ ✠ ✠

Two days later, posters went up everywhere:

ANOUNCEMENT

Upon the order of the Delegate for Resettlement Matters the Jewish Council in Warsaw announces the following:

1.By Sunday, September 6, 1942, 10 a.m., all Jews, without exceptions, remaining within the limits of the large ghetto are to gather for registration purposes, in the section bounded by the streets Smocza, Gęsia, Zamenhofa, Szczęsliwa, and Parysowski Square.

2.Jews are also permitted to move at night from September 5 to 6, 1942.

3.Food for two days and drinking utensils are to be taken along.

4.It is forbidden to lock the apartments.

5.Whosoever does not comply with this order and remains in the ghetto (outside of the above limited district) beyond 10 a.m., Sunday, September 6, 1942, will be shot.

JEWISH COUNCIL IN WARSAW
Warsaw, September 5, 1942

Chapter Four
Now I Am Alone

"THERE'S ONLY ONE THING we can do," the professor was saying. He hadn't slept much, and was gaunt and taciturn. Whereas, in the past, most adversities would make him irate and were—he maintained—in one sense or another, traceable to his wife, the last several days his eyes had taken on a different expression. In the past, I thought, whether in his conducting or away from the podium, I could always see a tiny glint of light in my father's jet-black eyes, like a minuscule fly of fury that danced around the eyes, even when he laughed.

But lately it was gone. Without the gloss of fury and high intensity, something had happened to the professor's vitality; I watched my father's eyes focus on a point and take on a dullness which reminded me of some old, wrinkled beggars who just sat on the stoops and stared.

"Only one thing," my father was saying. "I heard that this morning a transport will be selected to go to the labor camp in Poniatowo, near Lublin."

"Are you sure?" asked Rela.

"Not to Treblinka, Daddy?" I asked. I didn't have the heart to share the information obtained from my Organization.

"No. This comes from a good source—a Jewish policeman. I think this is our chance. Let us try to get on that one. That way, at least, perhaps we can manage to stay together."

"Don't you think we might wait another day or two," offered Rela, "to see what happens?"

Father was listening. In the past, I noticed, he never listened. He either agreed or disagreed instantly, for the professor treated life as an extension of his music. By general consensus he had a brilliant and uncanny musical instinct and, since his music was to a certain degree self-taught, he made instinctive decisions in life as well as in music. They almost always worked in his music, but not quite as often in life.

Now, I noticed, for the first time he was really listening.

"No," he said finally. "We couldn't survive another day or two in the street. We have no more food and we would perish. Those who volunteer for the labor camp, though, at least get a three-day supply of bread and marmalade. Maybe we will survive and stay together."

We walked toward the gate leading to the Umschlagplatz. En route, as we slowly traversed the four or five blocks, a living hell confronted us. As graphic evidence of the drunken forays of the SS and the Ukrainians of the last two nights into the "kettle," blood was smeared all over the sidewalks and the walls of the houses. Shoes, hats, suitcases, spilled open as if gaping in contempt, were all around. Here and there a woman's handbag. Further on were bodies in various positions: some still draining blood, others with their guts spilled open. Occasionally a crushed head or a limb had been severed from a body.

"Just look straight ahead," Father was saying.

Near the main gate stood a battery of Jewish and Polish policemen and, beyond, a few Ukrainians and SS. German gendarmes were manning the gate.

"Daddy, do you think ..." attempted Rela.

"Shhh, don't talk. Thank God for the gendarmes. At least, maybe we'll have some order," the professor whispered.

A large column of men and women could be seen waiting on the other side of the gate.

My father took my hand. Rela was walking alongside. She was nineteen now and looked quite grown. By contrast I looked small and thin. We approached the gendarmes.

"*Guten Morgen* [Good morning]," said my father.

"*Schneller, schneller, beeilt Dich, Mensch* [Faster, faster, hurry up, man]," said the gendarme.

He let my father go through the gate and put up his hand in front of me. Rela was waved on. Father attempted to turn back. It was too late.

"*Komm doch, Mensch, Donnerwetter* [Let's go, man, damnit]," exploded the other gendarme.

"*Aber, mein Herr, erlauben Sie, bitte, mein Sohn* ... [But, sir, allow me, please, my son ...]"

The gendarme grabbed Father by the collar and fed him a potent kick in his rear.

"You'd better go quick, mister, or else," advised a Jewish policeman.

I could still see my father wave at me. I thought I heard "See you later," but I wasn't sure. Some people bumped into me, yelling and shoving me aside. The human wave carried me back a few steps, and I just stood there. Up ahead, on the other side of the checkpoint, it looked like my father's head turned and bobbed in the undulating crowd through a few waves that clashed into one another. Then the head, too, disappeared and I stood there frozen, staring ahead. But I didn't see anything anymore.

A misty stupor engulfed me. *Now I am alone,* I thought. *In a way, it's probably for the better,* I mused, for I knew that together we had no chance to survive. Yet ... *Didn't even put up a fight for me,* I thought.

It was almost evening when I turned back. I was now alone. Actually, I didn't feel any sense of immediate loss. In fact, it was as if a tremendous responsibility had been lifted from me. *It's just as well,* I thought. I had known all along we couldn't possibly survive together. So now, finally, I can cast my lot with the Organization and take care of myself. I had no doubt that I could. After all, I looked Polish.

Chapter Five
Escape from the Death Train

HALF-CONSCIOUSLY, I ROAMED THE crowded streets. Here and there, a dead body was lying, many bloodied, a testimony to the nightly forays by the SS or the Ukrainians. Eventually, I had run into a few teenagers who, like me, had been abandoned or left bereft of families.

Night came and, in my dream, I relived crouching low with kids my age who had steered me to the attic of a building overlooking one of the Ghetto walls. Below us, the entire exterior perimeter was lit brightly with spotlights. Every fifty paces or so stood guards. They walked back and forth carrying rifles. Some wore black uniforms and leggings of faded yellow.

"Are they all Germans?" I asked.

"No," said one of the boys, "the ones in black are Latvians and Lithuanians; those in yellow are Ukrainians." I'd heard that the Germans had brought in Latvian and Lithuanian volunteers to guard the outside walls. Only the Ukrainians, however, were used for roundups and wreaking mayhem inside the Ghetto. It seemed the Germans trusted them the most.

The wall loomed right under us—maybe five feet—making it possible to make a well-aimed leap from the attic window right onto the wall. I was confident that I could make the leap, except that beyond stretched a brightly illuminated square, all but deserted save for the guards. Further on loomed houses where normal people lived. A street went off somewhere.

"Are you going to jump?" I turned to the kid next to me.

"Don't know," he answered. "Not much of a chance. You jump and even if you make it, you can run like hell—they'll get you. Got to cross the whole square. Too many lights. Seems if you don't make the jump, you'll break your ass; even if you make it, the bullets will get you."

I crouched there all night. There were a couple of scares; someone said "Ukrainians down below!" but in the end no one ventured all the way up. All night I was pulled back and forth internally: dozens of times estimating my planned leap. No doubt I would call attention to myself. I was measuring how many seconds it would take the guards to turn around, pull the rifles off their backs, and aim at me unobstructed; how many seconds it'd take me to sprint across the square, zigzagging. In the end, I had to admit that I didn't have a chance. For even if I leaped and evaded the guards, what would I do next? Walk the streets (I didn't know about the curfew on the Aryan side)? Where would I go? Where would I turn? Was there a place for me in this world?

In the morning I ventured downstairs and headed once more for the house where earlier I had found Ruth. This time she came to the door right away.

"Yes, what is it?"

"Ruth, excuse me, but I am all alone now. The family is gone. And I am looking for Zev. Please, is he here?"

"Er … yes, Zev is here, but he can't see you now."

"But, Ruth, what am I to do? Where do I go?"

"I can't help you. Where were you when we gave the order for everyone to assemble? We needed someone to run errands."

"Ruth, I told you, I was in the hospital. Later my father would not let me leave him for a second. The first chance …"

"And I already told you: right now we have to think of how we're going to take care of our leaders so that at least some of them survive to carry on. 'Can't leave my father … '"

She was closing the door.

"Ruth, wait, please, tell me where to go. Are you going to fight?"

"I don't know yet. If we do, it's going to be a fight to the death."

"Let me fight too."

"There's nothing for sure, yet."

"Where do I go, Ruth?"

"I told you: get on the train, on the transport, and jump. Then work your way to the Lublin forests. That's all I can tell you."

She closed the door. I walked downstairs slowly. "You mother of a bitch, I'll show you. I will get out on my own and then I won't need you anymore."

There was only one thing to do: head for the trains.

I ran into one of my former teachers in the street, a friend of my father's. The man, usually dignified, was speaking in a daze.

"Where are your parents?"

"They're gone."

The professor nodded his head. "I don't know anymore ..."

I joined a group heading for the Umschlagplatz. We passed the gate. There were perhaps a hundred in the group. I didn't see any children. The square was deserted; SS men, fully armed, strutted back and forth. Jewish policemen marched alongside us, shouting commands: "Look straight ahead. Do not talk, do not sit down. Remember, look straight ahead!"

A row ahead of me stood a young man with a horribly swollen face. I was able to see that the swelling had practically closed off both of his eyes. Suddenly one of the SS men spotted the man. He forced his way into the human row raining blows on the man's face with a rubber truncheon. I couldn't help feeling that what caused this heinous brutality was the German beast's apparent belief that, since the man had been brutalized before, he must be guilty of something. I only heard moans and thuds. No one dared turn their heads. SS men were firing their guns.

In a half hour, the group was marched and herded into a white stucco building. We were dismissed and told to disappear inside. I wandered from floor to floor, from room to room, trying to figure out a safe niche. All doors had been ripped out, all rooms were empty. People were lying everywhere on the floors, some bleeding from blows, others from bullets. Urine and excretion were smeared everywhere.

I learned that this building was situated just behind the Jewish hospital at the Umschlagplatz. On the other side were the railroad sidings where the loading was going on.

✝ ✝ ✝

A day and a night had passed. There was no food and no water. People were dying, people were lamenting, people were staring in blind stupor.

Several times a commotion could be heard downstairs, shots and curses in German and Ukrainian.

"They are loading," someone said.

"So why don't we go and get it over with?" I said.

"No, run upstairs. Many are beaten or shot before they even get to the train." We ran to the uppermost fourth floor until the commotion died down.

✝ ✝ ✝

On the second day, I decided to venture downstairs. Somehow I made my way across a fence and into the back of the hospital. The long halls of the ground floor were jammed with hospital cots. Upon them lay the wounded. Doctors and nurses were scurrying among them.

"Doctor, please, will you help me?"

"Doctor, I can't stand the pain anymore. Please, do something! Kill me, have it done with!"

"I can't help you: we've run out of anaesthetics."

"Do it without it—Doctor!"

I came upon a young woman, perhaps twenty-five, lying on one of the cots.

"Sonny, please come here."

"Yes, madam …"

"Sonny, please, get me some water. Water, please."

There was something special about this woman. A sensitive face, long blond hair. I promised and came back later with some water.

The woman had a bullet lodged in her side. Doctors said they didn't know when they'd get around to operating. People were brought in with battered faces, some gravely wounded. She was not on a priority list as long as she was conscious.

Her name was Helena, Miss Helena Szubiewska. She had come from Hrubieszow, in the district of Lublin, and she was a Polish Catholic. She had been visiting Jewish friends in the Ghetto with whom she was doing business—bringing in food and taking their valuables to sell. On several occasions she had climbed the wall, each time bribing the black-clad Baltics or the Ukrainians. This was to have been her last time, since she thought it was no longer safe to come into the Ghetto. After she had paid off the Ukrainian guard, he shot her as she was climbing the wall. She fell down into the Jewish side. She was taken to the hospital. In vain she was asking everyone to contact the Polish police; no one cared, no one bothered. Life was cheap. All life was ending, anyway.

"Please, sonny," she was beseeching me, "what is your name? Joseph?—Joziu, that's better. Oh, God, I am hurting so … please don't leave me, Joey, I beg you. You are my last hope. You have … oh, God, such beautiful blond hair and … blue eyes. You don't look Jewish at all. Please go to the Polish police. Tell them."

"First I have to ask the doctors to help you."

I tried. I pulled the doctors' sleeves; I pleaded. To no avail. There were many more urgent cases, I was told.

"She'll still live for a while. We have others who cannot wait. What is she, you said, Polish? What was she doing in the Ghetto, anyway? Probably smuggling. Why should you care?"

Helena had bits of food which she clutched. She shared it with me. Somehow I sensed that the door to my survival led through Helena's. I slept on the floor next to her bed.

The next day I said, "Miss Helena, I have an idea. Suppose you give me your cross; I'll go to the Jewish police and tell them that I'm your son. I'll ask them to take us to the Polish police."

"I can't give you my cross, Joziu. This is the last salvation to cling to, dear Jesus … help me. But go and tell them that you are my … relative from Hrubieszow."

"No, your son."

"All right … my son … you don't look Jewish."

I went outside and approached a Jewish policeman. I laid it on him. He took me to the Polish police precinct adjacent to the square. At the precinct they promptly locked me up in a cell. An hour passed, then two. I was sure that I'd be taken outside and shot any minute.

The door finally clanked open and I entered the precinct room.

"You, shithead!"

"Me, sir?"

"Yes, you! Come closer. Where're you from?"

"From Hrubieszow, sir. My mother is in the Jewish hospital here … please, she's wounded. Please, help us."

"What the hell were you doing in the Ghetto?"

I was stunned. I hadn't thought of that. I needed time to think of an answer.

"Excuse me, sir?"

"I'll give you 'excuse me, sir'! You son of a bitch! He knows very well what I asked him; he needs time to weasel out. Take off your pants!"

"Take off what, sir?"

"Down with your britches. *Now!*"

I did as I was told. The police sergeant took one look.

"A Jew bastard! Out with him!"

Now I was sure I was going to be shot outside—a matter of seconds. I was told to follow a policeman, the same one who had brought me in. In the doorway I turned.

"Sir, I'm sorry I lied to you. I am Jewish. But there is, truly, believe me, a Polish lady wounded, lying in the hospital. I only posed as her son after she had asked me to call the Polish police. I thought I could save myself, too. I swear, sir, please believe me. At least save her!"

"Take him out!"

The policeman took me back to the Jewish police.

"He's a Jew, that little bastard, he was lying."

"Sirs, I'm sorry I was lying—I wanted to save myself, too. But I swear there is a Polish lady lying wounded in the hallway. Go look! Please, at least save her. She'll die."

Nobody bothered about dying. There was death all around.

This time I wasn't allowed back in the hospital. Instead, I was thrown into the same white stucco building.

The next day, when shrieks of "*Heraus!* [Out!]" were sounded, I cautiously proceeded downstairs and joined a crowd being loaded after the last roundup. The trains stood ready to receive the load.

Earlier, through a window in the building, I had watched the procedure of loading the long column. I realized that survival depended on being one of the first to enter the cattle car; on being able to rush to the side opposite the sliding boxcar door, right under the windowlike opening wrapped in barbed wires, to get air into one's lungs. I had watched the other boxcars being loaded to their utmost capacity, with as many pressed inside as the rifle butts could produce. Survival meant air.

When my turn came, I stalled until the door to the next boxcar was pulled open. I had been a top sprinter all through my school days. When the command was given, amidst SS dogs straining at their leashes—"*Juden los! Verflucht! Noch mal!* [Jews out! Damnit! Once more!]" followed by Ukrainian curses: "*Skarey, yevreye! Yibi vasha mat'!* [Faster, Jews! You motherfuckers!]"—I was the first to jump into the next empty cattle car. Small of build, quick and wiry, I was able to shoot out through and under the barbed-wire opening. SS dogs were already gnawing into the laggards; whips sliced the air; moans cascaded and shots ricocheted. The SS got to those that didn't move fast enough. The Ukrainians were swinging their rifle butts, but I managed to leap aboard and scramble for the window.

☩ ☩ ☩

A good half hour had elapsed since I had asked the bearded man to help me jump.

The fat man was snoring; the bearded man's lips moved listlessly. He was praying. Nathan half-squatted against the wall of the freight car, his eyes dull and apathetic.

A stupor, like a heavy sleep, engulfed me. And then, suddenly, a creeping cold fear was upon me; I was scared to jump out, into the cold night, alone … at least here I was sharing my fate with others, there was the comfort of other human bodies to cling to. Out there: a wave of air that would hit me and sweep me into … other places, perhaps worse loneliness that would hatch more isolation, gaping, endless.

Then a few scrambled thoughts surfaced.

Ruth … that bitch Ruth who denied me my chance to fight for the Cause … I will show her; I will prove myself a good shomer. And then my mother looking at me with her special tenderness before I'd gone into the hospital and, as if sensing she would never see me again, saying quietly: "Remember, my son, if you are ever deported, ever put on those trains—with or without us—you must jump and save yourself. Promise me." I did. Then she gave me her autumn jacket to stay warm in the hospital, her quiet, doting eyes finding mine.

"When this is all over one day, you may be one of the few survivors … who knows, perhaps the only one. With your blond flaxen hair and blue eyes just like me, you could easily pass for a Gentile. Even most Jews take you for a goy." She paused. "You will then have a special responsibility to bear witness, to tell the world what has been done to us. Promise me, son."

I was still wearing her jacket.

✠ ✠ ✠

Something began to grow inside me … and the fear got weaker and I was shaking Nathan, saying, "Nathan, help me with the barbed wire. Nathan, will you make the jump with me? Please, Nathan, you and I, we are young, we've got to live. Nathan!"

Nathan opened his eyes a trifle wider.

"All right." But his expression had not changed. "Which way do you want to jump?"

"Well, there are two ways. I know from doing it on the streetcars. One: you jump in the direction the car is moving, that's if it doesn't travel too fast. But if it's going real hard, you face the inside of the car and swing your body toward the rear, you swing the right shoulder back. That's your best chance."

"But what're you going to hold on to?"

"Help me undo the wire; then we get pushed out and cling to the window with both hands. Get me up here, come on."

After repeated pleas, the bearded man agreed to hoist me upon his shoulders. I began to work the wire. My hands bled again but I kept on working.

In shifting positions and hoisting me upon Nathan's shoulders, we shook the fat man awake.

He murmured, "What're you doing? It's certain death out there! What're you doing?"

"Let the boys go," the bearded man said. "They are young. Let them save themselves."

The fat man was too tired to protest.

One by one, I twisted and bent the rotting wires. When I could go on no longer, I came down, and the bearded man hoisted Nathan up. Ten minutes later I was up again, and soon the small window stood bare and free. The entire opening was about two feet wide and a foot high—enough for a skinny kid to squeeze through; impossible for a grown person to negotiate.

"Which one wants to go first?" the bearded man was asking.

"I will," I answered instantly.

Then I understood myself. The SS and the guards who patrolled the train's roof might not notice the first boy dropping off, and even if they did in the darkness, there was a good chance they would miss him, but they surely would be on the lookout for the next one to shoot.

"Tell you what," I whispered. "I jump first, you watch me. I have more experience. Then you go. You walk back along the tracks, and I go forward. This way we'll meet."

"All right."

"Only make it fast. The tracks may be guarded, I heard."

I had heard that the tracks were guarded every 100 meters or so all the way to Treblinka.

"And whistle softly," I added. "That way we will know each other before we can see. Well, let's go. Get me up there."

I was hoisted up until I got hold of the lower frame of the opening. I looked out, barely getting my head through. The train was clacking through the darkness, wheels beating rhythmically over the rail joints. We were moving along a steep embankment. Up ahead I could see the contours of an iron bridge coming at us.

I was getting another push from below.

"Wait, stop. We're approaching a bridge. Can't jump now."

In a minute we were on the bridge, its trestles like a spider web in the night, menacing.

"Let's try feet first. This way it's no good," I offered.

The bearded man and Nathan lowered me, picked me up at the midriff. I held on to their shoulders and heads with my hands, moved my feet up the wall until they found the window. The two kept lifting until my torso was halfway through. Slowly and painfully I twisted around to face the inside and ease myself out. I craned my neck to look down: we were traveling along an open field.

"Now, Joseph," something said, "now, or you'll never have another chance."

A wave of air hit me hard, taking my breath away. The dark night waited to claim me.

Chapter Six
On the Run

I WASN'T SURE IF I could discern two small red lights of a disappearing train, or how long I had been lying there.

"Nathan!" I jumped up, and immediately felt a sharp pain in the back of my head.

It was dark and quiet.

Had Nathan jumped?

I withdrew thirty paces, then moved along the rail line. I walked for a few minutes and then whistled softly. There was no sign of Nathan. A fine mist began to come down. The pain in my head grew duller. It was dark and cold and I was getting scared. German guards might come out of nowhere at any moment.

I walked away from the tracks another fifty yards. Getting very tired, I saw a tree thick with branches. It seemed to offer safety, shelter. I lay down under the tree and covered myself with my mother's jacket.

Later I woke up, cold and wet, turned around, and to prevent being awakened again by the raindrops on my face, I covered my head with the jacket.

✟ ✟ ✟

It was light and the sun was bright orange. It had stopped raining but I was still wet.

Away.

I started to move further from the railroad tracks. About twenty minutes later I came upon a tall, unpainted fence hiding a farmstead. Looking down, I saw potatoes in the field. It was September, just before potato harvest time. "Food! Oh God!"

My hands trembled as my nails dug into the potato field. The potatoes were big. The wet dirt clung to them. I hadn't eaten in days except for the few bites of bread from Nathan.

A dog barked, and the gate in the fence flew open.

"Jesus Maria, you'll get sick from it ... eating raw potatoes." A hefty peasant woman stood there, one hand restraining the dog, the other hand touching her cheek in amazement. "You a Jew? Escaped from the train, yes?" It didn't take her long to put things together.

"Yes, *prosze pani*—Yes, ma'am."

"Well, stop eating these potatoes this minute, I tell you."

"I am hungry."

She gave me a sharp look. Then the look changed.

"You just wait here and I'll bring something out. Stay low now. And don't eat any more potatoes, for Christ's sake." She turned in through the gate. "Stay low, I say. My God, that's all I need. They're running around here like mad dogs all the time looking for Jews. You think you're the only one that jumped?"

She was back in two minutes bringing out a chunk of country-made dark bread, a fresh pat of white cheese wrapped in linen, and a mug of milk.

"Not so fast, Mother of God, Queen of Poland, you'll get sick." She looked around apprehensively. "They kill people here for helping Jews. Go when you finish."

"Where should I go?" I was afraid and began to choke on the food in my throat.

"Don't ask me, sonny. I didn't start the war. All I know—keep going. I can't risk my whole family for you."

I swallowed and managed: "Which way do you want me to leave?"

"Here, take the rest of the food with you, so you can eat it slowly."
She wrapped it up for me. "Now just sneak alongside the grove here:
then you'll find a wheat field. It's tall and you're small; walk west from
there on. And God bless you."

Chapter Seven
Surviving in the Countryside

AWAKENED TO FEEL MY stomach growl. I was hungry and finished off the bread and the cheese.

Then the cramps started. I squatted in the wheat field and moaned, and then rolled in pain among the tall weeds. The sun was hot, the tall wheat steaming after the rain. Cramps had seized me again. I was hungry again and ate a handful of raw grain.

Cautiously raising myself above the tall wheat, I saw barns in the distance. But I was too weak to move. Then, suddenly, I was seized by more cramps. Diarrhea. I used the wheat stems to wipe myself.

I was limp from exhaustion. But my stomach craved something, anything …

✠ ✠ ✠

I was at home in Łódź. The smell of spiced honey cake baked in the kitchen filled the whole house, and I sat with my mother and father and sister in the living room. The well-known poet Eli Blumenzweig was there. He and my father had been writing songs together. The wood in the great (upright, tile-covered) kilt crackled and warmed the room, and the chandelier sparkled with light.

"Tell a story, Daddy," I pleaded. "Tell how you got out of the army."

"Yes," Eli Blumenzweig was prodding his collaborator. "Tell the story, Srul."

"Well, in those days," Father began, "if a man was conscripted into the Russian Army he had little chance of ever seeing home again. The families never knew if their sons had died, or were rotting somewhere in Siberia. Sometimes they came back years, even decades later—old, without legs, without arms.

"World War I broke out, so the Czarist troops had picked up every healthy man they could find—and I was one of them. They took us to the recruitment center and the word was that we would be heading for Kiev in a day or so.

"I knew that I had to make my getaway. After supper we were supposed to stay in our quarters, but there was so much commotion with the new arrivals, a man could walk across the yard without being challenged.

"Now, luckily the wall around the center was built of rocks, and it was easy to find indentations for one's feet and climb.

"So I reached the top and peered over. There was this Russian guard, all shining in his uniform. They really dressed the guards up in those days, I tell you … I crouched low. A half hour went by, then what seemed like an hour. And then, a shikse walked up to the guard. Imagine, a shikse saved me from the Czar's service, maybe saved my life. She walked up to the guard provocatively, swaying her … hmm …"

"Iziu, please," Mother said, "the children are here." The professor froze his jet-black eyes on his wife and held them with fury.

"Go on, Srul, so … what happened?" said the poet, preventing an explosion.

"Together they walked to the left, she taking his arm. They disappeared behind a tree. I took one look and said: 'Now, Srul!' and just like that I jumped and ran."

"Then what, Daddy?" I asked, "Didn't you get hurt?"

The professor looked at his son scornfully for even entertaining the possibility. "Well, I ran and ran and then walked and asked some people. Then I reached a small train station and from there I got to Vienna."

"But, Daddy, you skipped all the details. Last time you told us much more ... And what about the SS, the Ukrainian guards, and the German gendarmes?"

No, these were not the gendarmes. These were Russian troops and it was World War I and my father stood nearby, getting ready to jump.

"Daddy, don't jump, don't, Daddy, they'll shoot," I wanted to shout, but I couldn't find my voice.

✠ ✠ ✠

I woke up in terror. Something hot and wet was touching my face. A dog. He was breathing hard and licking my face. When I sat up, the dog looked surprised, pulled his tail under, and sprinted away.

I fell back again. The stars were shining. At least it was not raining. I was hot all over. My feet were cold, but my face burned and my head ached dully. Where was I? I must be sick or something. Just like any other time when I was sick with fever and there were nightmares, usually a monster with a large black head chasing me and lurking, waiting for me behind the door frame ... then I would get well and everything would be all right ... like when Mother reprimanded me in the Ghetto once a couple of years ago for laughing and giggling, and I said: "Well, why shouldn't I? I know it's bad all around and people are getting killed, and we don't have enough food, but I am only thirteen, you take care of me, I still go to school—there is danger in it and we have to hide the books but that's exciting, and I have a roof over my head ... so why shouldn't I laugh sometimes? You want me to cry all day?" and my mother had to agree ... but now ... where was I ... I couldn't concentrate too well.

✠ ✠ ✠

My God, where am I? I know I must concentrate but just now I can't ... but I must ... try ... if I try I can scale the wall. Wait! There's my father, he's going to jump. Daddy, wait, Daddy, wait, Daddy, wait for me! I can't get up. Wait! I can't run, they'll see me and shoot me. I don't want to die! Daddy, wait for me, don't leave me, you left me when they put you in the line for the transport, you didn't even try to get me back.

☩ ☩ ☩

The sun was up again. A brown-speckled butterfly fluttered its wings noiselessly by and a fat bee buzzed along. The sky held no clouds. I looked up and into the blue. I could not move.

As I lay there I began to pray. "*Wo die Not am größten, ist der Gott am nächsten.* [When danger is greatest, God is nearest.]" That was a German proverb my father had quoted once—when the special restrictive rules for Jews had been adopted and we had first begun to worry about our fate.

"If you are there, God, listen to me! There is no one for me to talk to but you; if I keep talking just to myself, I'll go insane. Do you see what's happening? Do you see the slaughter of innocent people? Do you accept it? Well, we are taught that a silent person becomes ... what do they say ... an 'accomplice' to crime ... what about you? ... What about me, God? What am I to do? Where do I turn? I have no place to go ...

"I am sick, God, I can't move, I am alone, I am scared, I don't know where I am ... God, where are my parents, my teachers, my friends? I want to fight to preserve the dignity, the respect of my people, their honor ... for generations, the way I was taught ... How do I do it? I know I escaped ... well, what was I to do? My father left me ... well ... what was he to do? Do I matter to you, God? I know that I didn't have much use for you ... all right, so I didn't believe in you, ridiculed you ... I still did what I believed in, even if that meant not to believe in you. But if you are up there, make me believe; give me a sign, if you want me to live and to believe in you. What else am I to believe in? Why go on? ... Let's see now. What to do, what to do. God, I think I'll go crazy ...

"Why, oh, why didn't my parents know a single Polish family they could turn to in times like these? It was always "Jewish this, and Jewish that," and "we want you to associate only with nice Jewish boys we approve of" and "we don't want you to have anything to do with the *goyim.*" Damn them, it's their own fault. How can you live in a country surrounded by Poles, *their* country, and all but isolate yourself from them? Why, the only Poles I ever knew were our maid, Vala, and the few actors from the theater who came to my father for music lessons.

Serves them right. Now we could use a few Polish friends. Once I brought home a Polish friend, and I was told not to invite him again …

"But, my God, couldn't we just undo this? Couldn't we wise up and start all over again, this time making sure that we make a few Polish friends who could help us? When we need them? Like the games we used to play, or in sports: we would just stop—like playing ping-pong—and say, "This game didn't count; let's start all over again" … Couldn't we?

"Where do I go, God? Where do I hide? I don't need much, just a corner indoors—and something to drink—not milk, water will do."

☩ ☩ ☩

Another day must have passed.

The sun was up again. I didn't know how long I'd been lying there. My throat was parched. I managed to pick myself up and made my way through the field. As I walked, I remembered for the first time what Ruth had told me about the forests. Where were they? Near Lublin? They were east, I thought, fifty, perhaps one hundred kilometers away? But if I got there, somehow, starving and alone, working my way eastward, stealthily, what was my chance of finding the Hashomer? Would I go up to a farmer and ask, "Excuse me, sir, have you seen any Jews in the forest?" And even if I got there, what chance would they have, how would they resist?

A homestead loomed in the distance. Cautiously, hearing voices, I approached a faded gray barn.

As I passed the barn, I was spotted. There was a whole group of teenagers standing in front of the open barn door.

"A Jew! A Jew! Hey, what you doin' here, Jew boy? They catch you, they'll use you up for soap!"

Crude, loud laughter exploded.

Two swift, large dogs rattled menacingly.

"Come on, *owczarek*, (sheep dog) go get the Jew boy, get him!"

The two dogs sprinted right up to me. I could feel their hot breath an inch from my body. I was scared to move, scared to open my mouth.

"I am not a Jew, please, can you take them …" I heard myself say.

"He's not a Jew. Just look at him: a school uniform on him and a woman's jacket—what you do, Jew boy, run out of school in the middle of class? Didn't like the teacher?"

"Ha, ha, ha! And look at his hair, all shaved off."

A middle-aged man emerged from the barn, his open shirt covered with hay. He took in the scene for a moment.

"That's enough, knock it off," he said quietly. One skinny boy with dark freckles was still laughing. "Enough!" The skinny boy paled and moved away a few paces. His freckles darkened. "Come here, boy. Where you from?"

I was watching the dogs.

"They won't bite you. *Paszol*(Get out) he hissed at the dogs. Like the freckled boy, they, too, shied away, casting their suddenly peevish eyes downward, not daring to look back.

I weighed the answer.

"From the city," I attempted.

"What're you after?"

"I … may I ask for some water, sir?"

"Water? Wacek, run in, get a pitcher of milk and some bread."

The boy was slow. The man snorted angrily in his direction. The boy shot off as if catapulted.

"The rest of you knock it off. You, Marian," he turned to the freckled one, "don't let me catch you, or I'll rip the skin off you."

Minutes later, sitting on a tree stump, I devoured the milk and the bread. The man sidled up to me, wiping his hands against his shirt.

"You from the train?" he asked.

"…Sir?."

"Look at me." The man was weighing something in his mind. "You don't look very Jewish. Tell you what … Hmm … Your folks gone? … Yes? … I see. Well," and he took a deep breath, stretched, and exhaled slowly. "If I were you, I'd go to the priest at the parish house here and tell him you're a Catholic. You know any prayers?"

"Not many, sir."

"Well, tell him something. Tell him you want to be baptized. Then the Krauts can't touch you."

"Are you sure, sir?"

"They wouldn't dare touch you if you're a Catholic. I think so ... Well, I don't know. Go see the priest." He called out again. "Wacek, go get some sausage from Ma. Then take this boy and show him the road." He turned back to me. "Go about four kilometers and you'll see a church. Ask for the priest. Now go. Oh, yes, better not tell him you were here. Remember that."

✠ ✠ ✠

The priest heard me out and scratched his head. He was a burly man of stocky, peasant build. His mouth and eyes seemed disproportionately small in his large, square face. I had the impression the man had never helped or hurt anyone. The priest spoke haltingly.

"Hmm-hmm ... Not an easy matter. Too many Jews around here, all running around the field like rabbits. Tsk, tsk ... And then baptism is not an easy matter, either. Have to register each baptism with the German authorities, there are penalties. And I don't know about this ... seems to me you are still a Jew in their eyes, that's their law ... There was even a couple here, converted before the war ... good, practicing Catholics ... they're gone."

I looked at him with pleading eyes. The priest sighed.

"Well, anyway, you want to learn the faith; I can't deny it to you. Here is a prayer book, study all the prayers. Here. I'll mark down for you what you are to study by heart. You see: 'Our Father,' and 'Hail Mary,' and 'Credo': these you must learn by heart. Study the rest."

"But ... where do I go, sir?"

"Hmm ... Well, you are young; you can sleep any place in the field or crawl into the hay someplace. Come back in three days just to see me. I can't promise you anything."

On the third day, several of the prayers memorized, I went back.

"Well, how is my new Catholic? Ha?" the priest was jovial.

"I have learned the prayers, sir. You told me to see you in three days."

"It's enough to say 'Father' to a priest. If you say 'sir,' everybody knows you're not Catholic."

"Thank you, sir ... Father."

"Well, now," the priest squirmed uncomfortably, "I've thought about it. I can't do anything for you, son. Too dangerous. Too dangerous. You just go on, and ask some people for food, and go on, and perhaps you'll find someone, away from the main track, ask some farmer if you can help him out, for food and board. You see, too many people know me here."

I left. Tears were choking me.

Now the main thing was to think up a brand-new story of my background. Or else how was I going to ask for work? Where was I from? Was I an orphan? Where did I go to school? What street was it on? Wait, wait. One thing at a time. Let's see. I could say that my father was a Polish officer and didn't come back from the war. And that my mother died … from cancer … in the Łódź hospital … My God, I am going crazy. I simply must figure it out down to the last detail and memorize my whole new identity.

✠ ✠ ✠

It was cooler the next morning, and I set out in the opposite direction from the parish house. I walked across the fields, avoiding the people who worked in them. At noon I came upon a small stream. I drank its water and washed my face, after which I stretched out and fell asleep.

I woke up because my body itched. Large white lice were crawling in my clothes. Some, the larger ones, had dark spots in the center. There was nothing to do but pick them off one by one. Most of them I managed to kill by squeezing my two thumbnails together. This gave off a snapping sound. Another louse flattened out, and its blood was left on my nails. Some lice had gotten away from me, and I left them on the ground.

I got up and began walking. Suddenly I heard voices.

"I got her. I got her!"

"Oh, you beast, no, you haven't got me, no, you haven't got me!"

"Wojtek, come around the other way! Catch her! She got away!"

I woke up. There was commotion around me, and voices. Carefully I raised myself and looked up over the swaying wheat.

There was a clearing beyond the wheat field. Several boys, about my age and younger, were darting in and out of the field chasing a young, blond girl with a long braid. They were all barefoot. At times they would encircle her, catch her, tumble all over one another. All would be rolling over and falling over the entanglement of legs and feet. The boys wore short pants. The girl, I noticed, wore white cotton panties with peasant-style laces at the bottom.

Presently, the girl had gotten away again, and she raced inches past me. The boys, giving chase, breezed by. One of them spotted me.

"Hey … what …"

He called out to the others.

"*Ej*, Wojtek, Magda, come back … look what I found, come baaaack!"

Soon they were upon me.

"Who are you?"

"I'm just walking."

"What … what a funny jacket he's got … look at him!" said one of them.

"Look at *you*, you look like a beggar with your shirt torn!" snapped the girl back at him.

"Ha, ha, ha!" the others mocked.

"Maybe … hey, you know what … I think he's a Jew … my father says there're lots of them around now. They're running away. Look at his head, all shaved clean. You a Jew?"

"No, I'm not," I said.

"Hey, Wojtek, ask him a prayer," one of them said to the boy who had questioned me.

"Go ahead," he repeated.

"I pray to God, not to people."

"Oh, yeah?" said Wojtek menacingly. "Let me hear you say a prayer to your guardian angel."

"You don't know your prayers either, you stupid ass," said the girl, Magda. "The other day he got himself all fouled up in his 'Credo.'"

"Oh, yeah? I'm going to tell Father you used dirty words," complained Wojtek.

"You go ahead. And I'm going to tell your father you were feeling me all over when you fell on me."

"I wasn't. Liar!"

"Yes, you were!" She turned to me. "Don't listen to this stupid calf. Here, *you* catch me!"

And she ran away. I followed her. I had been a top sprinter in my school and the best all-around athlete. Magda zigzagged her way across the field with me in pursuit. Soon my legs gave way. I couldn't catch my breath and slowed down to a walk.

"Come on, catch me," she was calling. She turned back, brushing past me. I lunged; we fell. She smelled of fresh milk and earth. She pulled free just as several of the boys tackled me.

"Stop ... now, come on, boys!" I was out of breath.

Magda started swatting the boys on their backs, their faces, kicking them. They raised themselves up.

"You stop now, all of you, or I'll tell Father, upon Christ's wounds!"

"Let's go bake some potatoes," said the tallest boy.

"Yeah, let's go."

They ran off about twenty yards picking up raw potatoes from the ground. Magda kept her distance from me.

"You look different, though. Where are you going?"

"I'm looking for a job ... tending cows."

The boys made a fire, and soon the potatoes sizzled. The smoke was tickling my nostrils. I had been taught never to ask for food until offered.

"Give him one, too," said Magda. "What's your name?"

"Jòzef .."

Magda was unlike the girls I knew. Bold and lithe, she was gutsy and vibrant. All the girls I knew in the Ghetto were serious and quiet.

The meal was over and the sun was setting.

"Let's go back, or we'll get a thrashing."

"Yeah, we'd better go."

The group headed home. Magda turned back.

"Go down past the grove, on the left, there's a barn. Crawl into the hay. Tomorrow tell the farmer you want to tend his cows. He needs someone."

And she ran off with the others. "See you."

I watched her skip away, hopping twice on each foot, for merriment. I saw only her long beautifully curved legs topped by the gaily flowing laces of her panties and her long braid bobbing irregularly and reluctantly falling in with her sprinting pace. Then I was aware of being all alone again.

The sun was setting and the country odors were filling the air. A gentle wind carried them, at times separating each aroma, at other times blending them into concoctions of intoxicating strength.

I walked slowly in the direction pointed out by Magda, breathing in country smells I knew from my childhood. There was freshly cut hay somewhere off in the distance; the smells of horses nearby, of cows and of manure; the aroma of potatoes, of wheat and turnips.

Next to the barn was a spacious house. A dog snorted. The door opened and a burly man of fifty emerged.

"Praised be Jesus Christ," I said. I remembered people greeting the priest in this manner.

"For centuries and centuries. Amen."

"I wonder, sir, if you might need a boy to help around the house … take care of the livestock …"

The peasant eyed me for a moment. He scratched his back.

"Come into the house," he mumbled.

Over a large black stove where several pots simmered stood a woman, all encased in skirts, aprons, and head scarves.

"Old woman, you want a cowhand?" the man said, as if she were hard of hearing.

"I don't care. Why you asking? You know we can use one."

She turned again, this time eyeing me fleetingly.

"What can *he* do? Couldn't even raise a bale of hay."

"A cowhand, I said," the man shot back while seating himself imperturbably on a wooden stool and motioning me to do the same.

The woman didn't answer. She was setting the table. Again she eyed me.

"Himself from where?"

"Stuff them questions," said the man. "I'm hungry. Let's have the food over here, and a spoon for the kid. Talk later. Here," he said, handing me a spoon and inviting me to share in the meal.

Two strapping laborers walked in followed by a boy and a girl, about nine and seven.

Everyone sat down. In the center of the table the woman placed a large bowl of mashed potatoes, another bowl of dumplings, and, in front of each person, a mug filled with cold buttermilk. She poured melted lard with cracklings over the potatoes and the dumplings. The head of the household helped himself first. Everyone followed, digging into the two bowls.

There was hardly any conversation. The children did not speak unless spoken to.

After supper the woman sat down to sew. The man scratched the back of his neck.

"So himself ... where did you say you from?"

"From Warsaw, sir. I am an orphan, and I lived with my aunt, but she took sick. She will be in the hospital for some time, so I wanted to help out and maybe ... I can be of some use to you."

"Well, I do need someone to take the cows out and stay with them all day. You done this before?"

"Once, in summer ..." I was lying.

"Hmm ... we ... spend the night, and we'll see tomorrow. Old lady," he said, turning to his wife who had been listening without lifting her eyes from her sewing, "fix up this boy here over on the bench by the window."

The woman got up silently.

From the inside of a window box, which served as a bench, she took out a couple of blankets, spread them out. Then she fetched a large old sheepskin from the adjacent room adding that to the heap.

"There," she said.

Eventually, the kerosene lamp was moved out into the next room, and I was left alone to sleep.

The conversation in the next room kept up, at times becoming animated. Now and then the voices would drop. The young men were off to the barn to sleep.

Before they had left the room, I had knelt down by the bench, stealing a careful sidelong glance to make sure that my preparations for prayer were noticed. But soon I froze in my posture of prayer, listening for every word, every sound coming from the next room.

I strained but stopped short of sneaking up to the door to eavesdrop. In the event someone suddenly opened the door, being caught would be worse.

The woman's voice sounded more prominent. Now and then the man's voice would rise, seeming to reprimand the woman, but she kept coming back surprisingly strong.

It was very late when I fell asleep.

It was near morning. The man stood above me.

"Listen kid," he said. "I thought about it. You spend the night, so long as nobody saw you. In the morning you'd better go."

"But ... why, sir? ... I thought ..."

"It's better this way.

"But, sir ... have I done something ... please tell me ..."

"Well, I don't want trouble, that's why."

I sat nailed to the spot. Something was choking me. Outside it was raining.

"Goddamn woman. But I guess she knows what she's saying. You a Jew, right?"

"No, sir, I told you ..."

"Look, kid, I don't care. Out here not too many people come around. If somebody squeals on you, I don't know nothing. But I guess she's right.

"Right, sir?"

"Well, you just speak too good Polish, that's why. We've seen city folks here, we even had a boy from the big city once here to help out for the summer. They don't talk like you. You got to be Jewish; you speak too good. You got no papers, no nothing. I can't keep you. I would like to, but ..."

He got up and went outside, cursing.

☩ ☩ ☩

"And go with God!" the peasant called after me.

I crossed one field, then another. Two children were tending cows. They spotted me. When they came near, I recognized the girl with the long legs, Magda.

"Good morning, Magda," I said.

"Don't come near me, you hear?" shouted Magda. "I heard about you, you are a Jew. Why didn't you tell me then?"

She pulled the boy away with her.

Later that day I came upon a village, knocked at the first door and asked for food. A young peasant woman came out.

"Better get away, son. We just had German gendarmes coming through here. They're looking for Jews. Go, son, get away, hide in the fields."

But there was no time to get away. I saw green uniforms at the end of the road. I ran up to the first barn, climbed up and hid in the hay, and stayed there the rest of the day.

Later I pulled out the small prayer book given me by the priest and started reading the prayers. Some I already knew by heart. Others appeared mystifying. Each verse started with the name of a saint followed by the chorus "pray for us." I wondered what that meant. The long prayer, which ran for pages, was entitled "Litany." It didn't make much sense yet somehow it instilled awe and conveyed a hidden mystery. The prayer repeated itself time and again, with but small changes. I found comfort in the safety of the repetitions until it seemed that whoever heard them out could not refuse them. I slept in the hay that night. The next day I left the barn cautiously.

An old peasant dressed in a homemade wool jacket, buttoned up at the top save for a white collar, wearing a visored cap, walked by slowly.

"Praised be Jesus Christ," I attempted.

"For centuries and centuries. Amen," murmured the man.

"Excuse me, sir, have you seen the gendarmes this morning?"

The old man spat out, "They're gone, the Anti-Christs."

"Thank you, sir."

The man looked at me and swore again. "*Czort ich* … The devil should … What's come over this country?" He walked on shaking his head.

Two weeks passed. I slept here and there begging food and heading east toward the lands the Germans had not yet occupied. I had thought of heading for the forests in the direction of Lublin but did not know where to find the Hashomer there. What could I say, bound eastward, I asked myself again. "Have you seen some Jews, sir, hiding in the woods?" It made no sense. Still, the failure to search for the Organization gnawed at my heart.

Occasionally I succeeded in getting myself hired as a farmhand. But it never lasted longer than a day and a night. Invariably someone would get suspicious, questions would be asked, and I would be told to leave. No one harmed me. But the peasants were frightened. They could take no chances. The Germans had circulated their threats widely: executions or concentration camp for any aid extended to Jews, or for failure to report the presence of Jews in the area.

Chapter Eight
In the Forest with Soviet Partisans

DAYS CAME AND WENT. I kept getting away from the path of the trains from the Ghetto. By trial and error I kept improving my fabricated story of who I was, where I hailed from, and where I was headed. My hair began to grow.

I soon learned that in those parts of rural Poland a widely accepted custom was for every peasant and landowner to offer a night's shelter to a traveler, be he who he may. Usually it sufficed if a traveler mentioned a far-off village or town as his destination, asking for a night's rest en route and a hot meal. The peasants were under instruction to register a traveler with the village elder first and obtain a slip of paper from him, but those were given out for the asking.

I would sleep in one village one night, then walk on or rest and sleep in the field or in the woods. Whenever I came near my supposed destination, I would feel out the peasants for the name of a still more distant town, passing the name off as my new destination. I studied my prayer book, learning more and more prayers, litanies, and religious invocations. Winter came in November and snow covered the country. Still I trudged on, chancing the next house, and the next, until hundreds of farm lanes, doorways, faces, questions all merged in my mind.

There were times on the endless paths, in the infinite snow, when I was elated, when I thought with pride of what I had done—how I had survived; and I thought: *Wait till I tell them, Mother and Father. Just wait till one day I meet my father and my mother; my, will they ever be proud of me!*

One day, as I traversed a sparse birch forest, all snow white, I saw a woman approach. She kept looking at me as she passed me, and I looked back after her. The woman stopped and turned.

"Praised be Jesus Christ," she said.

I answered her.

"Where to … himself?" asked the woman.

She was in her late twenties, dressed and spoke like a peasant. I sensed something of a city air about her.

"Oh … to Bielsk Podlaski."

"And where from?" she pressed on, her eyes searching.

"From Zambrów. And you, lady?"

"Me too."

We stood looking at each other. Funny, I thought, we're going to the same place, yet we're coming from two different directions.

"Are you …?" I asked.

"Yes … and you?" she pressed again.

"Me what?" I was not ready to admit anything.

"Same thing you asked me." She was adamant.

"I don't know what you mean."

"Come now," she said. "You escaped too, didn't you?"

What if she is not Jewish, I reasoned, and I admit to it, then what? What if she denounces me up ahead, and sends someone after me? Better not rush with any admissions.

We sat down on a tree stump and talked for a while. Only after I made sure that the woman was Jewish did I reveal myself. We decided to travel together, passing ourselves off as mother and son. It felt good not to be alone.

We worked on making up our story. The woman's "husband" now became a former Polish Army officer (with innuendos, silent, to be sure, of "underground" activity) recently imprisoned by the Germans in Zambrów. Mother and son fled to avoid imprisonment, too. "We were out of the house when the arrest came." We wanted to get away some distance from Zambrow where people didn't know us, find employment on a farm with a peasant, and survive the war. Where were our papers? We had none. In our rush to get away, we couldn't get back to the house to fetch any papers.

The first night together we were offered a spacious barn and the hay to sleep on, but the hay itched, or perhaps there were fleas and bedbugs in the hay. After all, all kinds of cowhands had slept there. The woman and I ("call me Maria," she told me) were restless. I kept inching toward Maria for warmth, and she seemed to welcome it for it was November and the icy wind prowled the barn.

I had never been close to a woman. My legs and Maria's were practically intertwined. I vibrated inwardly with the softness of her thighs. She slept at last and I slid my hand along her thigh. It was fleshy, long, and it filled my palm with delight. But Maria woke up.

"What are you doing?" she demanded, drowsily, at first.

"Nothing. I was sleeping," I replied.

"Well, just be sure you are," she said.

Minutes later I tried again. This time Maria sat up.

"Joseph, I don't know what you are doing, but stop it! That's all I need now, to get involved with my 'son.' I tell you stop it, or I will not sleep with you again."

We had a hot breakfast with the peasants the next morning. It was snowing and work was limited. This was the time of year when peasants slept late, ate up their lard and the fruit of their harvests, waiting for spring to arrive. Conversations were long and questions curious. Maria was not well-versed in Catholic rituals, consuetudes, or prayers. The peasants began to exchange meaningful glances. I knew we had been recognized. We had to admit our origin.

The next day we had to move on. Our hosts would not shelter us any longer.

"If this was summer yet, see, we could have you milk the cows … the boy we'd send far out in the field. Nobody's business. Nobody see. Come night, go up on the hay, sleep it out till next day. But this way … what're we going to do with you? People drop in, out of nowhere, swap gossip, just look in. One look at you, they ask questions. Out here, you look and sound different, people get curious. God forbid, what's gonna happen? Best move on, spend here a day, there another. You always get a meal; people don't hold back on food out in the country. See?"

There was the country outside, endless spaces, sheathed in deep snow and cold, wet flakes that blurred the vision and made us sleepy and hopeless.

At night, if we slept together in barns or spare rooms, unheated, we whispered, searching for some credible pattern of fictitious origin we might latch on to.

"We keep going, here a day, here another, we'll look every day for peasant huts away from the village, till we find someone who can use us," Maria said. "I can sew and embroider, and you can help around the house."

But peasants were not buying our story. In summer, city folks would seek farm work for food and shelter. But who but escapees would wander across the open country in winter searching for jobs?

Each time we spent the night, we delayed our morning departures as long as possible. Usually we would start out in the early afternoon, brave the deep snow until we spotted another out-of-the-way house. We would knock and ask for shelter for the night.

More and more, too, we argued. Each accused the other of mistakes in conversations with the peasants, of inattentiveness. Mutual recriminations abounded.

Gradually, I began to resolve to dump my adopted "mother" at the first opportunity. My chance came soon enough.

It was past midnight when I was awakened sleeping on a bench in the kitchen of a peasant house. The dogs were barking and straining on their chains. The peasant came in from the other room, his sheepskin thrown over his coarse white nightshirt, kerosene lamp flickering in his hand.

"What in hell …" he murmured as he reached for the door.

Five heavily armed men barged in, forcing him aside.

"Old man, kielbasy and vodka," ordered one of them, a baby-faced man with small feet. Despite his looks, he was clearly in authority.

They were dressed alike; after they shook the snow off, I saw that each had three-quarter-high boots, parkas, and fur hats of a faded yellowish color. They spoke Russian. Each had an automatic rifle with large, round clips.

The peasant awoke his wife, and together they soon served plenty of bread, cold cuts, and jugs of vodka.

I remembered some words in Russian which my mother, who had attended a Tsarist Lycée, had taught me and, interlacing them with Polish, I asked the men who they were. They were Russian soldiers, they said. After the Germans had attacked the Russian forces treacherously in 1941, they were surrounded and separated from their units. Since then it had been the woods for them. They were still in the service of the Soviet Army as they turned into partisans, and Vanya was their commander.

"Please, may I go with you?" I said. "I am Jewish, and I speak some Russian, and I know many Russian songs, and I want to fight the Germans with you. Please, may I go with you?" The stream of words came out desperately.

The peasants appeared stunned that they had given shelter for the night to a Jew; for me, it was betting on the last card.

The Soviets talked about it for a few minutes. One of them, the tallest, a blond man, about twenty-six, with sensitive features and a gentle manner, was looking at me all the time, smiling. He was winking his eyes at me now and then.

"Yes, we'll take you with us," he said to me. "But not your mother."

"She's not my mother. I just picked her up."

"You gonna leave her behind?"

"I want to go with you," I insisted. "She's nothing to me."

"*Vot, molodziet* [Thata boy]," laughed Petya. "He'd rather go with us than with a woman, ha, ha." And he put his arm around me.

"Get your clothes together."

I reached for my jacket.

"What?" said Petya. "This all you gonna wear? In all that cold?"

"That's all I have," I said.

"Mister," Petya beckoned, "*Idzey siuda*. Come here. Get something warm for this boy here. A sweater and a warm jacket."

Reluctantly, the peasant brought out a torn sweater and an oversized gray jacket that buttoned up like a military tunic.

"*Vot u tiebia haroshy korman tiepier* [You sure got nice jacket here]," smiled Petya contentedly. "There you are, all dressed up."

Two hours later I left with my newly acquired saviors. I was now in the service of the Soviet Army.

As we were preparing to go, Maria approached me. "What about me? Aren't they going to take me, too?"

"Speak to the commander."

Maria tried to speak with Vanya, but he just shoved her aside.

"*Uhadziy.*" Get away.

Maria turned away and cried.

✚ ✚ ✚

That night we marched for a few hours. Then they picked a small clearing deep in the woods, made a fire, and lay down to sleep. Petya showed me how to face away from the glow while warming my feet at the fire. The Soviets were fearless and downright arrogant in their defiance of the Nazis.

That night and for several consecutive evenings, they sang Russian songs, drank vodka, and later fired several salvos from their automatic weapons in the air. Petya showed me the round magazines which were clipped to their arms, containing forty-five rounds of ammunition. He even let me pull the trigger once. I was not sure whether these salvos fired into the air were to defy the Germans, to bolster their animus, or to discourage German forays into the thick, forbidding Polish forests. The Soviets talked intermittently about *desants*—air drops which were meant for them. Indeed, at times distant roars of airplanes were heard, and then the exchange among the Soviets became animated. "The Nazis," boasted Petya, "are scared shitless of the forests; they'd never touch us at night. This is our territory."

They seemed to know exactly where they were going. Each night they would shift locations, marching ten to twenty kilometers through the woods, each time emerging in what seemed like exactly the right place, a deserted peasant house they were headed for. In some places, they seemed to have been expected. This was the Byelorussian territory of Eastern Poland, the country of Łomża, and several of the houses they entered at night appeared to have been known to the Soviets from their previous forays.

Toward the morning sometimes, they would enter yet another house where they would order just the type of breakfast and vodka they desired. They drank glasses of vodka in one gulp. One of the partisans was always on the lookout for surprise visitors. Anybody approaching the house was herded in and not allowed to leave until one hour following the Soviets' departure.

As a rule, there was not much chance of a subsequent denunciation to the Germans, since the peasants—few of whom were very sympathetic to the Nazi occupiers—were caught in the middle; if they resolved to report the Soviet "visit," they would be subjected to retributions by the Nazis should the ensuing grilling turn up any evidence of support for the partisans with food and drink; on the other hand, the peasants stood to suffer a great deal more from the avenging guerrillas in case they talked. The forces of the dark forests, be they Soviets, Polish partisans of the left or right political spectrum, various escapees roaming about more or less armed, or just plain bandits, returned sooner or later; and the revenge was always mighty: fire set to everything in sight or, worse yet, the slaughter of all the livestock, and even everyone in the family.

And so the dense, unending forests of the Eastern Polish countryside, especially during the long winter, offered sanctuary for every kind of outlaw, which covered Jews, Polish patriots grouped around several partisan organizations, and remnants of the Soviet Army, as well as plain bandits and criminal elements. There was little cause for any one of these forest bands to trust any other at a chance encounter and, indeed, a great many reasons for them to fear one another. Frequently, marauding bands fought with one another.

One night we came upon a group of Jewish women hiding in a barn. The Russians ordered the Polish peasant to lay out plenty of hot, mashed potatoes, melted lard, sausages and vodka. The Jewish women, crouching with cold and fear, were invited to share in the feast. There were about eight of them who had escaped from nearby small-town ghettos; some came from Bransk, others from Bielsk Podlaski. A few wore their best fur coats. They were silent and distrustful, but they soon warmed up after glasses of vodka which the Soviets insisted they down with them.

"Let's have some fun," the soldiers repeated. "Death to the Germans."

Later, everyone buried himself in the fluffy hay in the large barn. Food and drink filled my body and I fell asleep.

But during the night I half woke. I thought that I heard frantic whispers, accelerated breathing coming from several directions, deep moans and laughter. I even thought that I heard some Jewish voices praying and invoking God's mercy. But I was not sure.

Next morning one of the women approached me. She had deep shadows under her eyes.

"*Nu*," she said, "what's a nice Jewish boy doing with a bunch of animals—you *are* Jewish, no?"

"What do you mean, 'animals'?" I retorted. "Listen, lady,"—I tried to take on the recalcitrance of a Gentile boy addressing a second-class citizen—"better watch what you are saying; these are my friends."

"Friends? A *choliere* [cholera] should strike them," she swore in Yiddish. "You and your friends, *takie*, so now what's gonna happen when half these women get pregnant when they're on the run? *Goteniu, Goteniu!* [Dear God, my God!] Ha."

She shook her head, her sad eyes looking at me with tragic contempt. I knew that look. That was the way the Jews looked at the Polish hooligans who used to insult them in my hometown. I walked away quickly.

✛ ✛ ✛

The Soviets left soon after that, first entering the forest in their customary *tiralliere*: each man walking several feet apart. Some two hours later, Petya and Alex, a pudgy partisan, stopped in the deep snow to relieve themselves. As Alex pulled his trousers down, he revealed his bloodstained long underwear.

"Look, brother, got laid with a Jewess. Some great fucking, those Jewish women! Son of a bitch! You got laid all right?" he asked, showing off his underthings.

"*Da*, got fucked all right," smiled Petya.

"Look at me," gloated Alex, "son of a bitch! I got to fuck three of them. Two virgins. A real doubleheader. Yippee!"

I looked away. I felt guilty and ashamed yet stirred with excitement and desire.

Now and then I'd fall behind as I tried to relieve myself in the snow. I was still plagued by repeated cramps and diarrhea. Alex and Petya would turn back to look for me. They didn't want Vanya to get angry; the commander was complaining that I was not keeping up with the rest of them.

As I picked up the pace through the retarding snow, I felt proud of myself, after all. I was a regular partisan now, grown enough to keep company with big, fearless, and even cruel men; men who commanded the forests with their guns and ammunition; soldiers of the great proletarian army; men who were free to handle women in any way they chose. I was going to fight the Nazi beasts shoulder to shoulder with these big men, who smelled of earth, steaming woolens, and vodka. And I felt happy.

They walked all day and most of the night. I was falling asleep and kept asking how long yet, when will they finally stop and rest. But the Soviets kept going. Perhaps they felt that they had to shift location by many kilometers; maybe they had to keep an appointment. I was barely able to keep up and often fell to the rear.

I was half conscious when they reached a farmer's homestead after sixteen or perhaps eighteen hours of marching through the snow. I was stunned to find three other Soviets waiting for them at the peasant house. Hot breakfast was served, and plenty of vodka. The Soviets insisted that I drink and poured me first half a glass of homemade brew, then another. Everyone sang and coarse jokes were told. Huge waves of warmth enveloped me. I rested my head on my arms at the table and passed out.

When I came to, the sun was blinding and flooding the inside of the house. I was alone in the room. I tore myself up from the bench. The Byelorussian peasant entered from the other room.

"Where are my friends?" I exclaimed.

"Out there," the peasant pointed through the window, "the Germans are in the village. You'd better run, too."

I grabbed my jacket and burst through the door. Some fifty yards away I saw the last two of the Soviets wading through the snow on the run. I dashed after them. They had reached the first line of trees in the forest when I caught up with them. Turning back, I could see a few Germans in black uniforms among the huts of the village pointing their rifles at us. The Soviets took positions firing from behind the thick trees before they moved on to the deep safety of the forest.

Some time later I asked, "Petya, why didn't you wake me up? I almost got left behind."

"We did," said Petya. "We shouted at you. But there was no time. We had to get out. I thought you heard us."

✠ ✠ ✠

They reached another village by night. The peasant must have known them, for he seemed familiar with them and even called some of them by their names. Food and drink were served. Vanya and Petya got into a heated discussion. There was something in the air.

More vodka was gulped down. I tried to sip my glass slowly so I could listen in on the Vanya-Petya exchange. *Something must be going on,* I thought, *for I have not seen Petya so upset before.* Petya was always cheerful. His warmly creased face would cloud up only when he saw sadness or suffering in someone else.

And now Petya seemed downright angry. Presently Alex moved in next to me on the bench, which formed a ninety-degree angle behind a large wooden table that stood in the corner of the hut. It was as if Alex wanted to distract me by engaging me in conversation. Vanya and Petya moved away and continued to argue. At one point, Petya slammed his fist against the table. I wished I could fish out more words, but they were speaking fast and overlapping their words. Only here and there I thought I picked out phrases. "He's a child." "Stays behind us all the time," and then Petya said: "That's my business," and then a lot of words, and then Vanya saying "pig," and then I was getting hot and drowsy from the vodka, and then both men raised themselves from the table as if preparing to fight, the others restraining them.

By that time I had a lump in my throat, and cold fear was gripping me for I began to suspect the worst. Then the two men moved to the center of the room, and the dreaded word came from Vanya: "Jew!"

Petya lurched at him, and Vanya reached for his automatic rifle, with the others restraining Petya, and Vanya saying, "You son of a bitch, there are eight of us, whose lives are worth more?" And then there was a moment's silence and Vanya straightened up and said: "He stays behind."

All eight partisans hung their rifles on their shoulders, and I, as in delirium, followed them outside, the peasant following all. Vanya turned to me and said: "You stay."

"But, Vanya, why?"

"You stay. We can't take you anymore."

"Please, Vanya, what am I going to do? Where will I go?" I implored in my combination of Polish and Russian.

Petya, who stood immobile a few steps away, tried once more. "Let him go with us," he said to Vanya.

"Fuck you!" Vanya shouted. "I am the commander and he stays."

He turned to go. I attempted to follow.

"Please, Vanya …"

"Stay where you are!" He pointed his automatic at me.

"Don't, Joseph," said Petya, his voice sounding flat and lifeless, "don't, he'll shoot."

They turned, and their heavy boots squeaked upon the snow. In two minutes they were gone.

I did not move. The peasant led me back into the hut. Minutes later I broke down and cried, and cried.

"What am I going to do? Where will I go?"

"You Jewish?" asked the burly peasant.

I nodded.

"Well, go up the road about three kilometers. There is a big church and the monsignor. He's a good man. Maybe he can help. You can't stay here."

I stopped crying and eyed the peasant. I didn't trust him. I was sure the man just wanted to get rid of me.

But then my survival instinct awakened. I knew that I was the peasant's potential doom, for if caught by the Germans, I could always point a finger at him and brand him as one who'd sheltered the Soviets.

"No, you take me to the monsignor, or else if they catch me, I'll tell them the Soviets were here."

The burly man eyed me slowly. He was reasoning, almost peevishly.

"I can't take you there. Sonny, what d'you think? I'm going to stick my neck out so far? I have a family. You can't stay here. It's not my fault they left you behind."

"You take me to the monsignor."

"No, I can't. You want to lose both of us? I give you my word. I swear on the Holy Virgin. I tell you the truth. You go up this road to the left. And about three kilometers you come to a large church with two steeples."

"I don't know ... what if it isn't there as you say?"

"If I am lying, you come back here."

That seemed to convince me. I could always come back. I had a claim on the peasant, and I could blackmail him. It was my life, but also the peasant's.

Chapter Nine
Finding Shelter with My Savior

I TRUDGED THROUGH THE SNOW on a freezing moonlit night to reach the village of Piekuty Nowe. My feet were getting wet from the holes in my boots. Here and there a flicker of a candle was seen in a remote isolated peasant house, but the monsignor had told me to look out for the village and to count the third house on the left. "Ask directions of no one. Your arrival in Piekuty must go completely unnoticed. And when you get there, look through the windows until you recognize a young vicar. Knock on the windowpane and he'll come to the door. Father Falkowski boards with a family. They are decent people, but in these times you never know. The fewer people see you, the better."

The monsignor had leaned on the balls of his feet, his prominent belly—the insignia of his merited status in the church—providing much-needed frontal leverage. "If you see anything move on the road, get off into the snow and wait it out."

It was snowing steadily. Cold flakes floated toward me, sticking like glue on contact and soon melting into body sweat. The winter flirted dangerously with the uninitiated traveler, luring him to pause and entrust his weariness to its bluish-white blanket. But that, I knew, meant being buried alive; I'd heard many stories of people who died pausing to rest in the snow. To lie down to rest was never to awaken.

Once, when horses snorted up ahead, I jumped off the road and instantly felt myself sinking into the snow. But I stretched my arms out and eventually worked my way back up to the road with great difficulty. I spat some snow out and resumed walking. Three hours later I reached the village and located the house. The windows were glazed with frost. Only through their center could I see anything. There in the glow of a kerosene lamp was a young man reading at a desk. He was wearing a black soutane.

I could not bring myself to knock. Now there was hope. In a minute it might disappear; the open youthful face of Father Falkowski could turn hostile, suspicious, forbidding.

There was a crucifix in front of the desk and an open book. More books were stacked to one side. Presently the young priest looked up as I tapped the window.

Father Falkowski moved to the window swiftly, squinting to see beyond. Then he went to the door.

"Who is there?"

"*Niech będzie pochwalony Jezus Chrystus* [Praised be Jesus Christ]."

The door opened.

"*Per omnia secula seculorum. Amen.*"

I looked into a pair of warm brown eyes.

"Monsignor Perkowski sent me with a message."

"Come in but leave the snow outside."

I was taking my time. I had to sell myself and tried to play for time. Getting away from the door furthered the chance of the sale.

I said nothing until I faced the priest across the desk.

"So …" the priest was searching for something in my face. "Monsignor Perkowski sent you. You coming from him now?"

"Yes, sir."

"Who brought you down?"

"I came on foot, alone."

"Now? At night? Through the snow? Good Lord!"

"The monsignor has asked me to convey his regards and also told me to tell you my story."

The priest's expression softened.

"What is your name?"

"Jòzef Fajwiszys."

"Fajwiszys? Is this Lithuanian?"

I again played for time. Outside, the night was bitter and could kill. "Remember," the monsignor had said, "tell him everything about yourself from the beginning. If he hears your whole story, and likes you, he may help you."

"The monsignor told me to tell you my *whole* story."

"All right. How old are you?"

"I turned fifteen a month ago."

I took a breath. The coziness inside was worth fighting for. This time, at least, I won't have to be constantly on guard to preserve painfully every detail of my assumed identity, playing with mortal danger lest a single word, a wrong inflection—"Jewish" or "big city"— a misplaced gesture betray me. At least now I could talk freely. What a relief, to sell myself by telling the truth.

"Well," I started.

"Before you start, you must be freezing ... and look at your shoes; let me see them. Holy Mary, you have holes in your soles. I must get you something to change into and some hot tea."

"Well ..." I struggled against my careful upbringing, which required that I first demur any offer.

The young priest headed for the door on the left leading somewhere. *He's quick on his feet,* I thought.

"Franny! ... Is Franny there?" called out the priest into the other room and then disappeared.

I looked around, beyond the green light radiating from the kerosene lamp on the desk. Behind me, and next to the entrance door, stood a tall closet made of staunch wood. On the left, the door. Then an overstuffed bed with solid iron rails. Above it, a holy picture.

"How long have you known the monsignor?"

The priest was smiling at me.

"Since Saturday."

"You mean, just three days?" His tone was incredulous.

"Yes, sir," I said, wishing at once I'd said "Father." *So now he knows,* I thought. I took the plunge. "You see, *Father,*" I corrected myself, "I am Jewish."

The priest's voice lowered to a hush, and he curled his lips. "Oh ..."

Father Falkowski looked around conspiratorially as if to make sure there was no one else in the room.

I sensed I was there to stay. Presently, the red eyebrows furrowed.

"But ... Fajwiszys ... it's Lithuanian, isn't it? ... You see, I studied for the priesthood in Vilno and, well ... tell me your story."

There was a knock at the door. "Yes, Father?" Long blond hair, a dark checkered blouse, and a sunny face.

"Franny, this is Joseph. The monsignor from Hodyszewo sent him."

"Oh. How do you do. Welcome." And a smile.

"Sit down, Joey," said the priest. "Franny, a glass of tea for Joe too, if you will."

"Yes, Father, surely."

"I was born in Łódź. My father was a professor of music and a conductor. I went to school until the war broke out."

"What school was that?"

"The boys' branch of the Association of Jewish Secondary Schools in Łódź, it was called."

"Did you graduate?"

"Yes, in June 1939. Actually I started *gimnasium* there; but two months after the Germans came in, they closed all Jewish schools."

"You mean, it was a religious school? What they call a *heder*?"

"Oh, no, sir—I mean, Father—ours was just like any other school. We had all instructions in Polish, literature and history, Greek mythology and Latin, except that we learned Hebrew and the Bible, too."

"You studied Latin ... and Hebrew? Can you write in Hebrew?"

"Oh, yes."

"You don't say ... you see, I studied Hebrew at the seminary and I still know some. But you actually can *read* and *write* in Hebrew?" He looked at me with some incredulity. "Here, I still have a book, I think, there was a prayer written in Hebrew." He perused a few books perched on a shelf by the window, under the picture of Mary. Next to them was a strange piece of furniture that looked like a sawed-off portion of the prayer stalls I had seen in churches.

I fidgeted again. My feet were wet.

"Here. Can you read this?"

I rattled off a sentence in Hebrew. The dark eyes showed affectionate surprise.

"Can you translate it?"

"Well, it means: 'Rejoice, for your God, the Lord, shall always be with you, and even ...' I don't know this word ... and then it says—"

The surprise softened further into open admiration: "What is the word used for God, the Lord?"

"It says *Adonai, Elocheinu* because the word for God is not permitted to be used."

Another grain of suspicion was gone.

"That's right, that's what I learned in the seminary, yes. The Jews are not allowed to say Jehovah ... and what is this letter?"

"That's *alef*."

"Oh, yes, I remember. And that one?"

We huddled over the book, each craning his neck to follow the ancient characters.

The door opened. A swish of Franny's skirt and another cup of steaming tea. For a country girl, she had an unusually sensitive and kind face. There was warmth between Franny and the priest that conveyed some special closeness. I knew she liked him.

"For Christ's sake, Father, the boy is dripping wet snow on the floor. And here, his feet must be wet, too."

Franny made me take off my jacket and the boots with holes in the bottoms, and the stained, dirty, and sweaty rags in which peasants wrapped their feet.

I felt the need to explain. "I haven't always been dressed like this, Father. At home we had nice clothes and good shoes."

The priest smiled.

"Franny, get my old shoes, the ones with the wool lining. Oh, and the gray sweater."

"Father, I could not wear your sweater." I could not look him in the eyes.

"Why not?"

"I have lice."

The priest looked at me steadily.

"Don't worry about that. Later we will boil all your clothes. You have some tea now."

We were seated again after Franny brought the shoes and the sweater and had left discreetly with a knowing smile. The priest was carefully appraising me as I gulped down the hot tea.

"Joseph, are you sure you are telling me the truth? Because you know, I am going to see Monsignor Perkowski this week. And your story sounds incredible."

"Why, Father?"

"Well," the priest was almost pensive in his search for words, "for one, I have never met a Jew in my life who could speak good Polish. Are you sure you are telling me the truth … that you are Jewish?"

"Why, Father, why not? After all, you could see the monsignor any time …"

"Well, out here every Jew I've known—it's true I have known only the rag and trinket dealers going around the village and the storeowner in the village—but they spoke broken Polish."

"Well, you see, Father, Łódź is a big place—a huge industrial center. There were many Jews there who were well educated, who spoke good Polish, who were in part assimilated."

I went on, my feet in the priest's big socks, his sweater around me.

"And your family?" the priest said. "What's happened to them?"

"About my father and my sister, I don't know. They went with a transport and I was left behind. And my mother—my mother they had already taken. Her feet were very bad from frostbite because we had tried, earlier in 1940, to cross into Russia on foot, across the River Bug. And so in the Ghetto, the Germans took the weak first. They took her."

"Hmm," the priest said. His eyes turned misty. "I will pray for them." He paused, watching me gulp down the tea. "We'll have to figure out something for you. You'll sleep on the sofa in my room. And tomorrow morning when you meet Franny's mother and sister—their father is deceased—don't answer any questions about yourself. I'll talk to them. Then we'll see."

✠ ✠ ✠

The next day the priest said, "I have talked to my pastor today, Father Modzelewski, here in the village, about you. Tomorrow I'll take you to see him, but first I must be up early in the morning. Tomorrow is the feast of the Immaculate Conception, December the eighth. Peasants come from all over for the five a.m. prayers."

"May I go with you, Father?"

"If you wish. Only walk behind me, just in case. Stay in the church, pray to the Lord Almighty, pray for your unfortunate people, for your parents and your sister; don't talk to anyone. Oh, yes ... should ... if anything should happen, I only hope you will not divulge with whom you have been staying; say that you have been passing through the village and stopped by the church. If I get implicated ... well ... I have a parish to take care of."

"I never will, Father, I never ..."

✠ ✠ ✠

A day later, a large wooden tub was set up for me to take a bath. "You all cleaned up now, Joseph?"

"Almost, Father."

"Here's the towel."

"Thank you, Father."

"Oh, wait, Joey. Turn around for a moment. Let me see your, you know, your ... birdie."

"Yes, Father."

"I have never seen ... Just what is the difference? I mean, how could a Nazi ... in case something happened and they examined you ..."

"Well, Father, I have never seen a Gentile, either ... birdie, but from what I understand, the tip forms a skin and it folds over."

"I see ... well, if ever anything ... if they asked to see it, couldn't you just show it to them by pressing on the end with both hands ... to make it fold over?"

"I don't think so, Father. I mean, I could try, but what if they tell me to take my hands away?"

"I see ... well, you'd better put your clothes on before you catch a cold."

After we sat down in the priest's study, he turned to me, showing a caring look.

There are several ways, Joseph, in which you can avoid giving yourself away." Outside the wind was howling.

"Like what, Father?"

"Well, first of all, don't be too polite; don't excuse yourself so often as you do. Be bold, speak to the point, don't talk so much, don't qualify everything. Don't use your hands when you talk."

"Anything else, Father?"

"Yes. Now this strikes me as I look at you. Your lips. They are too pronounced, too, eh ... sensual. The Semitic race is supposed to have more sensual lips. You'll very seldom see well-developed lips on a Polish youngster. Their lips form a thin line. Your blue eyes are fine, your hair will get longer so that you will soon cease having that shaven, escapee look. But your lips. Now, look, Joseph, try to squeeze your lips together, like this."

"Like this, Father?"

"No, not completely, that's too much. Just like this ... Yes, that's better. Now try to always remember to hold them together like this. You look less Jewish that way."

"Yes, Father, I'll practice that."

✠ ✠ ✠

"Father, why are they persecuting us? Why don't we have the right to live any longer?"

"You see, Joseph ... you're reading the Holy Gospel which I gave you. How far have you gotten?"

"I am halfway through St. Luke's version, Father."

"Good. So you have read St. Matthew's version. And you remember reading Chapter 27, when Pilate said: 'Whom will you that I release to you: Barabbas, or Jesus that is called Christ?' And when the chief priests of Israel said 'Barabbas' and, in answering Pilate's query, 'What should I do with him?' answered: 'Let him be crucified,' and Pilate washed his hands of it—I believe it is line twenty-five: 'And the whole people answering, said: "His blood be upon us and upon our children."'"

"What did that mean, Father?"

"It meant that the Jewish people had murdered our good Lord and Savior, Jesus Christ, and that they had agreed someday to pay for it. Hence the persecution and hence the killing today."

"But, Father, haven't you been teaching me that a good Christian and a good Catholic loves his neighbor regardless of who that neighbor is?"

"Well, of course, those are the teachings of Christ, and a good Catholic will not have a hand in these atrocities. But the prophecy of the New Testament *had* to come true one day, and it—apparently—is being fulfilled through Hitler. God must have chosen him—in his eternal and enigmatic ways—to become his whip and an instrument of the prophecy."

"I had never heard that before, Father."

"Yes, dear Joe, God in his wisdom has evidently chosen you to learn the Truth and the Light. When this is all over, if you are alive, you may be one of the very few survivors, who knows, perhaps the only one. This imposes duties and obligations. You must pray to our Savior, thank him for his grace upon you, and beg him to lessen the punishments and the plagues being visited upon your unfortunate people. Beg him for mercy."

"But, Father—yes, surely I will pray—but, Father, my parents have never ..."

"And then, Joseph, also the Jews have been exploiting our nation for a long time, as merchants, hoarding money, lending money, what with usury ..."

"But, Father, my parents did not hoard, or do mean business, or commit usury, and many of their friends didn't ..."

"Yes, but many others did. And the rest must now suffer when God has unleashed Attila's whip ..."

✠ ✠ ✠

Two days had gone by. "Starting tomorrow, Joey, I shall be celebrating dawn Mass every morning at six, until Christmas. You can sleep, if you want, but I would like you to attend at least once."

"Why so early, Father?" I was asking.

"Well, it's a beautiful custom in this part of Poland. It's called *roraty* in Polish. Anticipating the Nativity."

"No, I would like to go with you, Father. But … is anybody in church so early in the morning?"

The priest smiled. He had a habit, in explaining anything to me, to assume the attitude of confidential whisper without lapsing into it vocally; instead, his brown eyes would darken and they would fill with a loving humility.

"People are very religious here, Jòziaczku."

Very few people besides my mother had called me by my diminutive, *Jòzieczku*, but Father Falkowski, almost from the outset, called me Jòziaczku, changing the fifth letter of my name. It came to mean something very personal and full of tenderness.

The priest continued. "There are men and women in our parish who get up at three in the morning every weekday during Advent until the Birth of our Lord. Some, the more affluent ones, drive their sleds. But you'll find a number of them, and some pretty old people, who walk up to two hours over the snow to and from church. Oh, yes."

✠ ✠ ✠

I was awakened at five-thirty. The priest was up and dressed in five minutes. I had been sleeping on the sofa in the same room. As a young priest, Father Falkowski boarded with Franny's family. He occupied one spacious room only, and I now shared it at night. Franny would make a bed of the sofa for me every evening. During the day, I stayed in the kitchen with Franny, her mother, and her younger sister. Whenever visitors came, I was directed to the priest's room or, if the priest had company also, into the bedroom.

"Up, up, Jòziaczku, if you want to come. I must be in church in fifteen minutes."

Before we left, the priest said: "Follow me by some fifty paces. Go right, then right again; left on the main road, and you'll see the church on your left. Go in, watch the others, do whatever they do, and after the service come around the back into the sacristy."

The night was dark and the snow crunched underfoot. So much snow had fallen that the huts of the village looked like little babies wrapped up in layers of white diapers.

The priest hurried ahead, and I could barely keep up at the safe distance behind. Twice doors opened and women in goatskin coats and mounds of wool scarves greeted the priest who was sweeping the snow with his black soutane.

The church was set back from the road in a circular clearing resembling a small town square. Two or three sleighs had arrived there already, their owners throwing heavy blankets over the steaming horses.

On the other side of the church stood a light beige modern stucco building put up by the parish just before the war as the new sumptuous quarters for the pastor. It now housed the local, six-man post of the German gendarmerie who had moved the pastor back to the old wooden parish house across the road from the church.

A small orange light was flickering near the altar and the sacristan; a good-looking fellow, about twenty-one, was lighting two more candles. I crossed myself and knelt down on the cold floor just to the right of the main aisle. Some people were already there kneeling and huddled in their coats.

I had been given a rosary by the priest and shown how to say the prayers, one Hail Mary at a time, by fingering the small beads. But now I was not sure whether I was doing the right thing. I looked around cautiously. A couple of people were praying using their rosaries.

I am safe, I thought. *At least I am not doing the wrong thing.*

But then I got fearful. Both persons fingering the rosaries were old women.

What if the rosaries are to be used only by old women, not men at this particular ceremony?

I forgot to ask that of the priest. I could only think of the division of men and women at the synagogue at Łódź; men prayed downstairs and the women upstairs. The two did not mix. What, I thought, if some law exists within the church where women are supposed to do one thing and men another? Better hide the rosary lest someone finds me out.

A tinkling bell was sounded and the priest, in white robes and preceded by two little boys, took his place at the altar. He was carrying the Host covered with an ornamental cloth, one hand under and the other over it. He placed it inside the tabernaculum which stood on the altar, a little golden house for the bread that would become the body of Jesus during the Mass. Then he faced the congregation with open arms, as if he were attempting to take them all into his heart.

A brief, silent service followed, enhanced only here and there by shrill and cheerful bells which the two little altar boys sounded from their kneeling positions on the altar's steps. Intermittently the people sang songs. They would follow the sacristan who would intone various hymns.

By the time the disjointed chorus of voices reached the second strophe, I had learned the melody. As for the words, I watched the people's lips and usually stayed half a word behind them. I was eager to learn my role.

The church was simple but warm. A dozen stained-glass windows represented scenes from the New Testament. The spaces between them were occupied by carved, five-foot-large stations of Christ's martyrdom en route to the Crucifixion at Calvary. The pews were in two sections of varnished wood. Two small altars flanked the center.

I would raise my head whenever the priest turned to face the congregation. I thought the Father looked directly at me each time. I felt safe and warm inside. It was my friend and protector conducting the prayers, leading the people in their supplications, their voices reaching out to God's mercy and protection.

In a way, it was very much like attending my father's concerts, I thought. For my father had also led a large number of people, all united in a chorus of common purpose. Their voices too would reach some distant power, so that they could be cleansed and guided.

"*Wo dein sanfter Fluegel weilt.* [Where your gentler wing abides.]" *Ode to Joy* in Beethoven's Ninth.

"*Gloria, gloria in excelsis Deo*" sang the country people in church.

"*Singt unserm Gott, und macht sein Lob bekannt,*" sang my father's choir in the original German from an oratorio.

"Sing to our Lord, and make his praise known ..."

I could almost see my gaunt father, his bones barely protruding from a year's starvation in the Warsaw Ghetto, conducting a full orchestra and chorus for as long as the Germans had allowed concerts—but only by Jewish composers.

And now Father Falkowski, my new protector, led men and women in prayer to an eternal power.

"From all sin … from your anger … save us, Jesus, from air, starvation, fire and war … save us, Jesus."

"Lord have mercy on us, Lord, have mercy on us …"

I worked my way into the sacristy after the service. I stood in the corner quietly as several peasants, all bundled up, came and went. Some asked for a blessing, some for medical advice, others poured out their problems to the priest, still others asked his opinion of the new German ordinances regulating the delivery of livestock.

The priest, whose face, in the minutes following the service, had still retained a subtle, ascetic look, gradually shed its otherworldliness.

"Father Janiecki is coming to visit me this afternoon, Jòziaczku," said the priest after the others were gone. "He's my old friend from the seminary, has a parish now nearby. I want him to meet you. He loves music and plays the organ himself."

"Should I follow you again, Father?" I asked.

"No, no, it's all right now. You can walk with me." He leaned close and offered confidentially: "You see, if anyone saw us together in the wee hours of the morning, they would know instantly that you are staying with me. But now it's fine. Anybody can walk with me. All kinds of people come to my house to visit and so on, you see?"

I felt happy, for I had read rejection in the priest's morning instructions.

There was hot milk with tasty dumplings for breakfast. The priest was served in his room, and I ate with Franny and her two women in the kitchen.

Later, in his room, the priest said, "Well, Joseph, how do you like it in church?"

He had a broad smile on his face. His smile was contagious.

I told him about the feelings the service had aroused in me.

"Yes, yes," the Father nodded quickly. "You see, my dear, your father's concerts *were*, in fact, a form of religious service. He searched and yearned for eternal beauty and harmony, a spiritual truth. And all this is part of man's search for God. Only, unfortunately, being an Israelite, he had not come to know the Light and the Truth of our Lord Jesus Christ. But in his way, too, he also strove for the Beauty and the Eternal, and he instilled it in others. You should be proud of it. Proud, also, that our Savior has chosen you to go one step further. For I firmly believe that it was no mere chance which brought you to me. Oh, by the way"—and he lapsed into a prankster's air—"did you see a middle-aged woman in a red shawl back at the sacristy?"

"I think so."

"Well, imagine that. She came to me and whispered into my ear: 'Father, who is that beautiful boy praying there, the one standing here in the corner now? … I tell you, I've never seen a young boy praying so beautifully, and singing, too. *Ojoj*, would that our youth were as religious and praying so nicely.' Ha, ha, ha!"

The priest shook with laughter, as if we both had outwitted half the world.

I forced my smile, for I was afraid that someone might have noticed me and gotten suspicious.

"Has anybody, Father … did anybody say anything else?"

"No, no," the priest was still shaking, "don't worry about it. Imagine, 'who is this boy praying so beautifully!' Ha, ha, ha!"

✠ ✠ ✠

The priest's friend, Father Janiecki, had stopped off to see the pastor and was not due for another two hours. The priest settled down to his morning breviary, Franny went out on an errand, and her younger sister attended to house chores.

Their mother, Mrs. Konopka, a devout and quiet woman, was spending a winter morning at a spinning wheel. Mrs. Konopka derived her family name from the village of Konopki—or was it the other way around? I learned that about half the population in the village was named after the localities where their ancestors were born. Some were related; others were supposed to have been.

I opened a book which the priest had given me earlier. It was an anthology of the lives of the saints. It made fascinating reading.

For there had been all kinds of saints: some were humble illiterates, others hailed from the country's aristocracy. There had been sinners and artisans, rich and poor among the church's chosen patrons. Each Catholic had a name given to him at baptism which derived from a saint's first name. The saint would become the infant's patron for the rest of his life.

I got engrossed in my reading. Mrs. Konopka's spinning wheel hummed. It was warm and cozy.

Every now and then I would raise my eyes only to catch Mrs. Konopka's glance. But she wasn't asking any questions.

"What am I to say if the lady asks me where I come from, and how I got here?" I had inquired of Father Falkowski.

"Nothing, Joey. We'll work that out in due time. We'll concoct a real good story for you." Little smiles danced around the priest's eyes. "Firm as a rock, you couldn't cut it with a scythe, ha, ha! ... Meanwhile, don't worry about it. Neither her mother nor Franny are going to ask anything about you, I took care of that. Just don't say any more about yourself than you have to. And remember, these people's lives are inseparable from their religion: hundreds of little customs and sayings. Read, observe, and listen, and speak up only after you are sure of them."

After a while Franny came home, her cheeks aflame from the frost.

"And what *are* we learning about the lives of saints, Joe?" she asked eagerly, sitting down by me.

"I have just started on Saint Thomas Aquinas."

"You are very fortunate, Joe, to have as your patron the Father of Jesus Christ."

"How ... do you mean?" I was not sure. I hadn't gotten that far.

"Well, St. Joseph. Surely ..."

Mrs. Konopka raised her eyes from the spinning wheel. I was quick to sense that a meaningful glance was about to be exchanged by the two women.

"Oh, yes ... of course ... yes. What I mean, I haven't read all about that yet ..."

Immediately I sensed that I shouldn't have said that. It made things worse.

But, just then, Father Falkowski appeared in the doorway, smiling widely.

"Upon Christ's wounds, I declare," Mrs. Konopka jumped up. "I bet Father Janiecki is here, hungry, and we're not ready with the food."

"Now, now, Pani Jadwiga." The priest was addressing her by her first name. "Just relax. The good father has lunched with the pastor. Don't let's get upset now."

He looked at me and the smile widened.

"Come join us, Joey," Father Falkowski said. "I would like you to meet Father Janiecki. I've been telling him about you."

I felt uneasy. As we crossed the small room separating the kitchen from the priest's quarters, I whispered, "Father, did you tell him—"

"Nothing to worry, Jòziaczku. Father Janiecki is like a brother to me. He was my roommate at the seminary. I trust him and so should you. Come."

A tall, lean man, wearing, like the priest, a black soutane, was facing us. I noticed his sensitive face and smiling blue eyes instantly.

"Hello, Joseph," he said, holding out his hand, which I kissed, as was the custom relayed to me two days ago by Father Falkowski. "I have heard about you from Father Staś," he used the priest's Polish diminutive, from Stanisław, "and very much wanted to meet you."

"Yes, Father," I answered. The new priest's eyes reassured me. I had learned to look for signs of danger by reacting to a person's expression immediately on the first introduction. For the eyes of an anti-Semite were the eyes of a hawk searching for prey, the compulsive eyes of an executioner scrutinizing his victim for any sign of fear. There were usually little ironic smiles dancing around such eyes at the sight of fear. But the eyes of the newly arrived priest were kind.

"Father Staś told me your last name—Fajwiszys—kind of unusual, isn't it?"

"Yes, I think …"

"Go ahead, Joseph, talking to Father Janiecki is just like talking to a brother," interjected the priest.

"How did you ever get a name like that?"

"Well, I remember my father saying that his father's name was Feivish. That's what he went by. But when, as a child, he played with other children, why, there were times when someone would get curious about him and say: 'Whose is he? To whom does he belong?' You see, in a small town …"

"Yes, yes," chimed in both men.

"And on those occasions someone would answer, 'He is Feivish's,' using the *genetivus possessivus* in Yiddish …"

The priests exchanged an approving glance on hearing correct Latin. Father Falkowski's look was saying, "Didn't I tell you?"

"And that's how it stuck. Later it became my father's family name: Fajwiszys."

"How interesting," smiled Father Janiecki. "Father Staś was fascinated by your knowledge of Latin. He also told me that you had composed poetry—nay, I hear that you had composed an original, long epic poem, your own continuation of the *Discharge of the Greek Emissaries* by Kochanowski. And in the Warsaw Ghetto, to boot. My, my …"

"Yes, I did, sir … Father."

"Amazing, amazing, simply incredible," Father Janiecki was saying, "and this from a Jewish boy."

The clerics asked questions, exchanged jokes, inquired about my travails. There was a warm, open, and trustful friendship between them. The priesthood was obviously a joyful life for them.

Then the tall priest turned to me again.

"We've heard, of course, of the existence of the Warsaw Ghetto, and for some months now the local people have seen freight trains going through here, loaded with Jews. We presumed they were being shipped to other ghettos, or maybe even to concentration or labor camps. But you were telling Father Staś about … executions, Joseph, even … gas?"

"Oh, yes, Father, that's definite, gas chambers in Treblinka."

"How … Holy Christ, in the twentieth century, a civilized nation, how in God's …" He turned to Father Staś. "One is completely at a loss for words.

"You mustn't mind us asking questions, Joey. You see, both Father Staś and I are country people. True, we've been educated and attended the seminary, and then underground, we've seen this and that. But we're both in our early twenties, our exposure is limited. In some ways, you have seen more and indeed, at your age of ... fifteen, are you, Joseph?"

"Yes," I nodded.

"That's what I mean: at fifteen you have even studied things, Latin, and Hebrew, and—Father was even telling me—you know English ..."

"Yes, Father, I have had two years of it in our secret high school courses in the Ghetto."

"You see, so—as I said—in some ways you even know more than Father and I. And, out here, with the German-controlled press and radio, out in the country we really don't know much, what with the carnage and the killing that's going on, as you say."

"Yes, Father."

Father Janiecki pulled his chair up closer.

"Your escape from the train, your wanderings through the fields and forests, your encounter with the Soviet partisans, how you came here—it's truly miraculous. What I want to know, though, how was it possible to live, to survive in the Ghetto even until now? I mean, being walled in, living in terror ... Where did the food come from, money?"

"We didn't have much money, Father."

"How so? After all, I hear your father was a conductor. Besides, I've always thought that Jews had money ..."

"My father always had contempt for money. He thought that it was below his dignity to even ask for his concert honorarium when it was due. My mother always complained. Money was a necessary ... well ... by-product of his music. When the war started and his income stopped, we ran out of money."

"Well, how did you manage in the Warsaw Ghetto then?"

"Father got something for conducting a choir. Then we were all doing what we could. Mother couldn't work; she had four toes amputated when we tried to cross over to the Russian side early in 1940. First-degree frostbite. My sister did some tutoring and I worked."

"What did you do?"

"My father got me a job at the Ghetto's post office. I helped out in the office at first, did some typing."

"Typing, too? Good Lord, how old were you?"

"Thirteen. I taught myself. I liked it. And there was an opening for a telegram delivery boy. I did that for a while."

"Telegrams? In the Ghetto?"

"Oh, yes, there was a wire service."

"Now, what kind of telegrams would the people in the Ghetto be receiving?"

"Essentially two kinds. One was a sort of coded message—I used to read them, because we had to fold them before delivery, and often there was a lot of waiting, so we would read them."

"Coded? How do you mean?"

"Well, mainly from Switzerland, even from America before she entered the war. All kinds of weird and funny words—like, 'Uncle Shmul sends his regards to Cousin Ryvke.' 'Brother Yankel is feeling better, his temperature is down to 36-1/2.' We knew these were stock market quotations so a person getting it would know what to sell or buy."

"You don't say. And the Germans … didn't get wise to it?"

I shrugged my shoulders. "I don't know. I suppose … what could they do? As long as it was legal to send them … the Germans observed the law."

"You mean *their* law … But you mentioned another kind of telegram."

"Yes. That was a bad one. These were messages, I should say notifications of death, to the families in the Ghetto."

"How?"

"People taken to various concentration camps. They would die, or rather be killed by the Germans. In each case the Germans observed the law, which said that the family must be notified of the death of the next of kin."

"And you had to deliver them?"

"Yes. Each day I would have ten or fifteen telegrams like that. We hated them."

"Well, I can imagine. Bringing those kinds of messages to families."

"Oh, no, Father. I mean, that, too. But then we all got used to that. Everybody expected plenty of death around him. Terror and killings every day. People starving in the streets. Homeless children freezing to death every night in the open. But I didn't mean that."

"What did you mean?"

"We hated delivering the telegrams because there were no tips in them. You see, the pay was very little. The whole job depended on tips. And whenever we delivered a message of death, the people would start crying and screaming, and praying '*Shma Israel*' and all that, so one couldn't very well wait and ask for a tip."

The priests looked at one another. There was silence.

"What did you do with the money?"

"I gave it to my mother."

"And did you work at the post office until … the end, Joseph?" asked Father Falkowski finally.

"It got to be too much walking. I walked many kilometers each day, after I finished attending the school courses. Then I had to study in the evening. There was so little food so I got weaker and couldn't walk so much anymore. Also, I got a better job."

"What was that, Jòziaczku?"

"As an office boy with JOINT. That was a branch of the American Relief Service, the Joint Distribution Committee. I was paid in packages of *ferfelki*."

"*Ferfelki*?"

"Oh, you don't know? Sort of like *kasha*, like barley. That's what we called them."

"I suppose the others weren't so lucky," interjected the tall priest.

"No, in fact, the food packages from JOINT—well, there weren't enough of them certainly for the whole population of the Ghetto so they were given out only—I think two a month—to officials and intellectuals, and artists, to keep them alive. We got two a month because of my father and two more because of my work there."

"And the others … were starving."

"Everybody was, except, I suppose, the very rich who bought things on the black market, smuggled into the Ghetto. But some were dying like flies. Every morning corpses were lying in the street—those were the homeless ones—covered up with newspapers. And then the cart would make rounds and pick them up. Children, lots of them, all skeletons."

"And their fellow Jews wouldn't do anything for them?" asked Father Janiecki.

"What could they do? There wasn't that much food. Every family fended for themselves. Nobody knew how long it would go on. The Germans wanted to starve us out. It made it easier for them ..."

I thought for a moment.

"Then there were the very rich, and the smugglers, and some of the police. They even had a nightclub. On Nowolipie. I used to go past it in the evening. Through the open doors you could see steaming dishes and fat men with their women going out, laughing. I hated them."

"You mean, Joseph, that the Jews of the Warsaw Ghetto would just starve to death without doing something, without protesting?"

I smiled. How was I to explain? "Well, people did what they could. Some sold their possessions to Polish smugglers in exchange for food. As long as they lasted. Others, strong men, volunteered for work details with faces horribly swollen from the beatings. I have seen them. Then there were hungry men prowling the streets on lookout for others carrying food packages. They would snap any package from a person's hand that might have contained food."

"What about the bystanders, passersby?" asked the tall priest.

"That was just it. People were so enraged when someone grabbed a food package from someone else, they would follow the thief and practically lynch him. Women especially would start screaming, crying—I remember one case, a woman had a loaf of bread, cried that she had just sold a coat to buy it, and others catching the thief, a bony starved man in rags."

"What happened?"

"Well, you see, anybody grabbing food from a passerby in the street would first dig his teeth into it, even while running away. So did this thief. And when they caught him, and were beating him, he had his mouth full of bread, and he was dripping blood from his mouth but he wouldn't spit out the bread. The remaining half a loaf was handed to the woman."

"You say, Joseph, that there was little organized resistance?"

"How would you resist? All locked up and guarded? Besides, the Jews, after centuries, didn't believe in resistance, only adjusting themselves to circumstances. Also, the rabbis have taught that bloodshed was a great sin. Except Hashomer Hatzair—well, I heard one or two other organizations."

"What was that?"

"Well, in a way we were like your Boy Scouts, but in addition we believed in the great Jewish tradition, that is, that our ancestors were a brave race, only the centuries in the ghettos of Europe had intimidated us, and then the rabbis considered any bloodshed a grave sin, so that they forbade resistance. While we thought that, if the chips were down, Jews should fight against the Germans, even to the death."

"But, Jozieczku," interrupted Father Staś, "what chance would a few thousand Jews in the Ghetto have against the German Army? After all, they have defeated our own country of thirty-three million people and the mighty French."

"Well, Father, you see, of course we wouldn't fight them until it became obvious that they were clearly out to exterminate us. Until then, we had to bear the daily killings and indignities, every day in the street. And for every German killed, they would pick a hundred or more hostages and execute them. But when we found out about the gas chambers, then we were going to fight."

"With what?"

"Well, we had friends, the Polish Home Army and the Polish Socialists. They were going to supply us with weapons, we hoped. We *had* to fight to save Jewish honor for centuries to come."

"What about religion?" asked Father Janiecki. "Was this a religious organization?"

"Oh, no, Father. We were agnostic, socialists. We believed in Darwin, Engels and Marx, and natural selection."

"But you say that that did not reflect the attitude of most Jews—armed resistance?"

"No, in fact, we had to work in secrecy before fellow Jews, as well."

"That's what I thought," said Father Janiecki. "I've always thought the Jews wouldn't fight." He appeared slightly embarrassed about having said that, and added: "What I mean ... years of tradition. Also, something about the character ..."

There was an awkward pause.

Father Falkowski interrupted quickly. "Joey, I forgot to tell you. Father Janiecki brought a violin. He plays himself. Would you play something for us? I was telling Father that you studied the violin."

"Oh, yes, would you, Joey?" chimed in the other priest.

From a beaten-up black case, which he opened with great care, he took out a full-size violin covered with a red mahogany varnish and handed it to me.

"What would you like me to play, Father?" I asked.

"Anything, Jòziaczku. Something you had composed, you were telling me. Anything you want."

I tuned up the violin, adjusted the tension on the bow, and placed the instrument under my chin. "I don't know how I will do on this. I was used to a half-size violin, and this looks more like a full one."

"Yes, it is," said the tall priest. Turning to Father Staś he said with glee: "How do you like this? He knows the difference."

"I will play something which I performed in my school in Łódź. But, please, you must understand, I haven't played the violin in three years."

Both men reassured me. I proceeded to recreate a small concerto which I had once performed with piano accompaniment by my father. When I finished, the priests asked for more.

I played some songs I knew, followed by fugues from an oratorio conducted by my father; I would play one voice and intone or whistle another. The priests marveled.

"Admirable, absolutely astonishing," the tall one was saying. Father Staś had a broad grin. He appeared very happy.

✣ ✣ ✣

Father Falkowski had to visit a sick priest nearby in the afternoon. The family had sent a sled to pick him up. When he returned, we ate supper and spent the rest of the evening talking. The priest introduced me to the Catechism, the Missal, told me about the lives of saints, the Passion of Christ and the significance of it for "every human being," born and unborn.

"You see, my dear, until the coming of Christ, your religion, the Jewish religion, was the only true one. And it was meant for the Jewish people only. They were the chosen ones, the protectors of faith. But all this changed with our Lord Jesus. For he had brought the happy message for all humanity. And thenceforth the Jews were no longer the privileged caste. Which they refused to accept. Perhaps that is why the world hates them. For they still feel superior though it is no longer called for."

I listened for a long time. I believed my friend and my savior. For I sensed much love and feeling in the priest, and tenderness, and caring. No one had ever talked to me so lovingly, except perhaps my mother on occasions. Certainly not my own father, who seldom had time to explain things to me and was too impatient to answer questions. My father demanded constant perfection from me in everything. I had to be the best student and sportsman in school, the best musician. This I accomplished. But the continuous effort required to excel in everything left me tense and restless.

I had been under constant supervision, not allowed any after-school activities open to other boys. As the professor's son, I had to shine and set an example for others. The slightest transgression would reach my father's ears in the teachers' lounge, and punishment was always severe and swift: I was belted; privileges were taken away from me. Many times I would simply be thrown out of our apartment, forced to sit out on the stair landing for hours, threatened with commitment to a correctional institution.

On the other hand, I was praised and extolled in front of strangers.

My father seldom, if ever, took time to explain codes of behavior to me, or, through reasoning, made me see the impropriety of some of my actions. Whenever I was involved in fights, he presupposed my fault. The rest of the time I was expected to know better and act accordingly.

I was never taught love and forgiveness, or charity toward non-Jews. Rather, I was told to behave, to display exquisite manners, because this or that was "proper" or "improper" or "civilized," or "as my son, you are expected to do this," and "what will others say," or that this or that was "human" or "inhuman," or "out of turn." The latter my father would usually couch in the German phrase: "*es passt nicht* [correct or incorrect, or unbecoming]."

I suffered greatly because of limited associations with boys my age. Whereas during summer vacations, when the family sojourned away from the cities, the rule was slightly relaxed, during most of the year I was not allowed to associate with any but two or three friends of whom my parents approved. Consequently, I often felt lonely and isolated.

Excellence—in art and in life, along intellectual and artistic lines—was the only goal worth pursuing. "That's the only thing that raises man above the level of the beast," my father would say, "this and man's ability to pursue the truth." I sprang from a chosen stock, I was told. Just look around you—the Jews excel in everything. Is there any doubt, any wonder? And so, I, too, must live up to it. And I'd better, so my parents could be proud of me.

But now I had an older friend, interested, understanding, who seemed to take much interest in me, who didn't reprimand me for things which weren't my fault, a man full of love and charity, a man who could explain so much of the world, someone who even provided explanations to the awesome holocaust, all the carnage, and parting and killing. He had an answer to all of that.

"To be a Christian, and a good Catholic, Jòziaczku, means to have charity in your heart for *all*. Not just for your own people, or your own family, or even your nation, but for all of the people. That's the meaning of the Passion of Our Lord, that's why Christ descended to this earth and assumed a human body, and suffered, for all of us. But the Jews didn't accept him. That's why they are being punished. Pray to him, Joey, beg him to shed further Light upon you, thank Him for having chosen you."

Weeks passed. I was studying the Epistles, the Catechism. I began to pray. After all, this is what my savior and friend was doing. And the Father knew the Faith and the Light and the Salvation.

✠ ✠ ✠

The next day, after a sumptuous supper, I turned to my priest: "Father, how can I ever repay you for taking me in, for everything?"

"You won't. Nor should you try. Just keep passing the good deeds on to other people. That's the mystery of the living Church. Good deeds unto one another."

I was taught the Decalogue, its deeper meaning, and ramifications.

"If ever in doubt, Joseph, remember what our Lord said when he was once asked what the most important commandment was. He answered that all of God's laws can be reduced to this: 'that thou shalt love thy God with thy whole heart, thy whole mind, thy whole soul, and thy neighbor as thyself.' That is the only thing in which you ought to excel in life. The rest is unimportant."

"But, Father, my parents also taught me to be kind to others ..."

It was late and we turned to rest.

✛ ✛ ✛

Christmas was coming. Women were washing and scrubbing everything in sight; the men chopped wood for the holidays, smoked meat, and watched while homemade brew dripped into jugs for the merriment that was to come.

Now and then Father Falkowski would explain the mystery of Christ's birth to me, along with the enigma of the Holy Trinity. About a week before Christmas, I had a dream. I was out of doors, looking up at the full moon. The moon was bright as day, and the moon suddenly turned into a six-pointed Jewish star. Then, while I watched, the star vanished bit by bit—as if it had been wiped away by the hands of a clock. In its place was the Christian cross, tall, shiny, and radiating blinding light.

✛ ✛ ✛

Three days before the holidays, Father Staś took me to meet his pastor, Father Roch Modzelewski.

This nobleman, just past fifty, carried his obesity with slow, deliberate dignity. His face betrayed long winter trips to the homes of his parishioners. I thought of a weather-beaten sailor's. It had been cut down to a network of blue veins by the stark frost and the many swallows of vodka the peasants insisted would keep him warm on the next leg of his trip.

His voice boomed all over the house. On meeting me, he spread his legs wide for good balance, lowered his head until his chin almost met his chest, raised his bushy eyebrows, and thundered: "So ... that's our adopted friend ... Hmm ... Hmm ... little fellow ... eyes look good ... you speak well ... no problem. It's all taken care of. Some good wine for my friend Joseph, Anna!" he shouted in the direction of the kitchen.

"Easy, easy, Father Pastor," coached the vicar Falkowski. "He's still a young boy."

"Won't hurt him a bit. Easier to cope with the devil this way." He pointed to his own glass. "You have wine; I'll have some homemade vodka. Illegal to make vodka these days, you see, you and I are in the same boat, both criminals together. Ha, ha. We may as well enjoy ourselves as much as we can." He looked around, picking out a chair for me, gesturing expansively. "Sit down, sit down, Joe, is it? Good name. Let it stay that way."

The room had been set up for dinner. Clean cloth covered a long heavy mahogany table with some ten chairs where the pastor often entertained. As he crossed the room, the floor trembled; I thought the walls would come apart.

"Now we eat and later talk. We have some company for dinner, Father Staś. Our gracious occupiers."

The young priest looked slightly alarmed. "Father Pastor, you have invited the gendarmes again?"

"Sure, got to get along. First they dispossessed me and moved me out of here. What if they move me out again, ha? Got to get along real friendly like." And he winked one eye at me.

"Gendarmes, Father?"

"Nothing to fear, young fellow. We'll have some fun. Play them for the fools that they are. Nothing to fear."

Minutes later, dinner guests began to arrive. First came the sacristan, the blond, good-looking fellow I had seen in church. He moved quietly, was respectful and well liked. Next came a married couple of—I gathered—considerable standing in the parish, for the pastor addressed them with deference.

The men wore their best suits on this Sunday preceding Christmas. Along with homespun woolens and britches with boots, they wore jackets fastened at the top by a tight collar which resembled a military tunic. The lone woman wore a long dress of modest, dark color.

Five minutes later the door swung open and two German gendarmes marched in, their booted footsteps reverberating boldly. One, who carried the insignia of a lieutenant, had a bottle under his arm.

"*Grüß Gott, Herr Pharer* [Praised be the Lord, Father Pastor]," said one of them with dead seriousness.

"Aaaa … *Guten Tag, guten Tag* [Good day, good day]," the pastor greeted them.

The Germans surveyed the field. One of them nodded at the vicar.

The pastor proceeded to introduce all present to the representatives of the German field police, *Feldpolizei*, the occupying authorities.

"*Mein cousin*," bellowed the pastor, pointing at me.

"So … *sieht anständig aus* [Looks decent enough]," acknowledged the gendarme.

"A fine boy," the pastor boomed, slapping me hard across the shoulders. I swayed forward under the impact, practically bumping nose-first into the German's belt buckle. "Sit down, sit down," beckoned the pastor. His cheeks were flushed as if he had already sampled the goods of his house.

I was seated between my priest and one of the gendarmes.

"Today, ladies and gentlemen," said the pastor in Polish, "we are singularly blessed by entertaining two mighty emissaries of the almighty Herod himself. The Gospel says: 'thou shalt render unto Caesar,' et cetera." To the Germans he added in German, "God is with us." And he raised his glass.

"Father, God is with us. Indeed, indeed. *Gott mit uns.*"

Everyone downed a shot of vodka. The other gendarme set a bottle down on the table.

"*Deutscher Schnapps.* For you, Father Pastor."

"*Danke. Danke schön,*" answered the pastor.

Food was served. Steaming dishes made their rounds among the guests.

"My cousin," said the pastor, pointing again at me, "knows a little English. My parishioner," he added, pointing at one of the guests, "spent five years in America. Speaks English, too."

"*Ach so,*" answered the lieutenant. "*Amerika. Kapitalisten.* Jew land."

The pastor had downed two more and raised a toast. He presided like a general at a staff meeting.

"*Roosevelt nix gut. Stalin nix gut.* Long live *Deutscher Schnapps.*"

Father Falkowski was nudging me with his elbow. The pastor was winking at me, too.

"*Heil Hitler,*" said the gendarme, stuffing himself with boiled beef and horseradish. His animus was getting the better of him, and he propelled himself to repeat the state-greeting once more, only louder and accompanied by the raising of his right hand. "*Heil Hit—*"

Just then his vocal cords failed him, while his right arm, holding the drink, froze in its upward motion. His eyes swelled up with tears, and a look of disbelief contorted his face.

"Horseradish," whispered Father Falkowski. For at that moment, the horseradish attack had ejected the gendarme's food out of his mouth. It hit the lieutenant in the center of his chest, splattering his medals with particles of boiled beef and carrots, and a thick brown sauce.

The officer was downing a shot of vodka, leaning far back in his chair. His throat clenched as he realized what had happened and he choked on his vodka. And then there they were, the two of them spitting, gurgling, coughing, food and liquid flying in all directions.

The lieutenant's eyes bulged and filled with tears; the veins in his eyes turned bloody.

"Damnit, you dirty dog."

Another crescendo of coughing seized him. The other gendarme followed up with a salvo of horseradish and a brown sauce.

"Goddamn ... 'Scuse me ..." he attempted to apologize.

The lieutenant's fury was mounting. "Such a beast, man, you have no manners."

And so they went at each other, the gendarme attempting to apologize, the lieutenant castigating him, until the officer realized that the master race was being watched by its vassals.

"You understand, Father Pastor, it's unbelievable, unheard of," he said.

"Of course," said the pastor. Anna, the maid, was all over the place, wiping and soothing, and replacing the dishes.

The pastor raised another glass. "Once more: God's with us. *Gott mit uns.*"

"The devil …" murmured the lieutenant, grudgingly joining the toast.

There were more toasts after dinner, and the pastor slapped the gendarmes' backs, profusely bidding them hearty good-byes.

"Now, young man, I am due for my nap," bellowed the pastor to me, "but I want you to come with me and tell me all about yourself."

"Go ahead, Joey," said my priest, "go ahead and talk to the pastor."

Anna led me into the pastor's inner chambers. The pastor was deep in downy comforters and wearing his caftan, open at the neck.

"Good," said the pastor. "Now sit right here next to me, pull up the chair, that's right."

I was still a bit shaken by the encounter with the uniformed gendarmes. The pastor sensed it.

"My boy, the best way to deal with a lion is from the inside of his lair, assuming, of course, he doesn't know you're sitting there. Something like that even in your people's old Bible." His watery eyes weighing heavily after the many toasts, he smiled mischievously. "Tell me about yourself, Joey."

"What should I tell, Father?"

"Start any place. Tell me how you escaped from the train. Fascinating."

He closed his eyes. Moments passed. I wasn't sure whether the old man had fallen asleep and whether I would awaken him if I opened my mouth. Then the pastor opened one eye.

"Start from the beginning," he said.

I began. Here and there I halted, unsure if the old man had lapsed into sleep yet. At one point the pastor's chest began to heave and loud snoring started to compete with my story. But instantly the snoring ceased. The pastor opened one eye. He knew exactly the point where I had stopped.

"Go on, I hear everything. I'm just resting," he said.

I resumed my story. The snoring came back, and when I stopped, the same response followed. The pastor wanted to know everything: conditions in the Ghetto, my role in the Organization, the aims of Hashomer. After a while I continued to talk through the old man's snoring. I was afraid to stop lest I be reprimanded for thinking the old man asleep.

"Your father was a conductor, you say," said the pastor at one point. "He performed on Polish radio, too?"

"No, Father."

"Why not?"

"Father was told he could conduct choirs on radio only if he converted."

"That so? Hmm. What'd he do?"

"He refused. He felt that was a betrayal of his people and—I remember him saying—he felt several men he knew who had converted to get ahead were men of little integrity. He had no use for them."

"Hmm ..."

Fifteen minutes later, as Anna later related, she found both the pastor and me fast asleep.

"Well, how long did Father Pastor stay awake?" asked Father Staś on the way home.

I recapitulated the afternoon for the priest, and both of us laughed over the pastor's unique ability to snore and hear everything at the same time.

The next evening the priest said, "I saw the pastor after Mass, Jòziaczku. He was quite taken by you—told me he wanted to see you again and hear more from you."

"Same thing again, Father?"

"You mustn't hesitate to visit him so long as he wants to see you. A fearless man, our pastor. A good man, too. And, too, we need him. Together, somehow, we'll take care of you, Joey. For, you see ..."

The priest paused and eyed me with warmth and seriousness.

"You can't stay with me much longer, my dear."

Something was choking me. "No, Father? ... Well, where ..."

The priest was pacing the room and stopped in front of me. "We shall place you with one of our parishioners away from the beaten track. But you can still see me on Sunday after church."

"I see." *They want to get rid of me,* I thought.

"That's the only way, Joey, if you are to survive. People are getting curious. You'd have to disappear from daily sight. The pastor is trying to find the right place for you."

"Father, am I not going to see you every day?" Fear and loneliness gripped me.

"Sundays, my dear, after church."

"Father …" My eyes welled up.

"Yes, Joey."

"I don't want to be Jewish anymore. I want to be like you."

"All in due time, Jòziaczku. You're not ready yet. We cannot rush it. Baptism must be an act of will *and* an act of faith. Now, wipe your face and smile."

"I don't want to smile. I want to stay with you."

"Now, now, Joey, trust us, we'll find a place for you. Remember, anything is right as long as it helps you to survive."

Chapter Ten
Tutoring in Hiding: First Confession

IT WAS A DAZZLING bright morning and the sun was basking in the snow. All church bells were roused in swinging motion, their sound raising spirits to elation, cheer, and hope.

The church was packed. The peasants wore their best clothes uneasily—the men sporting scarves, mainly white, and the womenfolk wrapped in fancy shawls, all smelling of mothballs and attics. They made their way to the wooden pews, exchanging greetings. Those already seated turned their heads to see new arrivals, swapping little confidences and whispers.

The young remained in the back, standing. Girls stuck together waiting for the boys in shining boots who'd move in next to them, laughing, and occasionally pinching them.

This was to be a festive High Mass celebrated by Father Modzelewski. He was aided by two little boys, all dressed in white tunics, slip-over vestments that looked to me like oversized night shirts. As the High Mass began, the pastor intoned Latin phrases, terribly off-key. He sang in a hoarse, low voice; upstairs, the chorus aided by the organ responded.

"*Deus, tu conversus vivificabis nos ...*" struggled the celebrant in a unison which tapered off before it rose on the last note.

"*Et plebs tua letabitur in te …*" answered the chorus.

The organist, I was quick to notice, suspended the last note in a fermata, quickly changing it to the celebrant's next first note in the hope of restoring the proper key. It was a vain effort, for the pastor started off with the very first pitch able to clear his cords.

"*Gloria in excelsis Deo*," sounded the pastor in a scale all his own.

"*Et in terra pax hominibus bonae voluntatis*," resounded the chorus in a reassuring confirmation of the basic laws of harmony.

I was crowded in with several tall, young peasant boys in shining boots and a few older folks, late arrivals. To the left stood a group of attractive young girls in their studied aloofness. They held prayer books and some fingered rosaries. The boys appeared self-conscious with their prayer books. They exchanged whispers and meaningful glances in the direction of the girls. Melting snow carried from outside made dirty puddles on the church floor. Several boys with a flair for elegance placed their white handkerchiefs on the stone floor each time they knelt.

"The old badger sounds like the creaky barn door before we fixed it," said one of the boys.

"Better that he sings the Mass and let the young one give the sermon. At least the vicar gives you a good gab," threw in another.

"What d'you say we move in on the girls," asked the first young man.

"Yeah, let's, we'll pass the time faster."

The two of them squeezed through the crowd.

"*Dominus vobiscum*," the pastor intoned in his recitative.

"*Et cum spiritu tuo*," thundered the organ and the chorus upstairs.

"*Oremus.*"

During the prayer a slight commotion ensued. A young woman in a pink shawl and a pert little nose began to move away from one of the boys. I could see them pinch her again, and this time the girl reprimanded them audibly.

"Stop it! Have you no manners?"

Some of the older folks who had come in late chimed in. "Manners? All they know is manure. You can smell it!"

"Watch it!" said one of the boys. "Easy on the manure: you live with it, you talk about it."

The other young man was defending himself. "What, *pani*? What did I do? You saw something?"

"Nothing sacred for the young bucks anymore," murmured the old woman.

"Some fine upbringing." The young girl was encouraged in her indignation. "Pinching girls in church!"

"Pinch your own ass," hissed a mustachioed peasant threateningly, "for penance!"

"Shhh!" others around them emitted.

The sacristan appeared behind them. He put his hands around the boys' shoulders. "Break it up, fellows. Fool around afterward, outside the church."

"To confession, they should go!" muttered the man with the mustache. "A few belts on the bare ass first, though."

Father Falkowski had just climbed the narrow spiraling staircase to the pulpit. The music stopped and all eyes focused on him.

"In the name of the Father, and the Son, and the Holy Ghost. Amen." The priest drew a slow but large sign of the cross in the air over the congregation.

The church responded with a loud murmur of voices.

"The Gospel for this day of the Birth of our Lord comes from the Gospel of St. Luke, Chapter Two. For those standing in the back of the church, there are still some seats vacant up front. You don't have to hide in the back, even if you don't go to communion today."

That last statement, as everyone knew, was directed predominantly at some of the younger fellows. The priest smiled, and the people in the church broke out with loud laughter. In the short time, little over a year, since Father Staś had become the vicar, he had overcome the parishioners' traditional suspicion toward a young priest. His admonishments, liberally sprinkled with humor, overcame the hesitancy of the older generation toward a young cleric, steeped in the suspicion that his piety would often be synonymous with a self-inflated importance and righteousness.

"At that time, there went forth a decree from Caesar Augustus that a census of the whole world be taken … And she brought forth her firstborn son, and wrapped him in swaddling clothes, and laid him in a manger, because there was no room for them in the inn …"

The church was quiet as the priest continued with the Gospel.

"And suddenly there was with the angel a multitude of the heavenly host praising God and saying, 'Glory to God in the highest: and on earth peace to men of good will.'"

He surveyed the church.

"Dearly beloved in Christ! 'Because there was no room for them in the inn,' says the evangelist. And the quotation from the Gospel ends with the words: 'Glory to God in the highest' or '*Gloria in excelsis Deo*,' as you are singing today. But there is another part of the Gospel which is not read in the official text of the High Mass on Christmas; it is verse thirty-four of the same Chapter Two by St. Luke. Simeon said to Mary: 'Behold this *child* is set for the fall and for the resurrection of many in Israel and for a sign which shall be contradicted.'"

He paused, his eyes fixed on the congregation.

"'There was no room for them in the inn ... this *child* is set for the fall and for the resurrection ... a sign which shall be contradicted.'

"We have all heard these quotations about the Birth of our Lord before. But do we all realize and remember the profundity of their message for all Catholics, for all Christians?

"What *is* the message for all of us that the evangelist has given us on this day? 'There was no room for them in the inn.' The Virgin Mary, accompanied by Joseph, was wanting shelter, and was turned away. Thus our Lord Christ was born in a manger.

"But there was no way for the people at the inn to know whom they were turning away. God, in his eternal ways, chose to disguise that fact from the people at the inn. To them, Mary and Joseph were just a couple of modest folks looking for a shelter.

"We must ask ourselves, every one of us: Were we there, at the inn, would *we* have turned them away too? Would we, today, turn away our brother, our neighbor, a stranger who came to us in need of shelter? Would there be 'no room' for him?

"And then the Holy Gospel tells us that this child, this Jesus and his teachings of love for our neighbor, will mean to some a fall from grace, and to others ... the resurrection; that those of us who follow him will be resurrected, and those who do not, will fall.

"Dear brothers and sisters in Christ. The message for today, in these times of distress, and war, misery and uncertainty—the message is clear: do not turn your neighbor, if he be in need, away, and you shall be resurrected; proclaim that there is no room in your house for another human who may need your shelter and your help, and you shall fall from grace.

"The evangelist, inspired by the Holy Ghost, also prophesies that this sign 'shall be contradicted.' Who, pray, is contradicting this sign of the child in our times? Is it the good Christian who extends himself in charity to his neighbor—be he who he may—is it the person who follows Christ's teachings, in whose inn there *is*, indeed, room for the strangers? Or is it the one who, in these crucial times, turns a cold shoulder on a fellow human being in need; one who, through his acts of commission or omission toward his neighbor, contradicts the sign?

"Which one is set for the fall? Which one for the resurrection? The answer, we know, is clear. It is how we live by this answer that we earn for ourselves the ultimate salvation of our souls.

"This is also a day of joy, of festivities, of food and drink, *in moderation*,"—a barely audible snicker of acknowledgement rustled the congregation. People turned to one another with amusement, nodding their heads—"which is rightfully ours *after* the communion, and I know that some of us—*especially* those who didn't have the *time* for a sacrament this morning—cannot wait for the end of the sermon to commence the traditional libation."

A wave of snickers swept the church followed by much shushing; it was a sacrilege, after all, to laugh out loud in the house of the Lord. One of the young fellows next to me whispered, "That's what I like, a regular fellow, he doesn't go on for hours like the old one."

"He's beautiful," whispered one of the girls to her friend.

"And so I leave you with this message today: emulate Christ and his teachings, love your neighbor, and only then can we truly sing: *Gloria in excelsis Deo and in terra pax hominibus bonae voluntatis.*

"There will be vespers celebrated at three this afternoon. In the name of the Father …"

The organ burst out with "Gloria in excelsis Deo," joined by the chorus and the entire congregation.

I followed the crowd outside. Three young boys surrounded me.

"What's your name?" asked one. He wore a Sunday peasant's cap with a shiny visor.

"Jòzef."

"Joseph what?"

"Joseph … Wiśniewski."

"Wiśniewski? … From where?"

"I live here now."

"Where?"

"I work for Mrs. Konopka."

"Ah … where the young priest lives?"

A tall young man of about twenty-three, with an intelligent, friendly face, had been standing near the group, listening in. He moved closer.

"Oh … you're maybe … a cousin of Father Falkowski. I know he had one …"

Two young boys joined the group, shook hands, and exchanged greetings.

The man with the friendly face said, "This is Joseph Wiśniewski," and then, extending his hand to me, said, "My name is Stefan Krasowski. I live in the next village. Hope you like the young priest. This parish is not the same ever since he came here."

Father Falkowski appeared in front of the church acknowledging the parishioners' greetings. He spotted me instantly and with his eyes motioned for me to proceed across the road to the rectory. But Stefan was already greeting the priest warmly.

"Praised be Jesus Christ. Respects to your reverence, Father."

"Throughout the ages. Amen. Good to see you, Pan Stefan."

The priest's eyes were fixed on me. They were posing an urgent question. I had no way of letting him know what I had already conveyed to Stefan about myself and our relationship.

"Loved your sermon, Father. Brief and to the point. The good father has turned many a young girl's head by now, ha, ha!"

"Now, now," countered the priest in a mock reprimand. His eyes were soaking up every expression on my face. "That's no way to talk."

"Would that Father preached every Sunday. The people love it."

The priest inquired about Stefan's family and shortly excused himself. As he took his leave, he nodded toward me in a deliberately casual way which could mean either a distant recognition of a stranger or a familiarity that takes itself for granted.

I entered the pastor's house. Father Staś was waiting for me. His reprimand had a note of alarm. He spoke in an excited whisper.

"You shouldn't be standing around talking to people after church, Joe. You could cause a great trouble for both of us including the pastor."

I explained my precarious position. I was on the verge of crying at the priest's reprimand.

"What did you tell the boys about your relationship with me?"

"They asked if I was your relative."

"And you—to that?"

"I didn't answer ... we were interrupted." I was fighting for control. I wanted to weep.

"You sure?"

"Yes." I was crying. "I ... give ... my word."

There was a pause.

"I believe you. All right now. Surely you can understand. We can both be given away if you don't watch out. It's a good thing it was Stefan, not somebody else."

There was a commotion outside, the sounds of several boots trampling upon the snow. The door opened and two young boys barged in, followed by a third. They were the same young men who'd accosted me earlier.

"A roundup, Father!"

"Gendarmerie from Łomża. Labor roundup!"

"The trucks are here! Hide us, Father!"

"Not here! Through the back door, to the left. Get out the back door and over the fence! Joey," he boomed, "in the other room, quick!"

The boys left snow all over the floor. I heard Anna come from the kitchen.

"*Ola Boga, (dear God)* sweet Jesus, what're they doing to my floor?"

"The hell with the floor, Anna. The roundup is on. They're picking up our men for forced labor in Prussia." The priest shook his head in disbelief. "And on Christmas Day. What profanity! An insult to man and God!"

The pastor appeared in the door. They were all standing in the hallway.

"A roundup? Hmm? Beasts!" He headed for the door.

"Holy Mary, Father Pastor, you'll catch pneumonia. You have nothing on," Anna said.

The door was flung open. Two gendarme officers entered. With them was the lieutenant of the local gendarmerie, the recent dinner guest at the rectory.

"Who are you?" demanded the taller one.

"I am the pastor of the church here," answered the pastor deliberately in Polish. He didn't flinch. He boomed like a general addressing troops.

"Correct," said the local lieutenant. "He is the Catholic pastor. There are no young people here as far as I know."

The taller officer shoved the pastor aside, walking into the dining room, taking it in. He surveyed all present.

"All right. Let's go."

The Germans went for the exit.

"Oh, *Herr Leutnant* [Lieutenant]!" boomed the pastor.

The officers turned in the doorway.

"Merry Christmas!" said the old pastor, bowing deeply. "You sons of bitches," he added, after the door slammed, in a traditional Polish expletive.

I soon joined the pastor, Father Staś, and Anna in the dining room, from which we could see outside.

Two trucks were jackknifed across the road. Some young men, in their holiday best, were already loaded onto the trucks. Others, herded nearby in a small group, were climbing up the back, stepping up on the back flap, which was down and open.

The gendarmes were holding back a group of women. The women were shouting and gesturing to their husbands and brothers. Some were wailing.

"Happened in Falki two weeks ago," said Father Staś. "Same thing. No young man has come near the church since. I expected it here, too, but … Lord Almighty, not on Christmas Day."

"Yeah," repeated the pastor. "Poland in chains. Nice times."

I stuck my nose to the window and scraped a thin sheet of ice from the inside. Anna stood behind me wiping her hands on her apron.

"Holy Virgin, sweet Jesus, Queen of Poland! What have we all done to deserve this scourge? The flower of our youth taken away ..." She crossed herself and started to cry. "Won't even let them pick up a bundle from home ... just the way they are ... not even bid their families ... some with children ... Holy Lord!"

A few of the gendarmes assembled in the middle of the road, apparently to coordinate their actions against the wailing and screaming women. Presently they moved against them urging them to disperse. With their attention thus diverted, one of the men jumped down from the truck and started to run away. Two more men followed him. But the second man slipped and fell. The third man fell over him. As they picked themselves up, I noticed the face of the first man. It was Stefan Krasowski who had befriended me earlier.

Just then the gendarmes turned. Something in the faces of the women who could see the men's attempt to break away told them what was happening.

"*Halt!*"

"*Stop! Verfluchter* [Damnit]!"

One of them grabbed a pistol, firing in the air. The second and third man stopped and turned, resigning themselves to captivity. Stefan kept running. He was turning into a path leading to the back of the church and the cemetery beyond. This time the gendarme aimed and fired. Stefan disappeared behind the church wall.

Other gendarmes approached the two men, pushing them back toward the truck. The two stumbled and fell. The Germans pinned them against the truck and hit them with rifle butts.

✠ ✠ ✠

Two Sundays later I stood in the pastor's study.

"Ha, ha!" Father Staś said. "Father Pastor would not believe! It's a riot!"

"He did say yes, though, didn't he?"

"Sure." He lowered his voice with his customary air of close intimacy. "You see, I approached him this way: 'You see, *Wòjt* Walewski,' I said, 'it would be a good thing for your boy, Staś, to get a tutor, someone his age, a nice fellow who excels in Latin and history—two subjects with which your son has problems.' You know, Father Pastor, how much you and I have tried to teach him. Nothing. What a blockhead! Nice boy, and all that, but vain—God's handsome creation. All he thinks about is clothes, polished high boots, and girls. Of course, I told the old man. 'Dear Wòjt,' I said, ''tis nothing to be ashamed of, every one of us has had his share of difficulty in his school years: your Stas with his Latin, I with ecclesiastic history. Ha, ha! Doesn't mean he won't grow up bright and useful.'

"'What does the good father recommend?' says the Wòjt.

"Well, I hesitated as if I searched for some remedy, and then I exclaimed: 'For goodness sake, Pan Wòjt, I have just the right boy for you, an orphan who knows his Latin inside out. If he could only board with you.'

"'Sure!' said he. 'Father's word is good enough.' I said I'd send him over today. Ha!"

The priest was rubbing his hands with satisfaction.

"The funniest thing is, you know what he told me at the end? 'Just as long as Father Vicar doesn't stick me with some kind of a Jew.' Ha, ha!"

"What did Father Staś say to him?" asked the pastor.

"'Not in a hundred years, good Wòjt. A rabbi, maybe, but not just any old Jew.' And we both had our laugh.

"Though he did say: 'Father, that wouldn't be funny.' I laughed, of course."

"So, now, Joey," smiled the pastor, "you're all set."

"A Wòjt?" I asked.

"Sure, the elder of a cluster of villages," answered the young priest, "good man, too, prewar Wòjt. He's playing ball with the German country *Kommissar* in Szepietowo; what can he do? But as much as he can, he tries to forewarn the local people of raids on the livestock, and so on. He walks a tightrope, but manages. You will be a tutor to his son, Staś—how about it? Good house, good food, stay out of sight … and … you won't have a thing to worry about."

He was triumphant.

"It's all right, I guess," I said. It sounded good.

"There's one other thing. I've given you a new last name for the time being. It's Kutrzeba. It is a very old Polish family; General

Kutrzeba of that family was a great Polish military hero who fought the Germans in 1939. So when you think of your new name, Joe, I hope you'll be a brave fighter, too. I told Wòjt Walewski that you'll be there today. You'd better get over there while it's still daylight; it'll take you a couple of hours through the snow. Then you can visit me next week; we'll talk."

✛ ✛ ✛

The road went right past the Wòjt's homestead. Halfway through it curved to the left past a small roadside chapel with a crucified Jesus. Frozen weeping willows hugged the road on both sides, each row leaning sadly roadwise.

The Wòjt was still away when I arrived, but Mrs. Walewska was home with Staś. The Wòjt's wife, reverently called *Wòjtowa*, was an attractive, somewhat emancipated woman with a high school education. She wore city clothes except when she helped out with a special meal, or during the harvest when all hands were needed in the field. Staś was my age, going on sixteen. He was tall and well proportioned, with a sturdy neck, flushed cheeks, long limbs, and flaxen hair. His steel blue eyes and a small nose, however, gave him a slightly stubborn look.

A spacious kitchen served as a day room. There was also a dining room, all decorated with holy pictures, but seldom used.

Later the Wòjt arrived. The Polish village official, like his wife *gimnasium*-educated, was in every way a model of landed gentry. Medium tall and heavily broad-shouldered, he had a thin mouth and a heavy head which sat directly upon his shoulders as if upon a snowman's trunk. He wore shiny cavalry boots and an expensive lambskin jacket. The Wòjt drank a great deal, was away most of the time, and spoke little when at home. He was impatient with his wife, but was most tolerant of his only son. On the rare occasions when he stayed at home, all kinds of people came and went, bearing problems that had mainly to do with the occupation authorities: livestock confiscated, a grown son ordered to forced labor in Prussia, and a host of others. The Wòjt would hear everyone, listening patiently and interrupting seldom; sometimes he offered words of advice, or a promise of intervention. He also offered vodka to every visitor, and was furious with his wife if she had turned anybody away during his occasional daytime naps which she tried to protect.

He was intensely nationalistic and had a constant look about him, seldom conveyed in words, of anguish and deep suffering brought on by the loss of his country.

The Walewskis, though several social cuts above the plain village folk, had a straightforward, direct manner of relating to their servants and neighbors. I was quick to notice the veneration and respect in which they were held. I was sure that, even stripped of his noble birth and appointive status, the Wòjt would have come into his position, were free elections to be held.

I was assigned a straw mattress in an attic above the kitchen. My few belongings were kept there, as well.

Mrs. Walewski and Staś ate in the kitchen with all the help at the farm. The Wòjt was seldom home in time for meals; when he did share a meal, carving out his spoonfuls of potatoes and *kasza* along with the others from one big bowl, a respectful silence prevailed at the table. Only his son, Staś, and the foreman felt privileged to address the Wòjt. He listened to the others but hardly acknowledged anyone else's remarks. When he did speak, it was with some ostensible effort, most sparingly, and so quietly that one had to strain to hear. Yet one had the impression that the man was capable of a violent temper.

The day after my arrival, I sat down to my first tutoring session with Staś. The young heir had not been privy to the great mysteries of the Latin declensions, particularly the third one with all its exceptions. It was rough going and required much patience, but there were advantages in putting up with Staś: he was fond of the young priest and so accepted me from the outset as his mentor, he did try to learn, and was not too inquisitive. In the final analysis, Staś was interested mainly in himself. There was one other advantage. *She* showed up with her mother the next day; they had heard of Staś's new tutor from Mrs. Walewska and wanted to meet me.

Marzena Janowska was a tall young beauty of fifteen. She had been to school with Staś before the war and now continued with her own private tutor, since secondary schools had been officially closed down by the Germans. Her father, an engineer and an officer in the Polish Army, was still off somewhere in a prisoner-of-war camp. The

Wòjt was alleged to have been making some progress in freeing him. Marzena—her name, I thought, was highly unusual as it derived from the Polish *marzyć*, to daydream—was a dark beauty of sharp, finely chiseled features. In many ways she was a double for her mother, who carried herself with an almost provocative, prideful indifference. Yet she displayed an air of deferring to men—traditionally a most coquettish combination among Polish women. To observe Mrs. Janowska and Marzena was to envision the numerous miscegenations throughout the centuries involving the invading Mongols of the thirteenth century— dark, Asian, olive-skinned—and the Slavic genes that produced long limbs in some and a coquettish aggressiveness toward men, disguised as elegant nonchalance.

Both Marzena and her mother, unlike the peasant women in the area, wore shorter skirts, carrying about them a citified look. Although Marzena had her own tutor, she asked to drop in on some of my Latin sessions with Staś. She was seductive yet attentive and possessed of an excellent mind and scholastic inclination. Often she exchanged looks with me when Stas' mind stubbornly refused to absorb the vicissitudes of foreign grammar. A faint aroma engulfed me. A girl and a woman permeated the air about Marzena, and it tantalized me from the first meeting with her. There were times when, pointing out a word during the class, I would accidentally touch Marzena's hand. Soon I would create opportunities to touch shoulders with her, to graze her hand, and perhaps even to arrange for our knees to meet under the table. Sometimes Marzena withdrew her knee; but there were moments, too, delirious in all, when she allowed her knee to remain there, touching mine, perhaps even—I wasn't too sure at first—to return the pressure under the table.

Officially, Staś was courting Marzena. He was, I'd heard, a frequent guest in her house; the Janowski family had their home upon a hill some two kilometers away. Staś was slow to catch on; but I was afraid that, eventually, if he suspected any tacit understanding between Marzena and me, he would turn on me. For Staś had accepted his limited intellectual grasp without noticeable rancor; his interests, after all, were more manly: shiny boots, physical prowess, horses, field and stream, as well as emulation of his father in "politics and administration." Study and learning were the required and necessary ways to grow up, and he was willing to coast along. But in matters of masculine pride, I was afraid to stumble on Staś' hard core.

Once when I found myself alone in the kitchen with Marzena, I took her hand and even once pressed against her legs. Marzena was leaning against the wall with one leg bent at the knee and I managed to touch her lower thigh with mine. It was then that she whispered: "Why don't you come over one day with Staś?"

"You wouldn't mind?" I asked. My heart was beating rapidly and I felt all my blood rushing to my head.

"I wouldn't be asking you," she said, casting a furtive glance toward the door.

"What about Staś?"

"I don't really care for him that much. I think he's stupid."

"Then why …?"

"Well, our parents encourage it and I … then there's my father still away in captivity and the Wòjt is trying to free him … you understand?"

Mrs. Walewska was coming back in, accompanied by Mrs. Janowska. We had just enough time to pull apart.

A few days later I managed to get rid of Staś for a minute when I asked him to fetch a dictionary. I touched Marzena's hand.

"I've been thinking of you," I whispered.

She cast her eyes down, then looked up and quickly kissed me fully on the lips. When Staś returned I couldn't concentrate on the lesson for a long while.

✠ ✠ ✠

A few days later a professional mating expert had brought a stallion over to pair him off with the Wòjt's mare. The stallion was kicking and bucking, fighting off the taut rope that was held with great force by two laborers. The peasants all stood by, some fixing their eyes on the scene with a keen anticipation, watching an event which, like sowing or ploughing, was at the foundation of their lives and prosperity. The younger ones, including Staś, had smirks on their faces.

The animal's black organ, sensing an anxious mare nearby, grew in size, revealing layers upon layers of inner, pink and dark skins, like a folded funnel sprouting out of imprisonment. It was frightening in its long dimension, growing and lengthening until it almost touched the ground under the stallion. Then, neighing and struggling, the animal was allowed to mount the mare which another laborer held: the stallion aimed and wiggled, mounted and failed, his front legs and trunk alternately slipping in an uncontrolled tremor, remounting until he finally entered the mare's flesh. Her body shook convulsively.

Slipping down the rear of the mare, the stallion thumped the ground with a clumping sound, his grace and vigor gone, his power quashed; he stood there, staring ahead stupidly, unbelieving. His huge organ, still extended but turning limp, hung under him out of control, like a broken pendulum.

A spell hung over the bystanders. Staś was smirking.

"Old boy got himself some good fucking," he whispered.

A brawny, bulldoggy peasant with a sticky, sleazy face turned: "Young squire, I see, got a good eye, ha, ha!"

"For good luck, Mr. Wòjt," said the foreman.

The Wòjt crossed himself. "Amen," he said.

☩ ☩ ☩

Staś was away with his father one day, and I hung around the kitchen reading a book while Mrs. Janowska and Mrs. Walewska chatted. Marzena was home with a cold.

"When she gets better, you must come over with Staś to visit," Mrs. Janowska said to me. Her smile seemed to last longer than usual.

From where I sat, I occasionally glanced up at Marzena's mother. She sat at the table, her legs crossed, her city skirt riding up above her knees. She had long curving legs, I noticed, her knees slightly dimpled. In a moment she recrossed her legs. I saw a glimpse of her thigh further up, a quick shadow and a fuller curve that enraptured me ... I thought of the mare, then I thought of Marzena and the softness of her thigh, and Marzena lying in bed, and a disabling, numbing sweetness came over me.

I caught Mrs. Janowska's look and pretended I was reading. She was smiling ... A minute or two later, she recrossed her legs again—

with a slight retarding action, almost deliberately, I thought. And she seemed to smile at me for an instant, as if she noticed my look.

I put the book down. A stiffness about my body, a powerful force tugged at me inwardly.

And Mrs. Janowska's legs ... I excused myself and went upstairs to lie down on my straw mattress in the attic and closed my eyes. Didn't the father talk to me about purity and the sins of the flesh? And then hadn't the Catechism also mentioned it? I could see the woman's legs provocatively poised, and the sweet roundness of her flesh. "Thou shalt not covet thy neighbor's wife ..." Well, I didn't covet her; it was just her legs ...

And now Marzena ... she was almost the same height as her mother, though the mother's shapes were more pronounced, as were her legs ... I felt another surge of the overpowering sweet numbness ... and my body was rigid ...

I heard steps, and Mrs. Walewska came up. She was looking for something in a different part of the large upstairs attic.

"What are you doing, Joseph?"

"Oh, just reading ..."

"Ah, all right. I mean, you don't have to go up on our account."

"No, *proszę pani*, I just thought I'd read here."

She left and I was left with my thoughts again. I wished that I were downstairs looking at Mrs. Janowska's legs, but it was too much to bear. I closed my eyes and presently saw Marzena's legs, then her mother's, and my hand found my stiffness. I unbuttoned my pants. Somebody could come up any time ... well, at least, until then ... I thought of Marzena again but, more and more, her mother's image was replacing Marzena's. It was her mother who smiled at me provocatively; she must have been aware of me looking at her legs, and the shadows between her thighs, as she recrossed her legs to taunt me more, and more, and more, till I was overcome by sweetness, helplessness, and an all-encompassing abandon, subjected to the stifling, mounting, fainting, pulsating feeling of giving myself up to her round legs ...

It was all over, and I lay exhausted. It felt quiet, and peaceful, but I wasn't sure what I had done. I felt guilty, though I didn't know why. Did I desire a married woman? No, I thought, I was just stimulated by her legs. What was wrong with that?

"Joseph, you hear me?" I heard Mrs. Walewska's voice. "Come on down. Mrs. Janowska wants to say goodbye to you."

"All right," I said.

I wiped myself off and came downstairs.

She smiled at me and I felt that she must have known. Her eyes showed a warm acknowledgement of my look. She seemed pleased.

"Give my regards to Marzena," I said, but inside I felt that I had betrayed her for her mother.

✠ ✠ ✠

Spring was coming and it chased the biting frost away. Mrs. Janowska came almost every day and sat at the same spot, often for hours, talking to her friend. She seemed to relish her exchanges with me; she asked me about my family, and smiled a lot. I often left her, went upstairs and gave myself to the image of her legs. I was sure she knew what was happening, and I could see a marked difference in the way that she carried her legs under the table. Sometimes she stroked her legs as she crossed them, and her glances thrown at me on those occasions were more and more challenging. I became addicted to her. Marzena did not hold any more interest for me. She had lost out to her mother.

✠ ✠ ✠

A couple of weeks later, I visited Father Falkowski one Sunday after church and asked him questions about aspects of Christianity I didn't understand: the Holy Trinity and the Immaculate Conception.

Father Stanisław explained the essence of these mysteries. In the end, he said, "All we can do is repeat, with Pascal—of late the devout, believing Pascal—'You are the greatest Mystery, O God. What my mind will not comprehend, my faith will sustain.'"

The priest seemed pleased with my reports about the way I was getting along with Staś and his parents, and even my acquaintance with the Janowski women, which I played down.

"Read the books I gave you, Joey," the priest was saying, "and save your questions each time when you come to visit me. Next week."

✛ ✛ ✛

I had looked forward to seeing Father Staś for a whole week. There was so much else I wanted to talk to him about, so many questions, so much I would unburden myself of. There were theological questions, questions about liturgy, certain prayers and customs I needed to know. The Walewskis were fairly educated people and devout Catholics; as one who had completed three years of gimnasium, I felt that considerable knowledge about the Catholic faith was expected of me. Too, Easter was coming, and I had questions about various rites and points of celebrations lest I give myself away to the Wòjt's family.

But the priest could not spare much time.

"Jòziaczku, not today." His dark brown eyes looked sad and tender. "A man is gravely ill, and they're sending a sled for me to administer the last rites. It's several kilometers away."

My eyes welled up.

"But, Father, you said last week ... I thought we would talk. I can't talk to anybody else ... the things I want to know, my doubts, the questions ..."

"I know, my dear, but be a man, I have duties."

"Next Sunday then?"

"No, I can't, my dear. I have an old mother, and it's her name day. I must go visit with her ... Now, now," said the priest, "don't cry—it's only two weeks. You'll survive. Read more books and get to know Staś better. He's not a bad chap."

✛ ✛ ✛

I walked back slowly. It had begun to snow again, winter's last flurry. Up around the bend in the road, near the chapel, I heard horses snorting and a large sled came into view. As it drew nearer, I saw the green uniforms of the field gendarmerie. I stepped off the road and took off my cap in a submissive acknowledgement, as expected by the Germans. There were six of them. As they passed me, I saw their flushed faces. They were loud and gregarious; they had been drinking.

"*Zhendobre*," roared one of them at me in his distortion of Polish "good day." I forced a smile. The Germans went on.

Well, now, I thought, maybe the father has a good point. The Jews do regard themselves as the Chosen People, they look down on the goyim, they consider them inferior, less intelligent. They ridicule Gentiles. They keep away from them. I had never liked that. It went against the humanitarian concepts imbued in me. Well, you can't have it both ways, I thought. Either you are a humanitarian and respect everyone for his human potential, or else. Perhaps, I thought, the "humanitarianism" of the Jews was a self-defensive ideology? Yes, there was no question about it; the Jews thought they were something special. And now all of this had come to an end. Christ, whom the Jews had rejected, proclaimed love and charity and forgiveness for *all,* and that included me. I wondered what would happen if things had been the other way around … if it were the Christians who were persecuted … how many Jews would risk their lives to save a Christian, in the name of love and charity. Not many, I thought.

And now there will be no Jews left in Europe anymore … their right to live has ceased … nobody wants them anymore … the Germans, and the Poles … And I can't be Jewish anymore and have a right to live. I must believe in Christ, in his love. But still, I am Jewish. Can I just give that up? My father didn't convert. But also my father—did he argue or try to help when they shoved me in a group for the extermination cars? No. So why should I care what he would have thought?

As the priest said, I was picked by the hands of God … to learn his Truth, to survive, to bear witness, to follow him … Christ … who forgives … who rejects none … who loves … who consoles the lonely and the downtrodden … unlike the Jews I've known who look down on everyone else …

I was approaching the Wòjt's homestead. One of the farm girls was drawing water at the well. I was overcome with a warm, good feeling.

"Yes, I do have a place to go, I do have a place to turn … It's Christ, who suffered for me, who loves me, and Father … he loves me too, he risks his life for me. If ever I were discovered …"

✛ ✛ ✛

The Wòjt and Staś were away, I was told by the farm girl who helped in the kitchen. The Wojtowa was asleep in her room.

I left the kitchen, for I did not feel up to chatting with the maid, who had been curious and asked too many questions. I resisted going upstairs to the attic, for there was just my hay mattress and the image of Marzena's mother.

In the dining room was a large picture of Virgin Mary and another one of Christ, showing his heart exposed, open to all. The room was small, just enough for a table with four chairs, and two more chairs propped against the wall.

I knelt in front of Mary's picture, and looked up at her.

"But then, once I've converted, that's it ... I can't be a turncoat ... I mean, to convert when you are convinced of the Truth to which you ought to devote your life, that's one thing, but that's just it ... one would burn all bridges behind ..."

"A Jew will convert for convenience sake," the father had said, "and will reconvert when it's safe."

"So here it is where my integrity is at stake, my honesty. Once chosen and admitted to the Eternal Truth, the Eternal Love and Mercy, I ought not fail him. And I ought not fail Father Stanislaw who loves me, who risks his life for me. It is up to me to prove that a Jew can be depended on, through thick and thin; that, contrary to established beliefs among Christians, a Jew can remain faithful ... whether or not it serves his immediate interests and convenience ... if it should ever come to pass ... if ever the Jews are no longer persecuted, I shall prove that a Jew can remain faithful. If I convert, I shall never become a turncoat to my Savior. (Also, my people would never accept me back; they would brand me as a traitor.)

"I have separated from my people before, but now I am leaving them for the Light, for God Eternal.

"Mother of God, Queen of Poland, look upon me. I am sinful; I shall not just repeat prayers from the book, but speak to you as I feel. Will you guide me, and accept me, and make me choose right? I want to do what is right. Father Falkowski says that you, in your mercy and love, will guide me to your Son, Jesus, the Almighty God, and his Father. That if I give myself to the Holy Ghost, give my soul to Him, He will accept me. I am alone, I want to be loved, I want your mercy, I want to live on, Holy Mother, dear Mother of God. You are Jewish as I am. No one would understand me better than you: are we Jewish, you and I, or are we Catholic? How can I be both?

"I want to do the right thing. I don't just want to be a turncoat, I will not convert just to save my life, to continue to deserve the father's efforts, to please him ... I will convert, with your help, because it is right, because I can help redeem the sins of my people who offended your son, who caused him to be whipped, and tortured, and pierced with a spear on the cross ... he who bled to death for our sins. If only we could have suffered similarly for Christ—to be beaten and whipped, and humiliated and killed, to save Christ his suffering ... Father Staś said that we should plead and beg to be allowed to have traded places with Christ—though it could not happen, though history could not be undone, he said that was the ultimate gesture of prayer. That nothing would please you more than this gesture of offering ourselves to spare your son ... if it were meant sincerely ... well, I do mean it sincerely ... if he be my God—the one who wants me, who saved me, who chose me to live, who forgave me, then I ought to want to have suffered for him, to give myself to you, of myself. Like when Mrs. Janowska smiled at me ... so kindly ... so warmly ... she looked at me so invitingly, as you do ... with understanding ... as if she wanted to convey to me that she waited for me and knew that I wanted her ... so I wouldn't be alone ... Is that something wrong, dear Mother of God? Please ... I don't mean any harm, or to be unclean, it's just *me* that I mean, I would not involve anyone else, or desire anyone, if it's wrong ... Oh, God, I feel so close to you, Mother of God, but also to her, Marzena's mother ... and her legs, like this, on my knees. I would offer this to her, but also, mainly to you, if you want me, if you will accept me, what I have to give you, to give of myself ... after all ... Oh, God, I feel it is coming, it is within me, and soon I will offer it to you, because it is part of me, and I am offering it to you, I am giving myself to you, holding nothing back, as I did to her before, upstairs. I have nothing else to give, to give of myself ... nothing shall I hold back, so you know, and see it ... it's going to be between you and me ... either way, you know everything, you are the Mother of God, either way you will know ... and now I shall surrender, to you, and also to her, her legs, oh, God, now and ... forever, oh, God ...

"Please, you didn't mind, did you? I didn't mean to offend you, or anyone, it's over, look, it's here, on the floor ... to show you my surrender. Thank you ... oh, thank you. If it's a sin, I beg your forgiveness. It's done."

✠ ✠ ✠

"Father, I am sure now," I said. "I want to be converted."

It was a Sunday in early March. I was talking to Father Stanisław in his study.

"You have progressed far, Joseph. If something should happen, I believe that right now you would face our Maker in the state of grace equivalent to the state attainable after confession and absolution for Catholics. As your priest and spiritual father, I have to make sure that conversion for you represents your own, free act of will, *and* of faith, as I told you earlier. If this keeps up, we will arrange it. But it's not so easy. The Church requires two witnesses and permission from the bishop."

"But, Father, isn't it dangerous for others to know?"

"Yes, it is, but let me worry about this. We can approach the bishop personally and confidentially—I believe you'd have to write him a letter."

"A letter, Father? What would I say?"

"Simply state in your own words your reasons for wanting to become a Catholic. Think about it, Joseph. As for your godparents— the witnesses, I might approach—I'll talk to the pastor about the lovely couple who were at dinner with the gendarmes—remember? They are good Catholics, and reliable, I think we can trust them. In fact," the priest pondered, "I might begin the conversation in this area. Quite personally," and he smiled, "I might tell you, I should be very proud of it myself—I think it should fare very well with my bishop" (he winked with an urchin's grin) "for this would be my first conversion, something every priest considers his primary calling, in the words of Jesus as given to us by St. Matthew: '[Going therefore, teach ye all nations: baptizing them in the name of the Father and the Son and the Holy Ghost.'"

"Father," I hesitated, "when I become a Catholic, I think I would never want to be Jewish again."

"Oh, no, Joey, on the contrary. Every man has his cross to bear, in his service to Christ, a responsibility peculiar to each one of us, inherent in his talents, and ability, his station in life, his background. Your particular distinction, your obligation to Christ for the mercy which he had shown to you—through me and through others—would be to become a living testament to his love for you, precisely *because* you are a Jew, and you have been *summoned* by him. This you ought to proclaim throughout your life, let the world know and, indeed, become instrumental in converting other souls, offering their souls to Christ, helping them see the Light and the Truth ... when it is safe again, of course, to be a Jew."

He got up and walked over to a bookshelf behind the strange piece of furniture that resembled a sawed-off portion of a prayer stall which I had noticed when I had first come in here on that cold night after my trek through the snow. I had since learned that the priest was saying his breviary there throughout the day.

"On page fifty-three in this book, Jòziaczku, you'll find a chapter called 'Examination of Conscience.' It goes on for several pages. Start on it. If you are going to be converted, you will have to go to confession first. This will help you prepare, examine your conscience, and confess your sins. And here, too, is a book on moral theology. It may help clarify some things."

"How far back must I go to confess my sins, Father?"

"The Church requires that all converts confess the sins of their entire life. But you need only state them in general terms. You only confess those you remember, and that will be sufficient for God."

Franny knocked at the door. The father had a visitor.

"Go now, Jòziaczku, and prepare for confession. Come and see me after church on Sunday."

I was taking my leave, backing out of the priest's room.

"Oh, and another thing, Joey. Remember what I told you about holding your lips together to make them appear thinner—because Jews have sensuous, more pronounced lips—and other things ... the characteristics that ... er ... your people have ... to avoid them?"

I nodded.

"Well, you're doing well in the other departments. Here's something else: don't back out of the room like this when you leave. It's too polite. People might get suspicious."

"Well, I was taught this, Father."

I thought: Damn my father with his Viennese manners. He taught me all the *Kinderstube*, instead of teaching me the true faith.

"Remember, I told you: don't be too polite; don't excuse yourself too often? Goes for the same thing. Bow, take your leave, and go out, don't back out like this."

"But isn't this the polite form, Father?"

The priest showed impatience.

"It is. As are many good manners. If they are implemented by a well-bred Polish fellow, city-bred, people out here will respect them, ridicule them, admire, scoff, or whatever, depending on the degree of their own upbringing. But when *you* use them, they'll get suspicious when they start putting other things together about you. So … the best thing is: be as plain and direct as possible. We must be very careful. One false word … now, Joey, pull yourself together and wipe off your tears. You can come to see me soon. I'll pass a word to you—a note in Latin. Now go and God bless!"

✠ ✠ ✠

I broached the subject of women next Sunday when I visited with the priest.

"It is said in St. Matthew's Gospel," explained Father Falkowski, "'whosoever shall look on a woman to lust after her hath already committed adultery with her in his heart.'"

My heart sank. So I had committed a grave sin but wouldn't dare to confess to the specifics.

Chapter Eleven
My Next Escape:
German Slaughter of Villagers

ONE FREEZING WINTER DAY two smugglers—ex-bricklayers—came to the Walewski's house to trade fine cloth, scarves, and a higher grade of vodka, all for foodstuffs they could take back to sell in the starving capital.

The Wojtowa was in the kitchen driving a hard bargain with them when I accidentally came downstairs. I wanted to avoid them, but it was too late to back out. She introduced me.

"You, gentlemen, are from Warsaw, so you might want to meet my son's tutor, Joseph Kutrzeba. He's from the capital, too."

The taller smuggler shook my hand. "Sieradzki," he said. The other smuggler, Zygmunt Kulak, only smiled. His eyes danced and ridiculed.

"Oh, where from in Warsaw?" he said. He was wiry, of medium height. On his small head with a receding hairline, he sported a dark blond mustache.

"From Ogrodowa," I answered.

I had often deliberated over the choice of a street in the capital, should I encounter someone who knew Warsaw. I had, after all, only lived in the Warsaw Ghetto and knew virtually none of the streets located in the Aryan section of the city. I had picked Ogrodowa, the location of our first residence in Warsaw, since one part of it lay outside the Ghetto.

Kulak looked up in amusement.

"Ogrodowa? Hmm? ... That was in the Ghetto?"

I forced a smile. "Oh, no! The other part of it."

"But close enough," said Kulak, "too close for comfort."

The Wojtowa was folding a bale of cloth. She heard it.

"Joseph's father, an officer, was taken prisoner. His aunt is ill, so he's staying with us and helping my son with his studies."

"I see," said Kulak, and he smirked again.

I avoided both smugglers from then on. The sight of Kulak filled me with apprehension, and whenever the two men were around, I took great pains to stay out of the kitchen.

Late in March the weather turned warm, and I couldn't force myself to stay inside. I put on a sweater and went for a walk around. The farm help was busy scrubbing and cleaning the barns and hauling out equipment for sowing. It would be Easter in another week, and the snow was melting. I walked along, trying to keep my shoes out of the mud.

Suddenly I looked up. Kulak had come around the side of the barn.

"Aha!" smiled the mason, "our compatriot from Warsaw." He seemed solicitous, almost protective.

"Good morning," I said. "How was your trip this time?"

"This time we've come to join the family for a while."

"Your family?"

"We're staying to build the Wòjt a real nice barn."

I was stunned. I felt a cold fear crawling out from somewhere.

"I see. Well ... very nice to have you, I'm sure."

"Sure?" The smile, which had held back a smirk, now gave way to it. It held and it challenged me to a reply.

"I don't understand."

"You will," he answered and went into the barn.

✠ ✠ ✠

In the following two weeks, the foundation for a new barn was laid down, and the men made their measurements: they jabbed little sticks into the ground stringing taut rope between them to draw up straight lines, as I observed from the windows of the house.

Two wheelbarrows had begun to make rounds from an open, flat box where cement was being mixed on the construction site, as the masons from Warsaw started laying bricks.

"Let's go help mix cement," said Staś to me one bright morning.

I tried to get out of it as I was feeling mounting distrust toward the masons; the way they looked at me caused me inner tremors—my instincts had come to recognize the rapacious stings in the eyes of the anti-Semite on a prowl for his victim.

But as Staś insisted, I followed him to the construction site. Outside the barn, two horses trudged in a circle harnessed to a log attached in the center of the circle to an automatic threshing treadmill.

"I'll go to relieve Antek at the reins," I offered. I feared being in proximity of the masons; they might again query me about Warsaw—where had I lived …

Antek was reluctant to turn over the reins to me. "Don't know if the Wójtowa would like this," he stalled.

"Just for a little while," I pleaded. "Go get a drink of water from the well."

"Well, for a little while, then," said Antek reluctantly, wiping his forehead. He came back a few minutes later just as Zygmunt Kulak approached me.

"So … how does the city boy like farm work, hmm?"

"I like to help out very much. I like horses especially."

"You do? Come on with me to the barn. I need to find some tools."

I hesitated. But it would be worse to avoid Kulak openly; he might get even more suspicious. Antek came back wiping his mouth.

"All right," I said, "be glad to."

I followed Kulak into the barn. Just as the door swung closed, Kulak turned on me.

"Tell the truth now; you're a Jew, hmm?"

I froze. Tried to force a grin.

"Pan Kulak is joking." I glanced at the barn door. Kulak sidestepped me.

"Let's see. Off with your pants."

I attempted to retain my smile while I felt my quivering lips giving me away.

"Off with them," repeated Kulak. He wasn't smirking anymore.

"I don't think that … I should … why do you say that?" I mumbled.

"Why? I wanted to see if you're a *Moyshe,* that's why."

He lunged at me, trying to tackle me. I dove around him into the bale of clothes. Kulak caught my arm and pulled. Both of us fell into the hay, struggling and twisting. Kulak ended on top. He started ripping my trousers off. I fought hard but he was strong; presently my pants were pulled down below my hips. In a desperate move, I yanked hard and twisted, managing to turn over on my belly, causing the mason to let go for an instant. I heard something snap. Kulak lurched at me; but I jumped, tripped, and fell again, rolled in the bales, Kulak swinging his arms in pursuit. But the mason was heavier, and with each lunge he was sinking deeper into the hay.

I managed to jump onto the cement floor, running for the door. My pants were falling off. I yanked them up and darted through the door while Kulak still struggled to dig himself out from the hay.

I ran for the nearby woods, and ran until I was out of breath. I dragged myself to the brook, slowly cleaned myself of the hay strands. My pants were torn. I knew I could not go back.

There was only one way: stumbling along the road, I headed for the village of Piekuty Nowe and the priest's house. Franny met me at the door.

"Joseph, Lord have mercy, what happened to you?"

"Nothing, Miss Franny, just fell down. Is the father home?"

"Look at you, face all scratched, and you're losing your pants … No, he isn't, but come on in, wash your face."

The priest was in church conducting the Stations of the Cross all week while the devout were singing and reciting litanies during Holy Week. It was quiet in the priest's study. The place was kept immaculate by Franny and her mother. Still numb with fear, I sat on the sofa, on which I had slept many times.

The vicar was both astonished and glad to see me.

"Well," he said, after he'd heard the story, "I told you not to associate with the masons and stay in the house … now it's too late."

He paced the room for a while, pensive. "Tonight you stay here. Let me talk to the Wòjt and the pastor. We'll see."

He wasn't angry, but he was troubled and closed in.

"Father, what if the mason has already talked to other people?"

"Nonsense, he knows where his bread is coming from. If he opens his trap, the Wòjt will fire him. Let me talk to the Wòjt."

✛ ✛ ✛

Two days later the priest told me in the evening:

"I saw the Wòjt in the church today. Nothing to worry about. Of course, I had to tell him … He only knew that you were missing and was worried to face me."

"What did he …"

"He was furious at the mason. Wanted to fire him. But he calmed down. I prevailed upon him to take it easy. Who knows what the mason is liable to do when he gets fired? The Wòjt wanted you back. I think he believes me that you're a Catholic. Said that was good enough for him. S'long as the Wòjt doesn't fire him, Kulak would not jeopardize his job by denouncing the Wòjt for 'harboring a Jew.' He knows, being a shrewd city slicker, that the Wòjt could denounce him in turn for being a smuggler. He also knows that the Wòjt is influential with the authorities; they would take the Wòjt's word. However," the priest was at the window, looking out, lost in thought, hands folded behind his soutane, "I agree that you should not go back there.

"I also talked to the pastor," he continued, "and we're in agreement that the time has come for your baptism, my dear. If anything should happen, at least you'd be baptized …"

I felt my skin curdling with fear. "'If anything should happen'?"

"We would like to write a letter to the bishop in Łomża, as I mentioned earlier. Permission for your baptism must be given by the bishop. Tell me, Jòziaczku, do you truly desire to be baptized?"

"Yes, Father, I do."

The priest studied me. "You understand, this has to be voluntary—an act of free will. The letter would be hand-delivered to the bishop; the pastor is going to Łomża, the seat of the diocese, right after Easter."

"A letter, Father? But what if anybody should read it?"

The priest smiled. "Have no fear, my dear. This wouldn't be the first time the Church has kept a secret. She is very good about it. Just sit down and write everything about yourself to the bishop. Oh, yes, address him as Your Excellency."

I sat alone in the priest's study.

"Revered Excellency," I wrote. "With the permission and blessing of the spiritual father, Father Stanisław Falkowski, I take the liberty to address Your Excellency in the matter of my faith and spiritual salvation … I have escaped from the train on the way to the gas chambers in Treblinka which, I trust, Your Excellency has heard of. Prior to this I had spent two years in the Warsaw Ghetto under difficult circumstances and much hardship. After many weeks of difficult life, trying to survive in the forests and villages, I met my spiritual father.

"Most of all, I wish you to know that I have been and am able to sustain my life through prayer and with hope for my eternal salvation through our Lord, Jesus Christ. I want very much, Your Excellency, to be united with him forever, with Your Excellency's approbation.

"I am fifteen years old.

"With deepest gratitude, I remain,

"Most Respectfully,

"Jòzef Fajwiszys (Kutrzeba)"

✠ ✠ ✠

Following the high Easter Mass, a tall man with a bushy mustache, blue wool jacket, and loose-fitting breeches stuck into high boots came into the pastor's house with the vicar after the Mass.

"This is the young fellow I told you about, Mr. Nowaliński," said the pastor, introducing me. "Now with summer coming, and plenty of work around the farm, I'm sure he can help you out."

The man stood holding his black visored cap, as a sign of respect.

"Well, I guess so," he said with hesitation.

"Mr. Nowaliński," interjected Father Falkowski, "has a reputation as a good farmer and a decent man to work for, so I have no qualms about referring our good friend to you here. Trust *he* will treat him well and reward him, ha, ha!" The priest tried to humor the man, addressing him in the third person, as the custom had it.

Nowaliński scratched his head—as the custom also had it. "How much will the young fellow want? ... Of course, he could mainly look after the cows. I don't know about the harvest ..."

"He's a good boy and willing to work. I'm sure Mr. Nowaliński can use him around the barn and even later in the field ... Well, room and board and a pair of high boots as a reward for a season's good work. Then, if he really pleased *him, he* can get him a new suit, perhaps, too. How's that?"

"I don't know about new boots; the father knows leather costs plenty these days, and it'd not be easy to get. But we'll get him something to wear in the meantime."

"It's a deal, *gospodarzu* [a complimentary expression to a landowner]," said the young priest, and the men shook hands. I never got the boots or the new suit.

✝ ✝ ✝

I went with my new employer in his horse-drawn wagon. Mr. Nowaliński, a man in his prime forties, lived on "the colony," as the homesteads were called away from the main village, some eight kilometers away from Piekuty Nowe, and adjacent to the village of Krasowo Czestki where Marzena lived with her mother. On the way down, we passed the village center.

"Our homestead is three kilometers away on the other side," pointed Nowaliński with his horse whip. Young people didn't speak unless spoken to.

The Nowaliński farm was a spacious building with barns and stalls for the livestock adjacent to a triangular yard. In the courtyard stood a well. On the other side, opposite the barn, the forest stretched for dozens of kilometers.

✝ ✝ ✝

"You enter the forest here," said the man, "and you can stay in it till you get to the other side of Lublin."

"How far would that be?" I was fishing.

"Ho, ho!" The man looked up, using the skies as an abacus. "A hundred, perhaps hundred and fifty. Never been there, the place is full of partisans."

"What kind of partisans, proszę pana?"

"From what I hear, all kinds. Some are our boys, the straggling Soviets after the German invasion, even outlaws, criminals, and Jews."

"Do they ever bother you?" There didn't seem to be a living soul in sight.

"You'll see. It's not always easy."

The Nowaliński family consisted of the man's wife and a growing son approaching twenty. They already had a live-in farmhand who didn't ask many questions. I was, after all, just another farmhand. I slept on the wooden bench near the entrance door, covered by sheepskins and a pillow.

✠ ✠ ✠

Days went by. The skies turned gray and unremitting, as sheets of rain came down every day. It lasted three weeks and then some. Each day I woke up loathing the day to come, for I never knew when Nowaliński would have me take the cows out into the field. There, huddling under a tree or a bush, I would spend eight to ten hours shivering in the rain under my mother's jacket protecting my head from the steady, fine mist that seemed to last forever. My feet were bare since my employers had prevailed on me to leave my only shoes behind. ("What will the father say when we let you ruin the only shoes you have? What will you wear in church?") So my feet would turn blue during the day, and stay cold throughout the night.

Sometimes, when it poured heavily, Nowaliński kept his cattle in the barn. After all, it was wartime, and the cattle meant survival. The Germans had counted his cows and, dead or alive, they wanted their mandated deliveries. With the cattle indoors, I had to help out alongside the coarse farmhand, a chubby boor of a man who told hideous dirty jokes all the time, pausing only long enough to sing a lewd song. I would help him milk the cows and shovel the manure. When all work was done, we would stand in the barn door for hours watching the rain. Nowaliński's woman didn't want anybody in the house during the day. She needed room to cook, she said.

"Stay in the barn," she told me, "and do something useful. That's why we keep you. Can't feed you for nothing. After all, we promised the priest to buy you new boots after harvest time."

Fever took hold of me one day, and I spent four days shivering under the sheepskins. Evenings I listened for whispered voices coming from the room where the farmers slept. I'd wake up at night amidst nightmares when I thought from scraps of conversation that they'd discovered me and would turn me out into the rain. On the fifth day the fever subsided, and they let me stay in the house for another day. The following morning I was sent out again into the fine mist with the cows.

✠ ✠ ✠

It had stopped raining. There were puddles on the ground; and the earth, already soaked to capacity, refused to absorb more rain. I had even stopped reading the books the father had given me. I'd lost interest—I was gloomy and desperate. But I was still saying my prayers at night. For one, I wanted to be seen kneeling down to pray.

I must have been asleep for a while when the dogs began to howl. Someone was banging on the door. Nowaliński came into the kitchen. He opened the door holding up his breeches.

Several young men dressed in assorted quasi-military clothes and high boots stomped in impatiently.

"Come on, Nowaliński, you're slow."

"Told you last time to get rid of this dog; this monster must hate the moon or something," chimed in another.

"Praised be ... Mr. Nowaliński," said a tall young man more respectfully. He wore a belted jerkin and a military hat adorned with a Polish eagle.

"For centuries and centuries. Amen," answered Nowaliński, scratching himself under his nightshirt. He hadn't come all awake yet.

"All right, get the old woman to fix up something for the boys. Sorry for this sudden visit," said a broad-shouldered man who looked like the leader of the group. He had a pistol stuck in his belt. The others sported a varied collection of weapons. "You know how it is," he continued, "can't send you a special delivery letter in advance. But if you sleep less, you get tired and maybe you make fewer babies, what with all the mouths to feed these days. You should be grateful to us. We're only staying till the morning—in the barn. My boys are all out there already staked out."

The man with the eagled cap, warming himself by the stove, was eyeing me closely.

"You look familiar. Aren't you from Piekuty?"

"Why, Pan Stefan!" I exclaimed. "Why, how ...?"

It was Krasowski all right, the young man I'd met in front of the church, who had subsequently evaded the Germans during the Christmas roundup, escaping from the truck.

He told about his escape. He'd been wounded but only slightly; the bullet had just grazed him. After that he joined the Home Army partisans, the *Armia Krajowa* (AK). The Germans didn't know who he was, but then a tragedy occurred. There was a pitched battle. The AK had been working alongside railroad tracks preparing to blow up a train when they were surprised by the Germans. The AK had tried to avoid the battle but were forced to protect their rear. I said that I'd heard something about this from Father Falkowski.

"God's will, it must have been. During the battle somehow I'd lost my ID card—maybe as I was crawling. So ... they found it."

"Good Lord!" I exclaimed, "What happened?"

"They came for me to the house. They shot my brother and deported my parents."

"My ..."

"Yes, well, what's there to do except to fight to the end now ..."

There were about twenty of them. After they had drunk and eaten, all but a few who stood guard camped in the barn. I talked to Stefan more, and he inquired about Father Falkowski.

"If you see the father next Sunday, I want you to give him this." He handed me a package with leaflets from the Home Army.

"Be happy to," I said, just as an idea gripped me. "Would it be possible for me to join you, too?"

That was up to the leader, replied Stefan, but he turned to speak to the broad-shouldered man, and came back.

"We'll be pulling out in the morning. You ready to go?"

I was joyously stunned. I was not prepared to leave without seeing Father first, and told Stefan about it. In the morning, after a few hours of sleep, Stefan told me:

"It's only right that you talk to Father first. In two days we'll be pulling into Baranowy, north of the tracks. If you decide to join us, be there. Memorize this name: Karpiński. Not a squeak to anybody but the priest."

I told Nowaliński that I had to see the priest urgently and walked over to Piekuty in late afternoon. I related to him the meeting with Stefan before, with keen excitement. The priest was stunned.

"Do you realize to what danger you have exposed us? Carrying partisan leaflets ... right past the gendarmerie outpost? What if they stopped and searched you? God Almighty!"

"But, Father," I argued, "these men are fighting for Poland, against the Nazis; I was sure you'd like to see what they're doing."

"I don't need Stefan Krasowski endangering our lives to send me the leaflets. The pastor and I know all there is to know."

"I didn't know, Father ..."

"Lots of things you don't know. We're pretty well informed, we're in touch with the Home Army. It's downright asinine of Krasowski to use you as a carrier of dangerous material; enough misery and tragedy he's caused already. A good boy but losing his ID card ... now he has his family on his conscience ... Christ Almighty!"

"Father, I would like to join the partisans."

"You mean ... what? The AK?"

"Yes, Father."

"Is this ... hmm, so that's what you came to tell me?"

"Well, I came to ask your permission, Father."

The priest held his look on me.

"You don't need my permission, Jòziu," he finally said quietly. "After everything you've been through, you can be your own man, if you want. There's no way in which I could or would stop you. But why, Jòziu, why?"

"I want to fight for Poland, Father. It is my country also; it's where I was born. And you have helped me, saved me, you risked your life for me, so now that I have a chance, I would like to do my share, and repay my obligation, and fight the Germans … Father, I'd been taught by my parents to pay back everything in my life; that one should receive only when one is willing to pay back; no taking without giving."

"It's your decision. But I must advise you against it. It's my duty. You are still young: you must study more, grow up and get stronger. You've been through a lot. It's a tough life in the forest. I don't know if you can pull through—summer, winter."

"Yes, I can, Father."

"I'm not so sure. You are still young, you must study some more, grow up and be stronger before you can risk your life under extreme hardships. So that's one. Then, and this is not a pleasant thought, Joziaczku, but it's true. There are some entrenched anti-Semitic elements among the partisans. They may be patriots but they are also of the extreme faction that wants to see postwar Poland, if it ever happens, free of the Jews. If they found a Jew in their midst, they'd 'dispose' of him. There's no appeal; it's the law of the forest."

"Even if I were a baptized Catholic?"

"Even so. And I couldn't protect you. You might let a word slip out—and there are some sharpies out there; you'd be doomed. They have the guns and the ammunition. I don't want that to happen to you."

"But, Father, please understand …" I was pleading desperately, more so because the possibility of my discovery by the partisans was putting a damper on this one ray of hope to escape the misery of everyday farm work, and the rainy days, and permanently cold feet, and the mental despair of living among coarse, half-literate people. I was pleading for something I already knew deep down I would have to give up.

"Father, you must see this. I have always been taught that life has no meaning unless it is subordinated to a higher purpose outside of man himself; otherwise it is meaningless. That's why I joined Hashomer. My father, he had that larger purpose: his music—striving for perfection and the purity of his music; to express man's highest aesthetic yearnings; to bring joy and beauty to thousands in his outdoor concerts at *low prices* who otherwise would be devoid of it ..." The priest, with his warm, compassionate eyes, was listening. "With Hashomer it was to struggle against the denial of human dignity by the Germans. Then *you* have taught me: sacrifice, among other things. As it was not meant for me to continue the struggle against evil under the Jewish banner, I want to continue under the banner of my fatherland: Poland. At the farm, I am growing desperate: nobody to talk to—just the cows, the rainy days, work, and manure ... how long can I stand this? Months, years? Will my mind endure? What happens after? ... I have decided, Father. I'll go with the partisans."

"If you have decided, of what good is it asking me for advice?"

"Father, with all due respect, one can ask for advice but still arrive at one's own decision after that."

"You *have* a larger purpose, Joziu, to serve Christ, to survive and to bear witness."

"Well, I came to tell you this primarily because I wanted to ask for your blessing, for baptism, in case something happened."

"We couldn't arrange for the baptism in one day, Jòziaczku; the bishop has not answered us yet. This must be carefully planned; the Church must be cautious—no one else may know about this. Only the sacristan and the two of your godparents whom we have to select, and they must be sworn to secrecy. It would take a minimum of two weeks. That is why, in summary, my advice is *not* to go. I want you alive, Jòziu, I have a responsibility for your life."

"Father, it wouldn't be your responsibility anymore; you wouldn't have me on your hands anymore, you have taken enough risks ..."

"A priest never takes enough risks in his service to God and mankind." His expression became tender. "I say, Jòziaczku, if you want to go, I can't stop you, but I hope you won't go. The pastor and I will continue to risk our lives for you, whether you go or not. If you were discovered ... But I'm sure that God doesn't want to squander away your life. The struggle for Poland will go on without your dubious contribution in the forests, exposed to fierce elements, and to sickness ..."

"I want to go and fight, Father."

The priest turned away. "Then go."

"May I have your blessing, Father?"

"You may."

I genuflected. The priest prayed silently for a few moments, then made the sign of the cross over my head ..."*In nomine Patris, et Filii, et Spiritus Sancti.* Amen." His eyes turned moist. "Go with God," he said with an unsteady voice, and he turned away. "I'll tell the pastor."

✠ ✠ ✠

Walking back to the farmhouse, I passed the gendarmerie post and decided to make a shortcut through the fields. It was also safer that way—without running into people. I walked a while, then, as the sun was at its zenith, I sat down on the ground to rest.

I didn't want to leave the priest. I had come to love him, and I should not cause him sadness by disobeying him who had cared and done so much for me. It was just that there was ongoing misery and no way out except to keep going—God knew how long? Years maybe. At least in the forest there would be a purpose, an aim, life would be exciting and I wouldn't have to toil in the fields. But, I loved him and he loved me ... perhaps I should stay, after all. Maybe I should ... and I wept for having offended my good priest and caused him distress ...

Something rustled a few feet away. I looked up. I heard another rustle. A fox, I thought, or perhaps a stray cow grazing. But the next moment I saw his face. Young, blond hair, military tunic open at the collar; sleeves rolled up, holding a rifle at the ready. Just then he saw me. No reaction, a bit curious, perhaps, in an impassive way. He must have seen and heard me before I noticed him. The uniform was of the special, not just ordinary, SS troops. I knew it instantly: they were the same as worn by the SS at the Umschlagplatz. Their hats featured the death's head emblem worn by the special *kommando* units, the *Einsatzgruppen.*

Slowly, I must act slowly, I told myself. Panic could mean death. I raised myself slowly and nodded at the SS man. There was no reaction. I took a few steps, and then I saw the others. There were three of them, then four more in the other direction, then I saw the rest of them— perhaps twenty, all spread out, rifles at the ready, tunics unbuttoned, ready for the kill. None said a word. The silence was ominous. Just standing or squatting, waiting … I was sure I'd be challenged instantly, perhaps shot … I stood, scared to move. None of the SS men had made a move in my direction. Minutes passed. There was no reaction from the SS men—just poised stillness. *It's,* I thought, *as if they were poised to intercept resistance fighters; a kid was ignored.* I took a few steps heading for the road. Nobody stopped me.

I reached the Nowaliński house, still shaking.

The farmhand was outside. "Seen any Krauts?" he asked.

"Er … many, back there."

"Didn't take them long."

"What d'you mean?"

"You don't know nothing? Get in the house."

Old Nowalińska sat huddled inside, her head all wrapped in a kerchief. She had been crying.

It took me several minutes but I finally learned the details. There had been an ambush. The AK detachment of Polish partisans, working their way northward, had apparently stumbled upon a wagon carrying six gendarmes. They were not the gendarmes from Piekuty Nowe but had apparently been sent over to investigate a shootout earlier and were returning by way of the village of Krasowo Częstki. The Polish partisans had pumped bullets into them yielding a number of Germans dead or wounded.

This morning, several trucks carrying SS troops had arrived from the country town of Łomża to carry out mop-up operations in the fields, which included setting up ambushes against the partisans. And I had stumbled into them.

"Christ, our Lord, protect us," the woman was mumbling. "I have a bad feeling this is not the end of it. The Schwabs are out to do something terrible."

✣ ✣ ✣

We could hear the shooting the next morning. It went on for an hour. In the evening, as the red sun was setting, a horse-drawn wagon pulled up carrying a man and his son from Krasowo.

"Horror, horror, Mr. Nowaliński," the man stuttered. "Something terrible." Then, haltingly, he told them.

That afternoon SS trucks rolled into the village of Krasowo Częstki. They encircled the village and ordered the *sołtys*—the village elder—to gather up all the inhabitants in the center—all 350 of them. It had been a large and prosperous village. The SS men told the soltys they held everyone responsible for the attack on the gendarmerie. Ordered them to dig ditches. Then they lined them up in rows and machine-gunned everybody. The man and his son had escaped.

The next day every man above fourteen from adjacent villages was ordered to cover up the mass graves and to harvest the ripe wheat, myself included. The cattle were driven to Łomża.

Nobody did much work in the days that followed. Old Nowaliński had gone again into Krasowo to find out more. He'd come back in the evening and sat at the wooden table, without touching the kasza or the potatoes. Every now and then he'd mention a few more names of those murdered—friends, families. The old woman just wept, huddled near the window, moaning and lamenting, rocking her body backward and forward, as if in a Jewish prayer.

The next Sunday I went to church with the Nowalińskis. A special Mass was being said for all the murdered. The priest's face was drawn like never before, but he responded when I approached him.

"You didn't go," he said.

"No, Father."

His eyes swelled up.

Later, at the pastor's house, he recounted some more details. Marzena was gone. Her mother was visiting in the neighboring village and lived. Many others whose names and faces I had gotten to know at church had perished.

"You see, Jòziaczku," the priest was saying, as if trying to get away from the horrors, "why I distrust the AK here. They are young, adventuresome, and irresponsible. Including Stefan Krasowski. After this tragedy, I doubt if they could show their faces around here again.

"Now, you see," he continued, "we must care for the living. Things are very tense—I pray that the AK will not get trigger-happy again, for they will only bring on more disasters. We are sending them a message. As for you, you must lay low for a while. It'd be best if you stayed in the man's house for the next few weeks. Don't move around, not even to see me."

He must have seen the misery in my eyes.

"But, I'm happy to tell you—permission for your baptism has come from the bishop. I can hear your confession later; we'll go to church together. Most of the local gendarmes are away at Łomża, and it's a good time."

"But, Father, I have not done the examination of my conscience very thoroughly, yet. You told me ..."

"Do the best you can. Actually, you're not required to go to confession before your baptism. Baptism is the *first* sacrament; you cannot be admitted to other sacraments before that. But there is no harm in confession, as approaching God in the state of bliss is highly desirable. At the confessional, go through each commandment and say what you remember. Spend the next two hours going over it now."

"Is it permissible to read from a piece of paper?"

"Yes, my dear, God will not mind."

I spent the next two hours reading from the book of catechism. I searched, questioned, and doubted myself lest I unwittingly cover up some past sins, thus offending God when I knelt before Him. I was still at it when the Father returned. The priest was smiling but he wore an unruffled composure as if he, too, had been praying.

"Father, I was wondering ... if my parents are alive somewhere, do you think they'd mind?"

"It is written in St. Matthew—Jesus said to his disciples: 'everyone that hath left house or brethren or sister or father or mother ... for my name's sake, shall receive a hundredfold and shall possess life everlasting.'"

The priest took off his cape, sitting down quietly.

"Let us hope they're alive, my dear ... They should be proud of you. Someday I should be happy to meet and talk to them. Perhaps they, too, would join you in the faith."

"I hope so, Father."

"Pray for them, my dear."

Chapter Twelve:
Struggling with Conscience

THE CHURCH WAS COOL inside. Residues of frankincense and perfume filled the tall nave. The mysterious altar was asleep—a tiny light burning—and the afternoon shadows cut a diagonal path across the main aisle. Small, huddled women were coming from somewhere. My priest was already seated at the confessional, audibly moving his feet against the wooden box and rustling his robes.

It seemed as if the church had always stood there, from the beginning of time. I knelt down at the side of the confessional, glancing through the grated opening. The father turned his ear to hear me.

"In nomine Patris, et Filii, et Spiritus Sancti. Amen," invoked the priest, adding a few words of quiet prayer. One sensed a stinging silence all around, and a pregnant hum in the air.

"Go ahead, Joziu, begin," whispered the priest. "Start with the commandments." After he listened for a while, he interrupted me. "You need only state your sins, not your doubts; those you can tell me later. The next commandment, Joziu."

"The sixth: 'Thou shalt not commit adultery.'" I felt perspiration running down my back, itching. "Well, I had some thoughts and even … deeds."

"Did you touch yourself?"

"Yes, Father."

"How many times?"

" Four, five, maybe more."

"Did you desire a woman?"

"Well … in a way, I …"

"Did you ever tell her that?"

"No."

"Anything else?"

"N … no. But I held hands with a girl and came close to her body. Also … I had impure thoughts and desires—a few times … Must I reveal her name?"

"No." My shirt was clinging to me as the priest made the sign of the cross. "In nomine Patris …"

"Amen," I said.

The priest got up and folded his stole. "You can pray for a while, then come over to the parish house."

He genuflected at the main altar, skirted around the railing with his soutane flowing behind him like a graceful banner in the gentle breeze. I raised myself. It felt so peaceful. Slowly I crossed the road into the pastor's house.

"Well, well, look who is here! Our young confessant! Welcome, welcome! They say the weight of the average person's sins equals thirty to forty kilos. But not our Joseph! … I'd say only ten kilos, ha, ha!" This, coming from the booming pastor.

Supper was served before sunset.

"You'll stay with me tonight, Jòziaczku," said the priest, "for tomorrow you'll be baptized."

"Really, Father? What about the farmer?"

"I'll take care of that. Yes, my dear, the time has come. Oh, you'll be pleased to know that we decided to let you keep your own name— Joseph. We thought there was something prophetic … symbolic in your name, with St. Joseph becoming your patron saint. As it says in Mark's Gospel, 'a voice of one crying in the desert.' Now you'll go to church a half hour early and lie prostrate on the floor before the altar in the sign of the cross until the time comes."

I was restless that night; it took me a long time to fall asleep. I prayed for a long time, even after the light was turned off.

✛ ✛ ✛

I had breakfast, which Anna had prepared, at the pastor's. She had a special smile as if she, too, had known my true identity. Father Falkowski led me across the road and into the sacristy.

"Now, one final question, Jòziu. Look at me; look me in the eyes."

"Yes, Father."

"You understand that your baptism is entirely voluntary; it must be so. If you want to change your mind, there's still time—that should be all right. You know that both Father Modzelewski and I will continue doing our best to save you. If not here, it'll be elsewhere. But I must know from you—from the bottom of your heart and mind: do you truly wish to be united with our Lord, Jesus Christ? Do you accept him as your Savior? Do you want to join his Holy Church? Do you?"

"Yes, Father."

The priest was looking into my soul, I felt.

"I think you do, Jòziu. If this war ever comes to an end, I hope that you will remain faithful to our Lord who suffered for you, and not betray him ... Well, you know it has been said of other Jews that they are opportunists; that they convert in times of stress but later, when it becomes safe, many convert again. The people say: 'A Jew will remain a Jew.' I only hope that ... this also being my first conversion, it's very important for me ... that you'll stay faithful and prove with your life that a Jew can be trusted when accepted into the faith."

"I will, Father, I promise. I will not betray Christ. Nor you, Father."

"Go now and humble yourself before the Lord. And pray to the Virgin Mary to intercede on your behalf."

I stretched myself flat on the cold stone floor before the main altar and the tabernacle. I prayed for help, for mercy, for faith. It was safe from the outside world.

As the priest entered in his festive robes of white and gold, he was followed by the couple I'd met at the dinner for the gendarmes. They were to be my godparents. The sacristan locked the main door; he was the only servant to the brief silent Mass which was to follow. The priest wanted me to accept communion right after the baptism.

I knelt on the steps of the altar, my head bowing low. "*Domine, non sum digno*—Lord, I am not worthy ..."

The priest spoke in a hushed voice. He motioned to the sacristan who stepped up bearing a container with holy water. He dipped his fingers in it and held them over my head.

"I baptize you in the name of the Father, and of the Son, and of the Holy Spirit. Amen."

"Amen," echoed my godparents and the sacristan. The sun peeked in through the tall windows.

During the Consecration, the sacristan merely touched the bells; he had been told not to ring them loudly—no chances were to be taken. When the time came to receive the Eucharist, I closed my eyes and, raising my head, parted my lips ...

I was helped from my knees. The two godparents were quietly congratulating me. The priest embraced me, and the sacristan shook my hand warmly.

I had accepted a new contract on my life.

Chapter Thirteen
Introspection: A Fateful Decision

SUMMER WAS AT ITS zenith. The wheat was ripe, and a dozen farmhands were enlisted to help Nowaliński with his harvest. They came early, just after dawn, sleeves rolled, women and men who sharpened their scythes. Then, patiently, they worked their way through the fields in slow and rhythmic movements like pendulums, moving one step at a time behind their scythes. They stopped periodically to wipe their brows, some spitting on their palms to get a better grip, reaping the fruits of nature which allowed little time while they lasted.

Nowaliński's son showed me the way with the scythe.

"Easy now, don't get impatient and don't work for speed or you'll miss once and watch your foot lying behind you. Take a swing—like this—and move your hands across, evenly. Never swing toward you."

I worked and a couple of times came near amputating my foot. Later I was told to follow the mowers and stack up fallen wheat into separate bunches.

Then came the hay—three weeks of it until it was all ready for stacking. Several men would brace themselves on their feet hoisting mounds of hay with their pitchforks onto tall horse-drawn wagons. It took great art to pick up just the right amount of hay and catapult it onto the wagon—all in one big sweeping effort, without dropping much hay, while the man on top of the wagon arranged it so the hay held fast, as the horses strained and pulled to get the wagon onto the road until their veins were taut, looking like a road map, I thought, on the verge of bursting under their huge muscles.

There was not much time for praying. Every evening after supper, just as the sun was setting, everyone lay down and slept loglike until the roosters told them it was time to start again. Work was halted only on Sundays or when it rained.

There were moments when I was glad to be alive: brief moments. But the merciless routine and the loneliness were weaving a pattern of despair, forlornness, and anguish. I had expected that, in the wake of my baptism, an inner peace and joy would come to me; that an inner repose would engulf me, a complete makeover that would fill me with hope and tranquility. But it didn't happen; instead, I faced hopelessness on awakening each day—a dark, gaping, futureless abyss.

☩ ☩ ☩

"Jòziaczku," said the priest the following Sunday. "I had a long talk with the pastor." His tone was gentle, but I sensed gravity in his demeanor. "Things don't look good. We have seen many German victories throughout Europe and the vise is tightening. The Ghetto in Białystok revolted, and the remnants of its Jews are being led to death. Jews are being hunted wherever they can be found. I must be candid with you, for you are very dear to us: I don't know how much longer we can keep you around, try as we might."

I felt my throat tightening, the familiar choking sensation. "Father … what are you saying?"

"Well, we've put our heads together, myself and the pastor. The best thing for you, we think, would be to go right into the lion's den."

"The lion's den?"

"Yes." The priest flashed an urchin's grin. "You know that, in addition to the raids on the population, the Germans have conducted a propaganda campaign all along to induce people to volunteer for labor in East Prussia, promising them good working conditions, good food, etc. We have a plan: if you should volunteer, your chances for survival could be much better. There, to the Germans, you'd be just another foreigner who speaks Polish. Unlike a native Pole, they wouldn't detect every nuance of inflection, or ask knowing questions about your background. You could tell them that you want to get away from home; that you want to learn a trade rather than work on a farm. Their propaganda trumpets that you could choose your line of work. We know that you are a city boy, not suited to farm work. It could be the answer."

"But, how, Father? ... I mean, what about identity papers?"

"We discussed that, too. It involves some risk; but, working together, with God's help, it might work. The Germans are now re-registering the entire population of our eastern district. New identity cards are being issued. Next week our village and the surrounding villages are to report to Stare Zochy, halfway over to Szepietowo. It's a simple procedure—coming from those who have gone through the registration before. The *Amtskommissar* will sit there; one or two gendarmes will take ID pictures, and the Wòjt. Now, they won't know you from Adam. They take the Wòjt's word; he's supposed to certify everyone."

"What about the Wòjt?" I shuddered.

"Everything will be taken care of with the Wòjt."

"And what if some of the villagers get suspicious?"

"That's taken care of, too. You don't go on the day the population of Piekuty is scheduled. You go the next day, with the other village. Tell everyone that you were sick the day before. The Wòjt will certify that. There's a risk, my dear, but, if it all goes well, you will have an official legitimate identity card. For you it'll be a passport to life. And with the new ID, you could volunteer to go to East Prussia."

"When do you want me to go, Father?"

"Sometime next week. I'll let you know."

✛ ✛ ✛

"Today, Jòziaczku, walk over to Szuby, straight along the road. It'll take you about three hours. When you see the queue, line up outside, give your name—Józef Kutrzeba—and say hello to the Wòjt."

He held and embraced me. "If it be God's will ..." and he drew the sign of the cross over my head. I kissed the priest's hand.

"Jòziaczku," he said as we parted, "if, God forbid ... don't involve us."

I looked at my savior. "No, Father, I'd rather die first."

✙ ✙ ✙

No one took particular notice of me. Peasants, stomping their feet to shake off the early snow, chatted sporadically as the waiting line crawled. A table had been set up by the roadside. I could feel my legs shaking. When my turn came, I gave my name and my picture was taken. Next, the gendarme took my fingers and rolled them in the black, sticky liquid, then affixed the fingerprints to a green form. The sołtys looked up.

"Who ... where you from?"

"From Piekuty Nowe, sir. Joseph Kutrzeba. I was sick yesterday."

"He's all right," interjected the Wòjt. Turning to the Amtskommissar, he added gravely, "I know this fellow."

The German signed the papers.

"Greetings to the father," said the Wòjt quietly.

Ten minutes later I had my legitimate identity papers, complete with a photo, and started on my way back. I walked slowly, thanking God and praying.

I reached Piekuty in late afternoon. Father Falkowski had stayed home all day awaiting my return. His eyes were moist.

"Father, I am now a citizen of the mighty Third Reich," I said joyously, "no longer a hunted animal."

The priest could not hide his joy. Years later he was quoting my words.

"In one week, Jòziaczku, you will go to Szepietowo and volunteer for work in Prussia, now that you have an identity card and an official right to live." His eyes were smiling and he even chuckled a little.

Chapter Fourteen:
Securing a "Legitimate" Document

THE VILLAGE OF SZEPIETOWO just missed being a town, though it was the seat of the Amtskommissar—for administrative matters—and of the *Landeskommissar*—in charge of robbing the peasants of their harvest and their cattle. Both worked out of adjoining offices. The father was rushing me, for it was vital to reach Szepietowo before the end of the office hours to report and find a place for the night.

An attractive Polish woman greeted me in the anteroom to the Kommissar's office. She sat behind the room divider, and she didn't speak the local dialect.

"Why do you want to go to Prussia?" she asked.

"I am an orphan, proszę pani; I have worked in the fields to earn my keep, but I would like to see the world and learn a trade."

"Why can't you do it in our own country?"

"Well, I just have the itch, I guess."

"Where're you from?"

"Warsaw."

"Oh, yes. So am I."

I tried to change the subject. "Would you let me speak to the Kommissar, please?"

"Not today. Tomorrow, maybe."

But she wrote out a slip for me to be put up for the night with a family across the street.

I faced the Kommissar the next day. With the secretary translating, I answered some questions and the Kommissar nodded his head. There would be no more transports to East Prussia for some days, he told me, unless more people volunteer. I was to stay put and check with the office every few days.

That was not welcome news. I was staying with the Polish family which had been directed to feed me. At mealtimes questions were asked. There was nothing for me to do during the day. It was not a good idea to walk around; people knew each other and I attracted attention.

A few days went by. Eventually, the Polish secretary, in between receiving and translating for various supplicants, would take notice of me.

"Don't hang around here. I'll get in touch with you when the time comes, I told you."

But I still came almost every day to make a "nuisance" of myself. One day the Kommissar noticed me as I bowed to him respectfully.

"*Acha, der junge Kerl mit der Wanderlust* [Aha, the young fellow with a yearn for travel]."

But the situation was deteriorating by the day. The secretary, I concluded, didn't want me around and was not much in favor of volunteers. Toward the end of the week I found myself alone with her. She lowered her voice.

"Damn it, what do you want to go there for? Are you crazy? Contributing to their war effort?"

"I told you, madam," I answered trying to control my desperation, "I want to see the world, learn something."

"And I told you: you can learn something here," she fired back. The door opened and the Kommissar entered accompanied by his two teenage children.

"*Ach so, unser Freiwillige ist wieder zu Besuch* [Well, our volunteer comes to visit us again]," he said with a smile. I thought I understood something about a volunteer and the visiting part. The official introduced me to his children. I decided to go for broke. The Kommissar had the secretary translate.

"Stay around some more, says the Kommissar," the woman translated. "The food is adequate, isn't it?"

"Yes," I said, "but—"

"But what?" she cut me off. "Don't bother us too often." The twelve-year-old daughter of the Kommissar said something to her father, and he turned to his secretary.

"The Kommissar wants to know if you'd like to play with his children. They don't have any playmates here among the peasants."

I was invited to a spacious house confiscated by the Germans where presently the Kommissar's children were spending their vacations, away from their school in Königsberg. I played ball with the children, picking out some German phrases and repeating some Polish words for them. Then I was asked to come again next day.

Early in the afternoon we heard a commotion and loud yelling in German. The Kommissar's children had me follow them outside to the porch. There we caught sight of a man in civilian clothes running away toward the woods. Two German gendarmes were pointing their rifles at him. Shots exploded. The man fell down, quivering.

"Oh, yeah," said the Kommissar's son. "They must have caught another Jew. That makes it one less, hurrah!"

✠ ✠ ✠

Several days elapsed. At times, I was asked to accompany the kids on their walk through the village; they were curious about several things. But we were also attracting the attention of the villagers. Again I stopped by the office and asked about my leaving.

"What's the hurry?" wondered the Kommissar. "Tell him my children like his company; they have no one else here suitable to play with and learn a little Polish. There's something refined about this boy—*gute Kinderstube* [upbringing]. Tell him to relax. As soon as there is a transport ..."

I felt the vise tightening. The Kommissar wants me around, and that carried with it ever-increasing risk of exposure. A week later an elderly peasant looked me up in the evening. He had a note for me from Father Falkowski.

"Word has reached me that you are still there. What goes on? Your further stay is highly inadvisable. You are endangering us. You can trust the carrier of this note. Please destroy it right away."

"Any reply?" inquired the peasant.

My thoughts raced in a circle. "Please tell the father that I'm doing all I can."

The next day I tried again lingering around the Kommissar's house until he came home for dinner. I used my best German beseeching him to let me go away.

"Maybe early next week," said the official. "Be patient."

I was in a trap. I could feel growing suspicion around me in the village that might, at any moment, turn into denunciation. I couldn't, on the other hand, just disappear and return to the priest, for by now the Kommissar would surely launch a search for me. Daytime hours turned into one continuous anxiety; nights I stayed awake trying to search for a way out.

"Tomorrow," said the secretary to me the following Monday after I was called into the office, "the Kommissar is going to Łomża. He'll pick you up with his car in the morning. Be here."

It was too good to be true. "So are his children," she added with contempt in her voice. "The school year is beginning."

The next morning I was driven in the Kommissar's plush Mercedes, after I'd taken leave of his children. The German took me straight into the office of the *Arbeitsamt* in Łomża and explained that he had tried to get me the best job available—that of an apprentice in an automobile shop rebuilding car engines. He made me promise to write and eventually to visit his children in Königsberg. I was processed, given a ticket and, together with another young Pole, boarded the comfortable train—not to Treblinka but to Germany, with a legitimate Polish ID card.

A three-hour train ride followed across the flat, northern fields of Poland. There was a routine check at the East Prussian border, and the train rolled into German territory heading for the city of Insterburg. There was death behind me, but there was also life ahead. Again, I was on my own; but I was also alive.

Chapter Fifteen
In the Lion's Den

THERE WAS A SPRINKLING of uniforms alighting from the train in Insterburg. A few civilians strutted across the clean and sparse train station. I carried a small bundle and looked around. Approaching me with a sly grin, pacing like a military officer during a casual inspection tour, was a middle-aged German.

"*Bist du eben aus Polen eingekommen?* [Have you come from Poland just now?]" "*Aus Polen, jawohl* [From Poland, yes, sir]," I answered.

"*So, denn. Ich bin Heinrich Toussaint.*" He looked me over. "*Sprichst du etwa Deutsch?* [Do you speak some German?]"

"*Ein bisschen* [A bit]."

Then he said something else; all I got was the word *Wagen*.

"*Wagen?*" I repeated.

"*Verflucht, wo is der Wagen? Wo ist der Pikalski? Komm, komm.*" (Damnit, where is the car? Where is Pikalski? Come, come.)

We came out onto a square abutting the semicircular sidewalk in front of the station. Cars crowded the small square. It looked very modern and worldly to me. The German stopped to speak to a railroad man, as if looking around for someone. I wasn't sure in what manner I should walk alongside the German who, for all appearances, would be my boss. I tried to recall what my father would have me do and decided that I should remain one step behind and to the left of the stout German. I switched sides.

"*Wo bist du?* [Where are you?]" the man demanded as he pirouetted to his right. Just then a hand waved from the side of the square. It belonged to a short man in blue overalls topped by curly, blond, receding hair. He was standing next to a small pickup truck. His bowed legs were firmly planted, as if supporting a weight three times his own.

The German snorted at him. "*Donnerwetter, Pikalski, wo bist du gewesen?* [A thunder should … Pikalski, where've you been?]"

"*Herr Chef mußt verstehen. Frau Chef hat viel Arbeit zu Hause für mich. Kom zurück spät. Ich nicht schuldig.* [Mr. Boss must understand. Mrs. Boss got a lot of work for me at home She come back late. I not guilty.]" It seemed to me that Pikalski strained for his best command in German. Chef wiggled his finger threateningly.

"*Pikalski, Pikalski, pass auf* [Watch out!]"

The German's broad, cheeky face was locked permanently into a thin lip line; but at the same time, he wore a faint frozen smile that seemed somewhat urbane, though scary. He'd come around motioning for Pikalski to lower the tailgate of the truck to accommodate me, himself getting into the front seat.

Pikalski, before urging me to jump into the back, lowered his voice confidentially:

"You Polish? From where?"

"Near Łomża."

"Well, you're lucky. It's not a bad place except for this sadist. But I can handle him."

"Pikalski!" the voice reached us.

"I'll talk to you later. Let's go to the shop."

"Are there many people there?" I intercepted him.

"Three other Poles besides me. You'll be all right."

My heart sank. I'd ventured into the lion's den to get away from being recognized.

* * *

It was a short ride. From the back of the truck I could see a wide avenue growing longer and paved with small, rectangular bricks, framed by medium-size buildings of clean stucco. Eventually we entered a courtyard and scrambled out of the pickup.

"*Geh mit Pikalski,*" bellowed the German.(Go with Pikalski)

Pikalski, who asked me to call him "Pan Staś—we don't go for formality here," led the way to a small ground-floor room with three wooden double bunks and two lockers. Inside, there was hardly room to turn around.

"This is it," Staś said as he closed the door. "How'd you ever get here?"

I expected the question. I couldn't very well say that I had been picked up during a roundup, for the German might tell him that I had volunteered. I had to go all the way on this one.

"I ... came to learn a trade, to become ... a mechanic."

"You what? You volunteered? You crazy?"

"Well, I am alone ... and wanted to see the world, learn a trade."

"Why in hell here? Why not back home?"

"Well, just itching to see the world, I guess."

"Well, well," Pikalski shook his head, "some itch. Better off having it up your ass."

"And you, sir—er, Pan Staś?" Trying to change the subject.

"Me ... ha!" he giggled, "They got me ... street roundup, in Warsaw."

He took a chunk of bread from a narrow locker. Then, from under a blanket covering a lower bunk, he pulled a piece of kielbasa, cut a small piece off, and broke the bread into two chunks, offering a piece of each to me.

"Here. What about your parents?"

"My mother is dead and my father never came back from the war. He was an officer."

"Well, who've you been staying with?"

"My cousin, the priest ... but I was getting fidgety—small village. So that's why."

Pikalski surveyed me. "The sadist told me to show you the place. Let's start with the pissoir." As we stood side by side, I was careful to shield my private parts from him.

"Don't you worry, kid," as he sighed with relief, "we'll take care of you. Got to go now, drive the bastard someplace. I'll ask him what he wants you to do. The others will be back from work at six. We'll get you a blanket later and a locker. No sheets. Only be careful of the old fart, Wojciechowski—he steals. Don't say I told you. You brought some food?"

"I still have some bread and kielbasa."

"Well, hide it."

Two hours later Pikalski came back, sat down on a lower bunk, and started.

"Got to give you a lowdown so you know what you're in for. This place is run by that fucking sadist Toussaint. Nothing happens here without his approval—in every nook and cranny; and all with this fucking smirk."

"Toussaint," I wondered, "French?"

"I once asked—he almost killed me. He or his family came from Alsace-Lorraine—the disputed French-German region—until the war, French. The Germans hate the French with a passion and vice versa. The bastard will know it if you even think it."

Over the next few days Pikalski, whenever he had a chance, seemed to be in his element to spill out his venom for Toussaint before me. Intermittently, he would draw for me the "potrait," as he called it, of the "Boss Supreme." Somehow, thus, I got the impression that he'd taken to me.

"I spend a lot of time with him," Pikalski resumed. "We are almost like two Satans who were born to hate each other. Yet, it's a farce which I've come to enjoy, else I'd go raving mad."

✠ ✠ ✠

A siren sounded at six o'clock in the evening, and within moments many feet were heard shuffling and stomping in the courtyard and outside the door. A tall, dark, and husky man barged into the room, followed closely by an older man with graying hair—both wearing dark stained overalls, their hands stained with grease and dark metal powder.

"I'm first, I'm first," the old man was yelling, lighting up the small gas range housing two burners.

"*Harasho* [Alright], Pan Wojciechowski," said the tall young man with a Russian accent. "I put my pot on the other plate." He spoke broken Polish, interlacing it with Russian, I thought.

I raised myself from the lower bunk in the center.

"Good evening. I just arrived today."

"Not now," fired the old man as he scurried out the door. "Got to wash my hands and put my potatoes on before the others rush in."

"I'm Victor," said the tall man, extending his dirty hand to me after his failed attempt to wipe it off with a dirty rag that hung from his pocket. "Byelorussian. I speak Polish like never hear before ..."

"My name is Joseph," I offered.

"The main thing is you understand me, or I help you," said Victor breaking into a loud roar of laughter. "Oh, *yibi Tvoyu mat', choliera* [Motherfucker, cholera-damnit]," excuse me ... I dirtied your hand. But," he added apologetically, "if you want to be automobile mechanic, you learn to dirty your hands, ha! ha!"

He picked up a towel from his bunk, turning in the doorway: "I only joking, *ponimayesh* [understand]? Excuse me, hmm?"

Two other men came in, both in their early twenties.

"What the Christ we got here?" said the huskier one. "The Krauts go for child labor now?" He grinned, his "r"s being uncharacteristically Polish. "Well, anyway, welcome to the sweatshop." He leaned forward like a bull ready for combat, extending his right hand to me. "*Servus*, my name is , Wacek by first name. This," he added, pointing at the other man behind him—a skinny midget with a large head marked by two wide eyes, with a self-effacing manner—"is the eminent candidate for the other world—Kazik Sikorski."

"All right, all right," nodded the skinny man, opening his locker and changing into a short-sleeved shirt. His mien was of someone used to tolerating Vacek's ribbing. Turning to me, he asked: "Would you like to share my locker with me? We don't have enough room in this chicken coop."

"Yes, thank you, sir."

"I don't know if you realize, but we sleep here on bare boards. We'd asked that Toussaint … bastard for straw mattresses, and we're still waiting."

Profanities didn't become Kazik; I thought that he strained for them to convince others of being one of them.

"But you'll get used to them," he added; "you get used to everything." And his face grew sadder.

"Coming through, coming through," chirped the old man, entering, his hair wet following his visit to the washroom. "Let's see, how are my potatoes doing?" He peeked under the lid. "Good, good, do you want to use the range after me, Mr. Kazik?"

Bowlegged Pikalski, the chauffeur, came in shaking his head.

"Old fart always the first one with the grub, never change."

Unperturbed, the old man faced Pikalski: "Hey, how about a little schnapps, hmm? Got a thimbleful still left, saving it for you."

"Trying to bribe me again, old fart? What is it you need now?"

"That'll come later; first you have a spot."

"I knew it." He turned to me: "See, I know the bastard."

"He's just the smartest of us all," threw in Vacek, "that fucker. And you fall for it every time."

"I didn't know Pan Wojciechowski can still fuck, ha, ha!" chimed in Victor.

"That's all right," grinned Pikalski. "I only let him outwit me when it suits me."

"Come to think of it," said the old man, with a chip on his shoulder, "new arrivals always treat. Got something with you from our mother country, young fellow?"

"I have some bread and kielbasa," I offered.

Pikalski pierced me with his eyes, shaking his head. "I warned you."

"That's all right, Mr. Wojciechowski, please help yourself."

The old man reached for my sausage. "Mmmm, good. I'll just save it for later and have it with my potatoes." He wrapped his piece in a brown bag, tucking it under his blanket.

That got to Pikalski. "Aren't you going to share your potatoes with Joe here?"

"Come on now," said the old man, with a mock grimace, "I only have three potatoes."

"You fucking bastard," intoned Pikalski. "You see, Joe, I told you."

The old man paid no attention. He had little pig's eyes surrounded by puffed-up lids. His movements were quick and jerky, yet there was a finality and thoroughness to them like a seasoned pickpocket's. His face, as now, showed a feigned, deliberate surprise, a studied astonishment which could turn into almost anything the next moment: clowning, ridicule, threat or violence. Presently he pondered the alternatives whereupon he took out the sausage and took a ravenous bite.

"Mmmm … good kielbasa. I do thank you, young fellow. See, when you get to be my age, you'll take anything you can get your hands on. Don't listen to him," he added, pointing at Pikalski; "you are earning my gratitude, you are. And that can be very important, as you'll see."

Pikalski stood between two bunks, feet planted defiantly on his bow legs, with hardly room to sparc, grinning sarcastically.

"I don't know about the gratitude part," Vacek (Wacek in Polish) sounded off, his feet dangling off the edge of the upper bunk, struggling with his overalls which he tried to shed, speaking with a hoarse, bemused voice. "But you'd better not bark up the wrong tree, old man. You're dealing here with an old knifer from Praga-Warsaw, if you fuck around with *Mister* Pikalski."

The latter stood there, his grin gradually turning into intimidation. "Someday," he hissed, "he's gonna get it, old fart—right under the rib, *tshhh*."

Wojciechowski's piggy eyes pondered his next move. Then he made a choice.

"Dear friend, Stasiu," he turned with an outpouring of faked warmth, "I would never want to be anything but your best friend. Why, I respect you, and everything. I wouldn't let a fly hurt you, don't you know?"

"See that you don't." Pikalski began to pull out of his overalls, too.

"Just to seal our friendship: how about one of my potatoes?"

"Fuck your potato." Pikalski was down to his long drawers, winking at me.

"Please, now, do me the favor; you'll make me personally very happy. A privilege, no less. Ha! If this were only back home, before the bastards got hold of me, ha! I would treat you to a feast, *Panie Stasiu*. Not only that, but I would fix you up with two fantastic whores: one would blow you, the other would rape you in the snout. Even Kazik, our intellectual—I would fix him up. And, except for his priestly looks, that would be no problem: he's got the biggest one of us all. Did you ever see his dick?"

Sikorski stopped in the doorway, a pot in his hand. His huge, childlike eyes looked sad, but his mouth was entertained, though it didn't become him.

"Before the bastards got hold of him ... listen to him," Pikalski was saying sarcastically. "You volunteered, old badger, don't give us this shit."

"So did you, for that matter," snorted the old man.

"For different reasons. I had to; the criminal police were after me. For underground activities. But you came to make money and—you're making it, upon God's wounds!"

"Yeah, for stabbing activities, not underground activities," fired back the old man sarcastically.

"*Niet Boha*, tovarish! [There's no God, comrade!]" boomed Victor, who had caught the last words coming from the washroom. "There is no God," he repeated. "You know there is? ... What you have, Mr. Wojciech? Two arms, two legs, and a big prick, *vot!*" Raising his fist bent at the elbow, he spat out: "*Bolshi huj* [big prick]!"—which sent him into a paroxysm of laughter.

"Hey, Victor," Vacek yelled from the door on the way to the washroom, as if the Russian were deaf. "Victor! Who created the world?"

"Big prick, that's who!" He clenched his fist upward again, elbow bent. I suspected it was part of an ongoing game: Vacek provoking Victor, only to hear the same answer.

"Now you're being vulgar, Russian," Wojciechowski butted in, shaking his head in pious wonderment. "Someday, God will ..."

"Why you say that, *Panie* [Mr.] *Wojciechowski?*" It was obvious that respect for the elderly was tipping the scale for Victor, no matter the good-natured expletives. "I mean no offense; I respect your religious feelings: you, Vacek's, Kazik's, and even my good friend's, the bandit's …"

"Look out, Victor, I'll give you 'bandit,'" shot back Pikalski, but it was apparent that he liked Victor.

"He, ha, ha! *Bratok* [Brother] *Stasiu!*" It was obvious that everyone here was afraid of Pikalski.

Sikorski had returned from the washroom. The old man meanwhile was bending over his potatoes at the gas range, and Kazik was unable to squeeze through past Vacek and the Russian.

"Do I hear, Victor, that you are blaspheming again?" the minuscule Pole asked good-naturedly.

"No, Pan Kazik, no, I swear I tell truth. I respect feelings of everybody, but is true: Pan Vacek ask me who created world. I say: *Huj!* A big prick! No? Who other? People fuck, and world is created. I mean, animals—same way, and so people. Not God!" And he took a step brushing his elbow against the handle of the pot: the old man's potatoes landed on the floor.

"You … fucking Bolshevik!" screamed Wojciechowski.

Victor stood riveted to the spot, holding his hand up to his cheek in genuine shock.

"*Bozhe Drogi!* Dear God! Forgive Pan Wojciechowski. I didn't mean. I am sorry."

The old man was frantically picking up the remnants of his potatoes. Victor stooped down to help him.

"I have some bread and lard; I will split with you, old man."

"Speaking of God, he punished the old badger," threw in Pikalski. "Come on, Jozek, follow me to the washroom. Got a towel?"

"No, sir."

"Use mine. And don't 'sir' me. I am, like he said—a knifer, a bandit. Staszek's the name."

I forced a smile. "Well, sir, er … Panie Staszku, I'm sure he meant it in jest …"

"The hell he did. I really am. I knifed many a man. I was a gangster; you don't believe me? In Warsaw, Praga. The criminal police was after me so I split here … Sure was. I don't bother nobody. But if anybody stands in my way, I slip a knife under his ribs, right here." He felt my rib cage. "Best place is between the second and third. Goes in smooth."

I shuddered involuntarily. We stood in a large room adjacent to the washroom.

"This here," Pikalski motioned, "is what the Krauts call *Gemeinschatszimmer*: means their fucking recreation room. The Germans come here to eat their sandwiches at lunchtime. You have overalls?" I shook my head. "Well, wear what you can tomorrow, then we'll get you something. Here are two blankets," he said later. "You sleep on one, cover yourself with the other one. Pillow, you have to 'organize' later, like everybody else."

✣ ✣ ✣

The lights were snapped on in the middle of the night. A piercing high-pitched sound was stinging my ears.

"Is there a fire?" I jumped up.

"All right, everybody up!" Sikorski was stretching himself.

"Fire? Listen to him," came Vacek's voice from the upper bunk. "Fire! Ha!"

"Is there?" I insisted.

"Will someone, please, explain to our new arrival where the fire is?" Vacek's feet dangled over my head for a second; presently he leaped down onto the floor. Pikalski was climbing into his overalls. He was grinning. The old man returned from the washroom, all washed up.

"What, what, what? Fire? Where's the fire?" He moved in a trot, shuffling his wooden clodhoppers.

"Boy wonder here," commented Vacek, moving his head toward me over the right side of his moustache, "thinks there is a fire."

The intruding sound had ceased. The old man looked up at me in feigned amazement.

"Ooooh ... I see. Yes, of course. Well, you can go back to sleep now; the fire will be put out. What say, Mr. Vacek, we'll take care of our boy and let him sleep some more, then bring him some breakfast, perhaps scrambled eggs and kielbasy? Fresh rolls? Nine o'clock all right, or should we wait till ten to serve His Lordship?"

"Don't listen to them," Sikorski said matter-of-factly. "This is the morning siren, five forty-five. Got ten minutes to get ready. Hey, Victor, get your ass up."

Pikalski was grinning. "Old fart, always pulling someone's leg."

"Are we going to work in ten minutes?" I asked in disbelief.

"Only if you need to earn some German currency, Your Lordship." The old man was bowing mockingly in my direction. He was hovering over the gas range warming up something.

"Come on, Jòzek," bristled Pikalski, "I got to take you around. Boss's orders. Show you the shop," he continued, buttoning up his fly. He had warmed up some German *Ersatzkaffee* hastily and was offering me a few sips.

We crossed the yard in the gray dusk, passing a few idle vehicles, some with their hoods up and gaping holes where the engines had been removed, and entered a huge, high-ceilinged workshop hall filled with all kinds of heavy machinery. Some twenty men were lined up punching the time clock, all wearing blue overalls. A few wore military caps.

"Pan Staszek," I turned to Pikalski, "who are these men wearing military caps?"

"These are our 'Jews,' we call them: French and Belgian POWs."

"Why do you call them Jews?"

The chauffeur smiled. "With their hooked noses and the way they talk with their hands, they're just like our Jews."

He punched his card under a time clock and turned to one of the two tall men observing the men punching the cards, who wore gray duster coats.

"*Herr Meister,* this is our new journeyman—the apprentice. Herr Chef told me to take him in."

I followed Pikalski into a glassed-in office built into a corner of the workshop hall. It overlooked the entire hall with the heavy machinery.

"*Wenn hast du denn da, Pikalski* [Whom do you have here, Pikalski]?" I heard from the corner of the cubicle office as we entered. I saw a teenage girl with a round, attractive face and large breasts. She looked me over.

"*In Ordnung* ["Alright]," she said, hearing Pikalski's explanation. "Go to work, I'll take care of him."

Pikalski left and the girl motioned for me to follow her out. "*Pass mal auf* [Watch out]," the chauffeur said, grinning, "he's under my care. And, for all I know, you're still a virgin, or ...?" The girl snorted playfully, feigning shock. She motioned for me to follow her out, through the gateway and into a row of clean, elegant offices. We entered one of them.

"*Sprichst du Deutsch?*" she asked.

"*Ein wenig* [A little]," I answered. She sat down and crossed her legs. Her navy-blue pleated skirt slit up her thighs but she ignored it. "*So, a bissel* [So, a little]," she repeated in her vernacular. She was studying me. "*Doch, ganz gut* [Indeed, quite good]."

I made a quick mental note: it was correct, in dialect, to say "*a bissel*." I'd been afraid to use any German phrases before hearing a German say them lest, unwittingly, I'd use a Yiddish phrase overheard in my childhood.

"What's your name?"

"Joseph."

"Hmm, Joseph. That's all right. Mine is Hannelore. You Polack?"

"Polish," I said.

"Well, I mean Polish. You look Polish. The others are Polacks. They're no good. We're doing them a favor by letting them work for us. Except ... well, maybe one or two: Sikorski and Schiller."

"Schiller?"

"I'll take you to him. You'll answer to him. He's ... well, almost like a *Kulturdeutscher*. The others are no good. Maybe Sikorski, too, though he's half *Humpelmann*."

"*Humpelmann?*"

She tried to imitate a clown with her body language. "*Wie in einem Zirkus* [As in a circus]." I joined in her laughter.

"How old are you?" she asked.

"Fifteen. Almost sixteen."

"I am sixteen," she said. She appeared a few inches taller than I and had the full body of a woman.

Hannelore filled in some forms. "If you need anything, come see me." Then she jumped up. "Come with me, quick, *der Alte* is coming."

"*Der Alte?* [The old man?]"

"Ja. Der Chef."

Heinz Toussaint peeked through the glass partition and came around. I clicked my heels. He nodded. The ironic smile was there.

He exchanged some words with Hannelore; soon she led me into the huge workshop past rows of various heavy machinery. The steady hum of over a dozen lathe machines filled the stifled air. They seemed to polish brass tubes; their reverberations echoed the shrilling lacerations of the smaller mills that dug into metal cylinders inside the engines that were mounted upon them. Some were peeling thin layers of metal at high speed. Together, they exuded a cacophony of buzzing, whining, and screeching. What stood out, however, was the roar of large truck engines installed on special stands. Every few seconds someone had to accelerate them—to test them, I thought. Men in overalls stood everywhere. We stopped next to a huge idle lathe. A man's head was buried inside.

"Herr Schiller," Hannelore accosted him, "Herr Schiller!"

A handsome, hawkish profile emerged with an effort. The man had short-cropped, curly and bushy blond hair, with piercing, watery-blue, immobile eyes shaded by brown, thick eyebrows. He straightened out slowly, annoyed at the interruption.

"Brought you a new apprentice," she yelled over the roar. "One of yours."

Schiller wiped his hands slowly against a rag, as if the delay in answering held in check whatever profanities he had contemplated.

"You Polish?" he asked in that language. It seemed as if he meant to ask a lot more.

"Yes."

"All right, leave him here."

I followed until we came upon a German with his light beige dustcoat. After words were exchanged, we stopped at a bank of vises.

"Ever done this?" inquired Schiller.

"No, sir."

He inserted a metallic object into a vise, lifted a hand file off the bank and showed me how to apply it. "Go ahead and do it."

"How long, sir?"

"Till I come back."

I took the steel file in both hands, braced my feet firmly apart, as I had observed Schiller doing it, and pressed the raw metal in the vise. The file slipped and scraped my skin.

"Steady," said Schiller, "and evenly—is the main thing. Don't rock the file." And he left me.

I applied myself to the job. Within a few minutes my hands were numb. A few more minutes and my muscles would not obey my will and I was sweating. The man in the beige dustcoat, referred to earlier by Schiller as "Herr Meister," was watching me. Presently he walked up to me with ill-tempered impatience and wrenched the file from my hands, applying it evenly against the metal.

"*Verstehst?*" he grouched, tossing the file on the bench. "*Also, los, arbeiten* [Okay, let's go, to work]. *Tüchtig!* [Apply yourself!]"

"How long will I have to do this?" I asked Schiller, who appeared shortly.

"Till you learn how to do it. A few weeks, maybe. The same as the German apprentices—what they call *Junggesellen.*"

"I mean … today?"

"We work twelve hours a day, sometimes longer in an emergency—when they tow a military truck in the middle of the night. And don't fool around. They watch us all the time. And I'm responsible for you."

A high-pitched siren sounded off then, like the one in the morning, rising above the roar of the machinery.

"Breakfast break," informed Schiller. "Fifteen minutes."

I followed him to the other, small hall used for storing engines. A German worker stood there ladling out Ersatzkaffee. Everybody was queued up with his own utensil.

"Here," said Sikorski, "drink from mine till you organize your own."

I felt hunger pangs. "Do we get … anything to eat?"

"Not now," said Pikalski. "You'll get your ration card, maybe in a day or two, that's Hannelore's job. Then you go to the corner store and buy whatever. Careful, 'cause it's got to last you a whole week. If you eat it in one day, you'd better stop eating for six days. Half a loaf of bread, margarine, half a pound of cold cuts, little marmalade, a few potatoes. Oh, twelve o'clock they hand out soup on the lunch break. That's all till six in the evening. For supper you scrounge up from your rations. Listen," he was burning his lips with the hot liquid and blowing on it, "watch out for that German broad. Don't fool around."

"Why ... I didn't ..."

"Just remember I warned you. She's sixteen, but she's got hots for everybody. Me, too. Probably a good lay but I wouldn't try. 'No cavorting with foreigners'—that's the law. And they enforce it, too, brother. You fuck with her, you'll get twenty-five on your bare ass, or worse: the camp. That bitch, she should know it, too, but she does it all the time, especially with foreigners—failing the war, she would have gone for international relations—degree guaranteed. She figures the *Ausländer* won't squeal, 'cause they'll get it. If you know what's good for you, listen to me. Better jerk off." With a grin. "Too dangerous."

I noticed that the chauffeur's grin was that of a little boy caught in a prank.

The siren sounded again. A middle-aged German walking on the balls of his feet was approaching us.

"*Ein Landsman?*" he asked, pointing at me. (Your countryman?)

"*Jawohl, Herr Wandt, ein Junggeselle aus Polen,*" answered Pikalski.

The German's head was square; it seemed attached directly to his trunk—his neck seemed nonexistent. As he was finishing his coffee, I noticed his hands were shaped like coarse paws—short and literally square. He put his mug down on the counter.

"*So. Bist du stark?*" (Okay, are you strong?)

I smiled self-consciously.

"*Hm?*" pressed Wandt. "*Kannst viel zwingen?*" (Can you lift a lot?)

I looked at Pikalski inquiringly.

"Wants to know if you can lift much." He turned to Wandt. "He learns quickly."

"We'll see," said the neckless German, strutting away.

"Motherfucker," hissed Pikalski.

"Who's he?" I wanted to know.

"He's the top dog here, next to the two Meisters. Works the number one lathe. Watch out for him all the time. Vicious bastard."

"Pan Staszek," I inquired, "Mr. Schiller, whom I've just met ..."

"What about him?"

"Is he ... Polish or German?"

Pikalski looked over his shoulder. Most workers had gone back to work.

"Shhh ... the devil knows. He's Polish, all right, from Poznań, like Vacek. But a *Volksdeutsch* [Ethnic German]. Supposed to be, like, in charge of us. Why?"

"Well, he doesn't wear 'P' on his clothes like the rest of us."

"Yeah, well ..." He cased the area with his eyes. "German ancestry, Polish-born, a good mechanic, so they regard him as one of their own. He is allowed to live in an apartment, with his wife. They wanted to make him a *Reichsdeutsch*—a citizen and all, but he stalls them—got to give him credit for that. He's all right, I guess, but I wouldn't tell him everything, just to be safe ... watch out!"

Schiller walked up quietly, motioning for me to follow him.

"Want to show you the rest of the shop, so you know, if I send you somewhere ..."

Presently we were passing Wandt's lathe. A huge bore was drilling through a cylinder block which was being cooled by a steady sprinkle of water from above.

"*Du!*" The German stopped us. "*Komm mal hier!*"

He indicated to me that he wanted me to lift another cylinder block, one of several on the floor. I bent down; the block wouldn't budge. I tried again, this time inserting my fingers into the openings on both sides. I strained my body with all my might until I managed to lift the large automobile engine a few centimeters. Wandt was watching me; Schiller stood to one side. After a few seconds, I had to let it go. The left side of the iron bulk crashed onto the floor. Wandt screamed. He'd gotten his foot trapped under the block. Schiller hastened to lift it, freeing Wandt's foot.

"Oooo! *Donnerwetter ... du Heilige! Scheiss!*"(Oooo, a thunder... you holy! Shit!)

In moments he had regained his balance, but barely—enough to whack me in my left ear. "*Du verfluchter Polack!*" (You damn Polak!)

And he whacked me hard in my other ear. He was saying something else, foaming at the mouth—which I could not understand. I felt a sudden dullness and buzzing in both my ears. Schiller pulled me away.

"Stay out of his way; he's got a gorilla punch. He started out as a smith in this business."

There was a painful buzzing in my ears until the siren sounded for lunch break. The soup was turnips with a few tidbits of potatoes floating loosely. Pikalski was away with the pickup truck; Sikorski told me I could use his canteen, "but only if you wash it afterward."

"Hey," he turned to the others, "why don't we chip in some bread crumbs for Joe here?"

Wojciechowski's piggy eyes blinked up. "I'm surprised at you, Pan Kazik. This is no poorhouse here. Everybody gets the same rations— old and young. You know me: I am for fairness."

"But he hasn't got his yet," retorted Sikorski.

"So ... he's like everybody else. When I first came here, long before any of you turned up, I went around for three days living on this soup and their shit they call coffee." He was munching on his bread, his face turning purple. "Nobody gave a shit."

"*Vot, svoloch* [swine], *Pan Wojciechowski*," butted in the Russian, "stuffing his belly full of this boy's kielbasy. Here!" and he threw me a chunk of his bread.

"Tsk, tsk, such language, you bolshevik!"

"Same as you, old man!"

"Me? When do I swear?"

Victor, a hulking man, raised himself up. "*Yibi tvoyu mat'!*" (Fuck your mother!)

"Only no '*yibi tvoyu*'! Fuck your own mother!" barked the old man.

"Wish I could fuck your own, old man! At this point, I'd fuck anything—and I mean anything!"

"Sit down, the two of you," intervened Sikorski, "for Christ's sake, two grown men ..."

"Well, don't let him swear at me," Victor said somewhat conciliatorily.

"You swore first!"

"Me? That was nothing; in Russia we say this only to color a sentence."

"Here, bolshevik, know my good heart; here's a piece of bread," making a conciliatory gesture to throw him a chunk.

"Fuck your bread and fuck you!" But Victor put on a smile; his school of life had taught him the politics of survival, I thought.

The old man shrugged his shoulders. "Wait till you come to me; he eats his rations all in two days, and he carries that shaggy dog look with him the rest of the week."

"That's right. I'm a Soviet man. When I eat, I eat; when I starve, I starve." He drew a familiar pause; everyone knew what was coming next: "And when I fuck, I fuck!"

"You're not going to last very long this way, Victor—ration yourself out," commented Sikorski.

"I don't care. Where I come from, they don't feed that … turnip crap to humans, only to pigs." Changing his tone, he turned to Wojciechowski. "All right, old man, I'll take your bread."

"Too late now; you didn't want it before."

"Well, I was what you call … modest." Victor was humoring him.

The old man broke off a piece of his bread. "Here," he said, handing it to Victor. The Russian divided the bread in half, tossing a chunk to me.

"No, thank you, Victor," I said.

"*Take it!*" he roared.

I accepted. At least on the farm, I thought, there was enough bread, milk and potatoes, even if meat was scarce. But this was going to be lean—survival time.

"Here, take this, too." Sikorski threw me a chunk.

"Here," echoed Vacek, throwing me a bite of his sandwich.

"I hear," Sikorski accosted me, "that you got a whack from Wandt." I nodded, trying to hold back my tears. "Well, just stay out of his way. You're not the only one. He does it to the young apprentices. They beat them—it's their way of discipline."

I was fighting my tears.

"You'll get used to it. We all do. In another day or two, you should get your ration card," he added, trying to cheer me up.

Just then the siren sounded to start the long afternoon.

Chapter Sixteen
Anguished Amidst My Countrymen

HANNELORE CALLED ME TO the office the next day, handing me a sheet of yellow coupons.

"*Deine Lebensmittelkarten*," (Your food ration cards) she said. "Be careful, don't lose them, and don't eat them all at once." She proceeded to clip out a good third of the coupons, keeping them.

"For your lunches that we cook for you here," she added. "Come see me again when you need something, but make sure the Chef is not here." And she smiled, seductively, I thought. I noticed the two top buttons of her blouse were unbuttoned.

I had to borrow money from Sikorski, as I was not being paid until the following week. Sikorski, I noticed, was the only other man besides me who knelt down at bedtime to say his evening prayers.

"Who you praying to?" asked Victor.

"To God."

"What's he do for you?"

"Hey, hey," interjected Wojciechowski. "Victor, remember, we told you: you be what you will, and let the others do the same."

"I guess his business," said Victor. "Only I cannot see a young boy going for the … 'opium for the masses,' like our great leader said."

Presently Vacek came in accompanied by a pretty, round-faced woman in her early twenties. She had a milky complexion, rosy cheeks, and a curvaceous figure. The old man and Victor raised themselves.

"Aaaa, Pani Marysia, what an honor again."

"Good evening, Mr. Wojciechowski; good evening, gentlemen," she answered.

"Marysiu," said Vacek, "this here is our new bedfellow, Joe What's-his-name. My wife." He called me to the side. "Jòzek, er … my wife works nearby as a housekeeper and once in a while she comes to … stay with me. So … we all go to bed, turn off the light and … you understand?"

I did. "Yes, Pan Vacek."

"All right. Good boy."

Marysia turned sideways as the men were undressing, whereupon Vacek turned the lights off. He slept on the bunk above mine and, as I was finishing my prayers to my guardian angel, Marysia planted her feet on my bunk and, as she was being lifted by Vacek, I caught sight of her thigh and her panties.

I tried to sleep, but I was kept aware of a whispered conversation that went on for a while. I was almost lapsing into nirvana when the old man's hoarse voice awakened me.

"Ehem … honeymooners. How about letting us sleep?"

"All right, all right, I know," answered Vacek from above.

"I don't care what you do, but a man has to get up at the crack of dawn."

"All right, all right," repeated Vacek.

"Otherwise, you know, one word, and the bride has to go."

I heard Marysia whisper something, and then it was still except the bunk still rocked sporadically. It was all exciting to me, and I tried to visualize exactly what they were doing and how. But then I became worried about my inappropriate thought and soon lost awareness.

✛ ✛ ✛

The next morning I promised myself that I would finally write to Father Falkowski. Thus, washing up after work, I ate my potatoes, lay down on my bunk, and wrote before the lights were turned off at ten.

Dear Father!

Much has transpired since I saw you last. To begin with, I spent a few weeks under the wings of the Amtskommissar. I could not help it, for there were no transports going to Prussia, and he insisted that I stay around and keep his children company. Well, you can understand the rest; what was I to do?

So, well, finally, it all resolved well and I arrived here three days ago. But ... there are four other Poles working with me here at this automobile repair shop, including some French and Belgian prisoners of war, and Germans. It doesn't seem too bad except that we work twelve hours a day including six hours on Saturday, and before this other thing that I mentioned before, I just have to be careful at all times.

Also, there is little food, in fact, very little. A half loaf of bread a week, and cold cuts and margarine to last one or two meals. There is here one gentleman from Warsaw—he's the only one who prays at night (I say my prayers, of course). I asked him about going to confession and he says there are churches in Insterburg and priests but my German is still poor (I'll have to write down my confession with a dictionary, so I wonder ...)

The man from Warsaw also cautioned me against confessing to German priests—what if they don't understand me? ... You know what I mean?

I hope this letter will reassure you that I have arrived as planned ... Please remember me to the pastor and to both of my godparents and I trust that I shall remain in your prayers, for the future is still ahead of us?

If you wish, you could answer me in Latin.

I remain with love and humility, gratefulness and respect,

Yours, loving,
Joseph

P.S. I am getting a little gift for you. When I finish it, I hope that you will like it.

P.P.S. We live on the premises of the shop, in a tiny room: six of us including a Byelorussian , and we sleep on double bunks of wood.

✠ ✠ ✠

A few days went by in which, it seemed, nothing changed: the same routine consumed our time, except that autumn brought cooler days and calmer nights.

One day Pikalski asked me to join him in some deliveries he had to make the next day. I was overjoyed.

"Will I get permission to go with you?" I asked.

"It's all set. I requisitioned you. Permission granted."

Pikalski liked to talk—or was it just to me, I wasn't sure. We had to make a few pickups of automobile parts. "The sadist is away for a few days so I catch up on my other deliveries and pickups."

"Are you sure it'll be all right with the Chef?"

"No problem. I get away with a lot. Besides, I need you."

"How come you get away with so much?" I was curious to know.

He let out his customary giggle. "In a strange way, I think he likes me—or maybe I know when to humor him. When I drive him around, we talk a lot and argue—politics, what have you."

I was amazed. "You argue with the German boss, Panie Stasiu?"

"Sure do."

"How come?" I wondered. "I mean, if anybody else …"

Pikalski giggled again. In a strange way, his giggle was scary. "Let's say, I know too much; I know where the skeletons are in his closet."

"Skeletons? How you mean?"

"It's an expression. I know where he gets his booze—illegally." He looked at me knowingly. "I drive him around, make pickups for him, certain visits …" Here he harrumphed. "I hold him … you might say, in check. Yet, I know my limits and he knows his." He burst out with laughter.

This was fascinating for me. I found it difficult to envision the relationship.

"Panie Stasiu, what makes the man tick?"

"Ha, ha! In him you get the miniature of this whole Reich, of Hitlerism. Thousands of reasons why we should hate them, those sons of bitches. You should've seen him ranting and raving when he picked you up from the train station."

"Why?"

"Why? His low-class—bicycle repairman—origin can only be overcome by his superiority complex. He is a perfect example of who runs this goddamn land: low-class hooligans whom Hitler has elevated into the middle class, giving them a little power, and drumming into them that they are supermen. They owe him everything."

"But ... why was he mad picking me up from the train?"

"Because he's too good to do this himself; one of his underlings should have done this—*but* he got a call from someone higher saying he should; you were supposed to be the protégé of the Amtskommissar in Poland. Were you?"

"Well," I hesitated, "he took me to the Arbeitsamt in Łomża. It was routine."

"I see. Anyway, the train was fifteen minutes late, and you should've seen him! He was foaming and, since I was nearby, I got the brunt of it. 'In Germany, everything should be *fahrplanmäßig* [according to schedule]. If the Duce could make the trains run on time, why can't we?' On and on he went. 'Too many good men are at the war front, and on the home front the essential utilities are run by third-stringers: old farts back from retirement, ready for the mortuary or maybe to be church attendants. Why in hell don't they put them in rest homes tending beehives?'"

I joined him in his laughter.

"Raving against the train engineer—who'd have some big fat excuse, or was maybe a saboteur. 'God forbid,' I said. '*Der Gott ist mit uns*,' (God is with us) he bristled. 'Even the Führer says that. I only hope that the Reichsbahn don't have one of these *Ausländer* types— the foreigners—running trains. These days you never know.'"

"I'm sorry you had to listen to all that," I stumbled.

"I'm used to that," answered Pikalski. "I am his garbage can. He gets all his frustrations out on me—it's safe, he thinks."

"But you are also a 'foreigner,'" I commented.

"We go at it all the time. I say, 'Herr Chef, but I am also a foreigner.' 'You are all right, sometimes,' he says. 'But most of you Poles, you are an undisciplined lot, and querulous—even among yourselves. You require constant supervision.'"

"Is this why we are allowed to live on his premises, instead of at the *Arbeitslager*, like all other foreign workers?" I wondered.

By that time we had made all the stops heading back to the shop. Traffic was light—mostly military vehicles.

"It took some doing for him. He had trouble with the Labor Office, but he has friends at the Gestapo—five minutes from the shop. He convinced them that, since he fixes trucks and cars for the military, he needs his workers all the time, even in the middle of the night. Lucky for us. My friends at the camp, on the fringes of town, say it's hell: the German guards often beat them for no reason at all. They are driven to and from work, and seldom allowed outside. Not like us; in our free time we can walk all over Insterburg. Only thing, you have to wear the letter 'P' sewn up front of your clothes. Don't let them catch you without it."

"How come you don't wear it now, Panie Stasiu?"

"I told you I get away with a lot. As long as I stay in the truck."

"What is it Victor is wearing?"

"For him, he's another brand of animal; all Russians, Byelo-whatever—have the letters 'OST,' meaning East. But he is especially ranting against the POWs: his Belgians and French."

"Why?" I wanted to know.

We were approaching the shop, entering the courtyard. "Watch out. I'll tell you about this the next time."

✠ ✠ ✠

Two days later I was helping Pikalski again.

"Why against the POWs?" asked Pikalski after my prodding. "Except for two Belgian mechanics who are semi-civilized, he says, the 'Gypsies,' he calls them, the French are even lazier than us Poles; with their hooked noses, they look no different than the Jews—for whom, thank God, our Führer has found a solution—whatever it is—and the

Führer should be taken at his word. At least, in the strafication on Europe's so-called nations …"

"You mean: *stratification*?"

"Whatever—don't interrupt! … the Poles and all Slavs can do some useful work, if you watch them all the time, that is. Though they are mostly stubborn and chauvinistic—which is laughable. After all, they are still half pagan …"

"Panie Stasiu," I interrupted him, "what's with the POWs?"

"I know I got off the subject—only because that bastard up front cut me off," pointing to a military vehicle. "Oh, yes, he calls them 'the untouchables.' 'You can't work them overtime, and what's worse, our *Wehrmacht* protects them—*verflucht!* They get their fancy French food from the Red Cross and those stinking French cigarettes—while our own men can't get enough smokes. What kind of war are we fighting? *Scheiss!* Some kind of wiseass parlor game?' He said that a Wehrmacht officer had explained to him that the Allies were holding some German prisoners of war—so we have to, he said. Otherwise, they would piss on the Geneva Convention instead of pampering those Gypsy or Jew peddlers, as he called his POWs.

"Oh, yes, he called them the laziest tribe, with their dark hair and hooked noses. 'Some civilization,' he called them. 'And listen to them talk—a regular flood, and all in that guttural language. Brrr! …' he foamed, to think that some of his ancestors—thank God, only *some*— spoke those horrible sounds! '*Verdammt!*'"

I was fascinated. Also pleased that Pikalski was confiding so much to me. The chauffeur had found himself a listener, I reasoned, and I couldn't be happier.

"But why does he call us half-pagan? … After all, we are all Christians, like them. Has he ever been outside Germany?"

"He was—once, in Poland, after the Blitzkrieg, he told me, to look over some machinery for his shop which he brought here. It's better for their war effort, he said, for the Poles don't know how to get the most out of their machinery; they just don't understand German productivity, *nicht wahr?* The son of a bitch likes to provoke me."

"What did you answer, Panie Stasiu?"

"I let him choose his own answer. They say: give him enough rope … He knows he has to do with Pikalski," he replied proudly.

"Well, what did you say to him?" I insisted.

"I said—what did I say?" he replied absent-mindedly, having to slam on his brakes in traffic. "Oh, yes, I said: 'Herr Chef is always right—but not always! Ha, ha!'"

"What did he say to that?" I probed.

"He said: '*Pass auf*, Pikalski! One day you're going to get it—you with your arrogant Polish snout!'"

✛ ✛ ✛

On yet another trip I asked Pikalski: "Has Toussaint always had this shop?" That got him started.

"I found that out bit by bit, over time. Imagine, this bastard, as you know, only had a one-man bicycle repair shop. After Hitler came to power, he got government money to expand to this huge shop. Thanks to the Führer. He told me with disgust about the prewar times and about the mess his country had been in. His ancestors, who had originated in Alsace-Lorraine (*Lothringen*, he said), settled in East Prussia two generations ago. And you know, the Prussians are the worst Pole-haters. They still, five hundred years later, cannot forget their debacle at Grunwald. But, he said, they always regarded themselves as Germans and, to assert their patriotic identity, moved to what was then the heart and soul of the nation: Prussia under Bismarck. And then came World War I: betrayals, defeat, and the Weimar mess."

"The mess?" I asked.

"Sure. He told me that the *Junkers* of Prussia …"

"The *Junkers*?" This was a lesson in history for me.

"*Junkers*," stated Pikalski. "The entrenched aristocracy of Prussia. The Junkers owned the land; but they were losing political power, what with—the sadist called—the decadent intellectuals and 'humanitarians' of the Weimar Republic, which apologized no end to the Allies who bled Germany, extracting humiliating reparations. It seems to me," commented Pikalski, "that Toussaint could not get very far, since he was not able to penetrate the Junkers; to them he was always 'the stranger from the West'; but the main thing, as he said, was the international Bolshevik-capitalist-Jewish conspiracy. Thank God, who had brought us the Führer, and work, and food for the body and soul, full employment and *Lebensraum* in the East.

"The bastard got himself rich on imported labor, cheap. In fact, he got himself off military service as his 'skill and management of a vital industry' was essential to Germany's conquests. Those in power saw to that," continued Pikalski. "His comrades at the SA."

"SA?" I asked, to be sure.

"The gangsters, *Sturmabteilung*, Hitler's original bodyguards before they lost out to the SS; they simply put them—their SA leaders—against the wall and shot them. Ever since, the SA keeps a low profile. I found out, by the way, that some of his former comrades are with the Gestapo."

"Is that what he's wearing on holidays?" I asked. "The SA uniform?"

"Right you are; this is when he strides across his shop like a fucking peacock."

"Now I know," I mused.

"And let me tell you, he has an uncanny instinct for viewing his shop and instantly knowing who works diligently and who—which he loathes—does *herumbummeln*—in plain language, fucking around. A man, he told me, must keep busy and be efficient—especially now, in wartime. And the woman's place is in the three *K*s: *Kinder, Kirche, und Küche*—children, church, and kitchen. In that sense, they're right, of course, no?"

"I guess you're right, sir," I replied. But I was glad that he was giving me an overview of historical and political matters.

✠ ✠ ✠

One day, before picking me up at my usual workplace, Pikalski walked up as I was busy filing, pointing at my vise.

"Now what in hell is this?"

"It's a cross."

"Don't be smart, I can see it's a cross. Who told you to do it—the Meister or Schiller?"

"Neither." There was no point evading it. I looked down. "I'm making a cross out of spare brass."

"For whom?" he insisted.

"For my cousin, in Poland."

"That priest?" By now everybody knew about my "cousin." He was the only "family" I had. I nodded.

"Well, better watch out; if they catch you, it'll be your ass."

I had begun to shape a cross out of a piece of raw brass I had found; it was to be a gift for my priest—a crucifix for his desk with a small square base. When finished, the base would have three steps leading to the cross—all made out of one piece of brass. So far, it was a closely guarded secret—only Sikorski knew of it. In the shop, I was able to steal minutes at a time to work on it. Sikorski had told me it would look more impressive if made out of one piece, but such a job was much more time-consuming. I kept the object in my bench drawer. However, the task posed some dangers: next to my vise was the closed door leading to the engine room, with the Belgian mechanics.

Toussaint had a habit of surprising me and the few *Hitler-Jugend* apprentices by suddenly barging through the door, although, whenever possible, the Belgians knocked on our door indicating the boss was approaching ... The German youths also had a system: feigning sneezes, for there were times when Toussaint would smack them in the face for *herumbummeln*. Sometimes they gathered around when they thought Toussaint might be away; they'd take me into their group and even ask me questions about Poland. They were my age, and some even seventeen, apprenticing after school. Toussaint, when he caught me or even his Hitler-Jugend, would slap us in the face or penalize us for working overtime on Saturdays. Thus, for self-protection, the German youths and I tried to be loyal to one another.

✠ ✠ ✠

The noon siren shrieked. There was a rush of blue overalls to line up for the soup. Ours was water with a few bits of cabbage floating in it. There was a separate line for some five German workers who were fed soup containing chunks of meat and beans. Among the twenty-five-odd foreigners lined up, the French were openly contemptuous of the Germans. Their loud derisive jokes purposely included some

German words, venting their sarcasm against the quality of the soup, and just about everything else. They seemed completely unafraid.

"Just don't get an idea that you can talk like they do," interjected Pikalski. "They are protected by the Geneva Convention. Us, we're protected by shit. One word out of us, and we've had it."

Schiller approached us—composed and calm, as always.

"Cleaned your vise before going to lunch, Joseph?"

It suddenly hit me. I had left the piece of brass in my vise, with the cross in the making. But it was already too late. Meister Gruber was approaching our group holding my brass in his hand. He turned to Schiller.

"*Wissen Sie, was das bedeutet, Schiller?*" (Do you know what that means, Schiller?)

He addressed Schiller in the third person, a sign of basic respect. Everyone else was *du*.

Schiller was imperturbable. "*Wo kommt das her?*" (Where does it come from?)

"In his vise," said Gruber, pointing accusingly at me. Schiller slowly turned to me.

The siren sounded summoning us back to work. We returned to my workbench. The German apprentices, lazily resuming their work, must have sensed something wrong from Schiller's attitude.

"*Was ist los, Herr Schiller?*" (What's the matter, Schiller?)

Schiller was regarded as a *Volksdeutsche*—an ethnic German—and thus was owed respect. They addressed him as *Herr*.

"*Gar nichts. Lasst uns alleine* [Nothing. Leave us alone]." He turned to me. "You're lucky. Gruber must've gotten laid; he's in a good mood today. All the same, he wants me to keep a personal check on you from now on, meaning: don't you dare to do your own work on *their* time again; do it after hours on Saturday—half a day. Also, from now on, you stay at your vise all the time. He made me personally responsible for you. If you want to go to the latrine, you report to me first. Understand?"

"Yes, sir."

✠ ✠ ✠

A few days went by, and we had Saturday afternoon off. I needed working overalls and went down Hindenburgstraße to look for a clothing store. There I also noticed knee-high white socks, the kind I saw the Hitler-Jugend wear with their uniforms. I loathed having to wear the letter *P* on my clothes, especially after the mandatory wearing of a white armband with the star of Zion in the Ghetto. With my meager cash, I bought a pair of socks. Then, back in the room, I put on the white socks, ripping off the *P* (at work, we didn't have to wear it). All of a sudden, I felt a new assurance and even smugness surging up within me; I could conceivably be regarded as a German—no foreigner dared to wear white socks. I also felt added confidence inasmuch as I had picked up much Prussian dialect from the young Germans in the shop. Thus, "*Ich weiss nicht*" became "*Ik veet nusht,*" and so on.

I walked along the wide avenue framed by neat if sickly trees. Presently a German Luftwaffe corporal approached me raising his hand in a "Heil Hitler" salute. (Following the aborted assassination attempt on Hitler's life, all military personnel—and not only the SS— were ordered to extend their right hand accompanied by "Heil Hitler." Military salutes ceased.)

Unlike officers' riding boots, his were loose-fitting.

"*Du, Kamerad,*" he winked confidentially, "*weisst du von einem Puffhaus in der Nähe?*"

"*Puffhaus?*"

"*Ja, ein Puffhaus,*" he repeated impatiently. "A house with women."

I'd heard of it, on the fringes of town, but no one dared to even think of it; mixing races—*Rassenschande*—let alone any intimacy was punishable with a vicious whipping at the Gestapo, if not a concentration camp.

"Aaa ... of course." The airman was casting furtive glances about him, as if on the lookout for the gendarmerie. While, apparently, being taken for a Prussian, I had to choose my words carefully.

"Go straight ahead, *ein Schtickchen,* and ask somebody else. Good luck," I added. The German appeared grateful.

"That's a big help, danke schön," he muttered.

✠ ✠ ✠

I decided to look for a shirt at another clothing store. My only shirt had several sewn-on patches of different fabrics. Sikorski had taught me how to sew and darn socks.

Next to the store was a cinema; the posters featured a well-known German-Hungarian star, Marika Rökk. The proprietor looked over my ration card. "It's all right for working overalls."

"How about a shirt?" I asked.

"In about three months, perhaps. Also, you don't have enough coupons." I had used them, it seems, to buy the socks.

On the way back I looked up the only Catholic church in town. The tall Gothic nave was cool and pastoral; it had an unused look about it. Two old women and a man sat in contemplation.

"How do you address a priest in German?" I had asked Sikorski earlier.

"Herr Pfarrer."

On the way out, I approached a tall man wearing a soutane.

"Excuse me, Herr Pfarrer, can you tell me how I could prepare for confession? My German is not fluent."

The priest handed me a small prayer book which he'd picked up from a stack at the entrance.

"You will find it here. Fifty pfenning." I handed him the required change.

That evening I sat two hours in the washroom writing down my confession in abbreviated Polish, then attempting to translate it into German. I had saved some words for Sikorski, who would supply the translation later. I planned to go to confession the following Saturday evening.

✝ ✝ ✝

My roommates had a visitor that evening who had brought a bottle of vodka. Wojtek Kobylak, Pikalski's friend from Warsaw, was a tall skinny man endowed with an ashen complexion and prematurely turning bald. He lived in the foreigners' camp on the outskirts and walked to his factory every morning at five-thirty. His camp consisted of a barbed-wire compound of barracks which was guarded day and night by German guards in black uniforms. Each infraction by the inmates—and often, no infraction was necessary—was punished by severe beatings.

"You guys don't know how lucky you are," Kobylak was saying. "You live in peace, and you pretty much can come and go as you please. And no guards."

"Come and go," repeated Sikorski sarcastically, "except when the old man gets a shipment of parts or when they haul in some broken-down military trucks in the middle of the night. Who has to get up and slave away?"

"That's better than having drunken guards roam through our barracks at night. I tell you, we're at the end of our rope there. Terror all the time; you never know when your turn comes up next. I dream of Sundays when we're allowed to get away."

I didn't hear any more, for I sneaked out into the washroom. I wanted to take a shower and this was a good opportunity. I had to be always on guard lest someone see me naked and find out I was circumcised.

Vacek was out with his wife. Victor, who'd been with some buddies, arrived late, his speech halting and eyes glassy with vodka. The Germans considered the Ukrainians and the Byelorussians one notch better than the Russians; the former two enjoyed more privileges in moving about and some extra ration cards.

Later, as the lights were turned off, Vacek retired to his upper bunk with his wife. I was restless and hungry, yet I listened to the movements and the sounds above me. I tried to visualize a woman's body and her responses. My body ached ... I had found myself but, to hide it from Victor on my right and Wojciechowski on my left, I gathered up my knees and raised them up high. I tried to pray but the sensations of my body fought my prayers. Unwittingly, I closed my eyes and surrendered to my vision of Vacek's wife up above, and myself ... down here, alone. It helped me forget my loneliness and my misery.

Chapter Seventeen
Getting Acclimated

A LETTER FROM FATHER STANISŁAW arrived a few days later.

"My dear Jòziaczku,

I am writing in Latin which I know you'll understand—
just in case somebody gets nosy—you know ... We have lived
in apprehension for many weeks over your fate. I am happy,
again, that you have finally gotten there. From your letters
(thank you) I surmise that things are hard at times, but you
have a roof over your head—which you had not always had in
the past.

"Pray hard, my dear. Pray to the Virgin Mary; she has
always had a special relationship with her son and will
intercede whenever possible. Pray, too, to your patron, St.
Joseph, and to your guardian angel. Go to confession often,
if you can, even if you must do it in simple words. Just be
careful. You'll draw new strength from the sacraments.

"I am sending you a food package—just some bread for
you. Write to me. Regards from the Pastor. He's with you, as I
am, all the way.

With love,

Yours in Christ—Stanisław."

The package arrived on Friday. Wojciechowski stood over me as I unwrapped the brown paper. The large, oven-baked bread loaf still had some leaves stuck to it. As I picked it up, it broke in half revealing a long string of kielbasa camouflaged in a matching opening within the loaf.

"Celebration, everybody, celebration!" gloated the old man. "Quickly, young fellow, get the large knife over there." He proceeded to cut up the bread and sausage, handing out chunks of each to the other roommates.

"What are you doing?" exploded Pikalski. And to me: "Don't let that old badger take food from you."

"Please," I said, "I want everyone to share."

Pikalski shrugged his shoulders: "Just don't let me hear of your hunger cramps tomorrow." But he accepted a piece. "*Na zdrowie!*" (Your health)

On Sunday I dressed again in my knee-high white socks and walked down the main avenue. There was a queue outside the movie house with the feature starring Marika Rökk still playing. Soldiers and airmen chatted and smoked cigars, roaring their approval of dirty jokes. The few Hitler-Jugend were in their black uniforms—short pants and white socks. I knew foreigners were strictly forbidden to enter a theater. But I walked into a gate of an apartment house unstitching the thread that held my letter *P* to my clothes. With a beating heart I took my place in the queue. I hadn't been to a motion picture theater since before the war—a good five years. A thought flashed through my mind: what would I do if discovered? Well, I'd plead ignorance, unless there was a chance to sneak out.

The lights went out, and the newsreel came on to the sounds of martial music. German soldiers were battling the Red Army. Their faces were unshaven during—as the narrator said—a "tactical withdrawal." They grinned with confidence, the Führer pinning medals on their chests.

A few minutes after the main feature had started, the house lights came on abruptly and the feature ground to a halt. Two Wehrmacht gendarmes and a civilian were going up the aisles, subjecting everyone to close scrutiny. Now and then they entered a row of seats studying the faces. Germans, as always, sat obediently mum after being told: "Nobody move!" Now and then they'd have someone identify himself. I felt trapped. I said the Lord's Prayer and Hail Mary three times, frozen in anticipating the worst.

After they'd worked the rows and came to the row just ahead of me, they stopped and left, just after I vowed to the Virgin Mary never to go to the movies ever again. After the feature resumed, I only remembered a series of flashes on the screen—still numb inside.

Later I told Kobylak. The little man shook his head.

"You were lucky this time—very. But next time your luck might not hold out. Twenty-five lashes with an iron-tipped whip at the Gestapo. That's the going rate. And if you scream, you get more."

☩ ☩ ☩

The following Saturday Kobylak, Pikalski's friend, came over. He moved slowly through the door, pale of face, easing himself with great difficulty into a lower bunk (we had no chairs).

"Give me some water," he gasped.

"What ... the fuck is the matter with you?" Pikalski squinted his eyes in disbelief.

"They got me," gasped Kobylak after a pause. He'd drunk the whole glass.

"They ... who?"

"Gestapo."

"How?"

"Last Sunday ... at the movies."

"At the movies?" yelled Sikorski. Pointing at me, he added: "He was there, too."

Kobylak turned to me, wincing. He had trouble moving his body.

"You too?" screamed Pikalski. "What the fuck were you doing at the movies?"

"Nothing happened to me," I replied.

"They got me," whispered Kobylak. He looked at me. "What feature, the early or the late?"

"The early."

"I went to the late one. The bastards got me. They checked everybody's ID."

"Well … what happened?" asked Wojciechowski.

"Took me to the Gestapo upstairs, around the corner here." He paused, trying to catch his breath, then continued in a toneless voice. "Twenty-five." Everybody gasped. Silence. "Had to drop my pants. In the middle of the room. Told me to bend down, touch my toes. After a count of three—I had to count—I rolled over and hit the wall. Told me: if I scream, I'll get more." He winced again, trying to shift his body.

"Pull my shirt," he said to Pikalski. "Go ahead." He grimaced as the chauffeur pulled his shirt slowly over his head.

"Christ's wounds!" exclaimed Vacek.

"*Yop tvoyu mat'!*" (Motherfucker) gasped Victor. Kobylak's back was covered with many huge welts of varying shades, some swollen like large sausages. Dried blood and the flesh around them had discolored the rest of the man's body.

Sikorski was white in the face. "You all right?" asked the old man. Sikorski shook his head. "Get some water, quick!" the old man hollered at me. I ran to the washroom and back.

"You been working this week?" asked Pikalski.

"Have I? The old bastard found out what happened, made me get up to work. I was lying in bed like I was dying. He sent someone over, said if I don't report for work, it's deportation to the camp. Yeah … had to work all week. Thank God I didn't scream. They finish you off if you do. They're killers."

✛ ✛ ✛

That night I prayed very hard; I thanked God for sparing me, promising never to go to the movies again. I also prayed for all the suffering in the world and for all those whose bodies were tormented, and for my parents and sister, and for Kobylak's health.

It was the same routine all over again the next day: a long haul from six a.m. till six p.m. The only diversion was the latrine. Within a small cubicle there was only one closed compartment for all the workers in the shop, and one coarse urinal. Nevertheless, at times ten to fifteen men crowded the small area waiting to use the private compartment, and smoking, to break up the routine tedium, or squatting down to rest their feet.

But cigarettes were hard to come by. Foreign workers were entitled to cigarette rations, but the stores were mostly out of them. Pipe tobacco could be obtained more easily—if one were sixteen; I had just made it. One pack a month. At first, I rolled it in cigarette paper, when available (the French sometimes shared it with us). But the crude tobacco would puncture the paper, so I "organized" a pipe somewhere. Smoking was permitted in the shop.

Several times during the day one of the two Meisters or Wandt, the foreman, would stick their heads through the latrine door, especially if they needed a missing worker right away. It was not advisable to be thus spotted more than twice in a day. Not the Belgian and the French POWs. They came as often as they pleased and stayed at will. They seemed secure behind their prisoner status. A few times I witnessed a Meister reprimanding a POW who'd yell right back at the German—mostly in French, or threatening, in broken German, to report harassment to their German Army officer in charge. Not so with the German and Polish workers; these smoked in a hurry, casting furtive glances at the door.

A few weeks went by, and my work on the crucifix was nearing completion. Now and then, during regular working hours, I would take it out of my drawer to give it final touches. One slow afternoon, right after a midday break, the door to the engine testing room burst open and Toussaint barged in wearing a white apron. I bowed, attempting to hide the brass in my vise.

"Guten Tag, Herr Chef," I bowed. The German hardly nodded. He was smirking as usual, his manicured hands clasped behind his back. He leaned down to inspect my vise.

"*Was haben wir da?*" (What do we have here?)

"It's a ..." I stuttered. The German straightened up. The smirk was still there, but his mouth clenched up. Within moments he returned with Meister Gruber. The Meister's blank, bespectacled face quivered with controlled fury.

"He's working on a crucifix—something for a friend in Poland. I told him he could work on it in his own time, *not* in his working hours."

Toussaint turned to me slowly. His mouth unclenched, but he was not smirking anymore.

"What do you say?"

I had nothing to say. The German slapped my face. Gruber wanted to say something, then changed his mind, took a swing and slapped my other cheek. The German apprentices stopped working but only for a second. Then they frantically resumed their work, filing away at a heightened pace. Schiller came up next, watching me work for a while.

"A good number you are, you *cholera*," he said finally. "From now on, I'm sure not sticking up for you anymore."

That evening Wojciechowski shook his fist in my face.

"You little shit." His mouth curled up in an ugly twist, showing a couple of missing teeth. I learned that, in retribution, Toussaint had summoned Schiller and Pikalski and told them they were all collectively penalized by having to work all day Saturday because of my "loafing." "He's one of you. Now control him."

Wojciechowski had only begun his vendetta. "You just wait—we'll teach you a lesson. You're not going to do this to us. Oh, no! We'll beat the living shit out of you, first."

Pikalski had come in, in the midst of this.

"Easy with the shit, old man. He's just a kid," retorted Pikalski. I noticed that even Sikorski was mad; he never said a word—it was his way.

"Personally, I don't give a shit," said Pikalski. "Everybody gets into trouble sometimes, and I got nothing to do on Saturday. But you go on like this," he scolded me, "and I won't be able to stick up for you no more."

"I won't do it again, Panie Stasiu," I said to my protector. "I'm sorry, please believe me."

Pikalski was uncomfortable. "Never mind this 'sorry' business. Just you remember."

✠ ✠ ✠

The next few days I felt very lonely and had a constant lump in my throat. Hardly anyone spoke to me. In the evening I had to wait till everyone else had cooked his meal. The old man would shove my pot off the gas range regardless of my turn. He was riding and deriding me for every slightest trespass. My only escape was to write to my priest. I was unable to do so, but eventually managed:

"I so much try to be a good Catholic, Father, so that I could deserve God's graces and blessings, but it isn't always easy. When I try, I sometimes achieve the opposite effect. Is it my fault or the fault of others? That is why I so much wish you could be near me so I could ask your advice and consult you ... Must one always present the other cheek? When can a person assert himself? When should he? Do many Christians struggle with the same problem or is it just me? How do you choose between these opposites? How does one live up to his faith? I mean, just go to confession and start all over again? Or do you follow your conscience? What if it is wrong? How do you shape your conscience? Although I went to Mass and to confession on Sunday, there was much that I could not say in German, and much that I dared not say. Even after I was absolved, I felt a heavy load, still.

"Father, I feel that I must live to serve God; that I have a *contract* with him, and when I cannot fulfill it, I am nothing. Please, help me, Father, for I know not what to do ..."

Chapter Eighteen
Encounter with Gestapo

IT WAS MY SECOND year in Germany but it seemed like several years. I finally finished the crucifix and managed to mail the package to Father Falkowski. He wrote saying it had brought him much joy, that he treasured it, and that it had since rested permanently on his desk. In responding promptly and warmly, he wrote:

"As to your problems, I am very pleased that you unburden yourself of your doubts and uncertainties ... well, who among us is free of doubts? St. Thomas of Aquinas—one of our greatest—and St. Paul—both were beset by gnawing *Verzweiflungen* [doubts] (just to show off my German). So you see, my dear, a little vanity, like all human foibles, is inevitable—ha, ha!

"I do hope that you will not indulge in what is known as an 'overscrupulous conscience,' for it can become a terrible drain and burden that corrodes the soul, as many of us know who hear confessions. Splitting hairs, is what it is.

"As for your attitude, none of us can help that. That, as someone once said, is a reflection of our souls, a silent one. *Assuming* the other person possesses the correct receiver to read your soul. He may be a person of poor or blocked spirit whereby he reads the wrong signals. And while each of us should work constantly to ennoble our souls—

through our Savior—we can only control our words, usually no more than that.

"A tailor, similarly, selects a bale of cloth and, unless he selects an inferior material, he does not concern himself with the makeup of each single thread, as long as the whole appears good to him. Then he measures, and cuts and shapes it until the finished garment pleases his eye and sense of beauty. But the wearer of the suit must also take care of it—clean it, fold it at night, and press it. You are both the tailor and the wearer of the suit; at the same time, you cannot help the overall image that others get from viewing you—real or imagined ..."

✠ ✠ ✠

One day I went into the shop office to see about my ration coupons. Hannelore had her head next to the radio. When she spotted me, she uttered a loud but subdued whisper.

"Did you hear that?"

"Yes." I heard the beginning of the Fifth Symphony by Beethoven. At once I was sorry I'd said that; as a country boy, I shouldn't know Beethoven. But she paid no attention.

"I didn't mean *that*." She eyed me as if making up her mind if she could trust me. "That was London. The BBC," she said quietly.

"But I thought it was illegal for you to ..."

"Are you kidding?" she whispered. "They just said Rome has fallen."

The news didn't make much of an impression on me. Rome was planets away.

"Germany is losing. Don't you understand?"

I still did not get the connection.

✠ ✠ ✠

Back in the shop, Pikalski walked up to me in his swaying, bowlegged strut. "Just don't get any ideas, hmm?"

"What do you mean?"

"You know what I mean. You know what you get for fucking around with a German broad? Twenty-five at the Gestapo. And you don't even have to stick it into her. Remember Kobylak, smart ass."

✛ ✛ ✛

Toward summer, Sikorski took to making a battle map in our cubicle, sticking pins into it to keep track of the German front line. The latter was derived, after all, from the *Völkischer Beobachter*—the Nazi party premier newspaper, available to all.

"I'll be a son of a bitch," he said with amazement.

"Don't be a *skurwysin* [son of a bitch]," parried Victor, who liked to impress us with his Polish. "What's happening?"

"The Russians are inside Poland. The Red Army."

We gathered at the map. It was true. Some towns allegedly "given up for tactical reasons," in the official German Army vernacular, were inside the Polish border.

We were not in a jubilant mood, however. The war was coming to us. Slave labor was one thing. Bombs and guns another.

"I just pray that I live long enough to see the gangsters' asses whipped," Vacek said softly.

"What you gonna do, Victor," Pikalski was provoking him, "when Daddy Stalin liberates you?"

"Oh, Pan Staszek, big trouble, big trouble for me. You know what Russians say? When you let Germans take you prisoner, you are enemy of the Russian people, automatic! What they gonna do to me? Shoot me or, if I am lucky, send me to Siberia."

"So what you gonna do, Victor?" Vacek insisted.

"If I fall into their hands, this is my end." He flung out an arm: "Goodbye world, goodbye women and vodka, for here comes one Victor Ivanovitch Paramov, man of courage and hot blood, a fucker of women with big breasts—*na sorok!*—and hard drinker, a Byelorussian patriot and a friend of his Polish friends, who died true to his destiny, without grudges, leaving behind all the good food, drink, and women, and a song or two."

"Hey," grinned Sikorski, "what about good liverwurst?"

"Wait, brother, don't interrupt. This is my goodbye poetry written in advance. Fuck German liverwurst; who needs it? They make their own in hell, for this is where I'm going: into the grips of the devil and, I hope, a whore!" He exploded into a paroxysm of laughter.

✠ ✠ ✠

There were more signs of German troubles. Disabled army vehicles camouflaged for combat were being shipped from the Eastern front for overhauls in increasing numbers. The shop went on a full six-day schedule, with two shifts around the clock. One could volunteer for the night shift and so did I: from six in the evening till six in the morning. Food was a problem, as during the night no soup was ladled out; I would eat whatever food I could scrounge up. But at least I could smoke my pipe undisturbed. Soon a new addition came to the shop: a hulking six-footer who never smiled; his job was to wander around the shop all day, watching everybody work. We found out that he was totally ignorant in the mechanical field and named him "the Spy."

✠ ✠ ✠

On July 15, 1944, a letter arrived from Father Falkowski. It was brief and hurried:

> I am writing sparsely in the hope that my brevity and alacrity will still enable the note to get through to you. From the way events shape up, this may be my last communication to you in a while. As you know, events are getting ahead of us.
>
> May God bless you and keep you, my Dearest Jòziaczku, and help us unite in the future. Pray and trust in our Lord, for he is your last resort, and salvation, and refuge. He is your way and your consolation. Reach out to him whenever you need him. Pray to Mother Mary, Queen of Poland, if you need her to intercede on your behalf. Until we meet again,

> Your friend in Christ, always
> X. Stanisław

P.S. I'm sending you a food package under separate cover.

The package never arrived.

✛ ✛ ✛

The chief escape from work was a visit to the latrine. The French POWs made the most latrine trips to smoke their *Gauloise* cigarettes. A sticky day came and everyone seemed sluggish due to the heat. After lunch, I felt as if my eyes were going to be glued together. When four o'clock came, I was on my third trip to the latrine. I was surprised no one was there, so I sat on the stool in the cubicle and fell asleep. I woke up when the Spy entered shouting my name. As I emerged, the Spy grabbed me and pushed me into the shop. But within a half hour I was back smoking a pipe. Two Frenchmen came in, smoking.

"Don't make it long," said one of them. "The Spy is vicious today." I had barely finished when the Spy stood in the door, filling its frame with his huge gorilla's body, his eyes scanning those present.

"You are going with me," he declared.

To the office, I thought, but I still asked: "*Wohin?*"

The Spy told me to wait in front, right in the gateway, where I could be seen by many in the shop. Then he came out, motioning for me to follow him.

"Where to?" I asked while something gripped my throat. The Spy had left his dustcoat inside. He was dressed in his suit.

"*Wirst schon sehen,*" came the answer. "You'll see."

I had halted, and the towering Spy turned around.

"I am not going any place till I speak to Herr Chef first."

"You're going with me; it's official." He grabbed me by my shoulder, yanking it forward.

As we reached Hindenburgstraße, the Spy turned right. The worst hunch was about to come true for me. Halfway down the block we reached a plain stucco building known as the Gestapo headquarters, a four-storied building, plain, with high windows, indistinguishable from any other structures on the block—down to the absence of any sign up front. Except everybody knew about it.

Victor, Vacek, and I had been walking by one day when Vacek had pointed to a third-story window.

"What?" asked Victor.

"There, there!" Vacek was tilting his head up high.

Then we saw him. He was standing on the parapet of the third-story window, his foot leaving the ledge, one leg raised as if to take a step in mid-air, halting, then the body following his upraised leg in a floating motion, frightening in its awkwardness. It was as if his will had resolved to jump but the body was laggard. At once his arms fluttered wildly in the air, tilting to one side till the man came down hard as a rock. It seemed that his legs had suddenly collapsed, the trunk following. The man toppled and rolled over, lying there for a breath or two. But, miraculously, he somehow scrambled to his feet, stumbling, rising, and hobbling away in the direction of the railway station.

Earlier, while the man had still been suspended in mid-air, Vacek said that he saw two heads peer out the window and heard screams from within. As the man limped away, Victor burst out: "Better get away from here."

Now, it seemed, it was my turn.

"Up the stairs," said the Spy.

So that's what it looked like inside: a narrow, curving staircase, a carpeted hallway—almost like visiting a private home. One encased bulb was throwing off murky light. I felt a helpless sensation through my spine, wishing it all had been a dream. But it wasn't. One last chance, this time pleading.

"Herr Meister," I gulped. He followed me, holding on to the shiny balustrade. I was looking at the bald spot on his head. The skin on his bald spot was creased. I wanted to get close to it, plead, even hug it.

"Up, up, come on," he prodded me ahead. "*Los!* Go!"

"Herr Meister, perhaps ..." I had barely found my voice.

"I want to apologize. I really mean it."

"Los, los, Mensch, that door right there." But he sounded less angry, perhaps even regretful? There might be a chance. And then it came out of me—in a rush.

"I'm sorry, Herr Meister. I really didn't mean it. I felt so tired today, maybe I'm getting sick. I promise I'll work more diligently, and I won't go to the latrine at all ... er ... I mean, but not to rest at all, please, can we go back now, I won't do it again!" I tugged on the Spy's sleeve in supplication; perhaps I should even kiss the man's hand? But the Spy withdrew his sleeve.

"Nein, nein, too late now. We already telephoned them. Better go in."

To the side of the door I noticed a small shingle: *Geheime Staatspolizei*—the Gestapo. The door was narrow but leather-draped and quilted into diamond-like sections. *To muffle the sounds,* flashed through my mind. *Will I ever come out of there?*

A nondescript face appeared in answer to the buzzer. The Spy said a few words—nothing reached me, as I was scanning the room frantically. Then the Spy left.

I saw two large windows facing the door. To the left, a desk placed diagonally across the corner by the window. The civilian with the blank face presently seated himself down behind the desk, absorbed in some papers. The room was large and empty save for a tall wooden closet next to the door. There was another door to my left. I didn't dare to move.

I stood at attention. Seconds went by, then minutes. I was still alive, unharmed. Nothing was said. The man kept reading, leafing through some notes. Then, suddenly, someone let out a shriek from beyond the left door, followed by harrowing moans. More moans, another shriek. Then a prolonged scream. Then quiet again. No reaction from the man behind the desk. He must have heard the piercing screams. But he read on, unaffected. Outside, car tires hummed a quick tune. There was a world beyond, with traffic and people pursuing their business, without measuring each second of their lives approaching the inevitable ...

So it's come to this. Finally. Well, it had to be: Wojciechowski must've squealed ... All along I was afraid in his presence, the way he looked at me; I think he suspected who I was. They wouldn't have brought me otherwise—not just for Herumbummeln in the latrine ... But the face of the civilian does not seem to be that of a sadist, a killer.

How do they beat a man here? Do they just start, without a word? Could I take it without screaming? But why is that man not doing something—as if I was not in the room? Could this be part of the treatment, at first? To let me stand here for hours till I collapse?

Someone screamed in the other room. And again. Aaaaaa!! Three moans again, then some pleading and one thud after another, another voice yelling, rising at the end of each expletive—German—with an arrogant finality.

If the old man *had* denounced me, wouldn't they at least check me over? Yes, I would have to take my pants down, for sure. And the interrogation—Polish identity papers ... who had helped me, sheltered me? Everything.

More screams from the other room. A scramble, as of a body falling down, an echoing thud. What do they expect me to do? Stand at attention? The man keeps writing—no reaction to the goings-on ... What if I thought of an excuse ... for spending too much time in the latrine? Beg? Promise to do better? Would that spare me? Naw ... they don't bother with people pleading; it makes them more vicious.

What if ... well, no. But, what if ... what have I got to lose? If the old man had not denounced me ... if he had, nothing matters anymore. But if he hasn't ...

"*Ich bitte um Entschuldigung*, pardon me, sir," I said, clearing my throat.

The man kept writing notes. Seconds went by. Didn't he hear me? Perhaps not. Is he deaf? But how can a deaf man work ... I might try again, louder.

"*Verzeihen sie mir, bitte.*" Please, excuse me ...

No reaction. The man turned a page. This time he must've heard me—do they have deaf Gestapo men? Or are they short of personnel? But what did the Spy tell him before? I couldn't make it out ... If the man is deaf, it might even be better, for then he can't hear me scream if I am going to get beaten, and they won't punish me more for screaming, like Kobylak said.

Minutes. More minutes. I stood at attention. Tires drew out sustained notes on the asphalt outside. How long have I been here?

"What do you say?" The man was looking at me.

"Please, sir ..." *No*, that was wrong! To request. "May I say something?"

"What?"

"Please, sir, I think I know why I am here; it's because der Meister caught me twice in the latrine smoking. Yes, sir, that was wrong, I admit, I'm sorry. But please sir, if you will, sir, I have a reason ..."

That's a chance, it might ...

The man was looking at me—no expression. An empty, blank face, with small ears.

"You see, sir, I am volunteer. I like it here very much, in East Prussia I mean. I came on my own you can check that I volunteered. I really did because I wanted to learn a craft and see *das schöne Reich* in Germany and I like it here but … But I do what I can and perhaps I admit I didn't do the right thing but could be begging your pardon if only the Meister wouldn't call me names at times; at times he calls me 'you damn Polish pig'—*du verfluchter polnische Schwein*—and please sir it hurts me because I can't help it if I am Polish and if he calls me that I perhaps don't have all of the enthusiasm that I had when I came here from Poland, when I volunteered, please, you can check that …"

One of the ears grew larger as his head turned sideways watching me. I stood at attention. Time went by. The man was still looking at me.

"How old are you?"

"Sixteen, sir."

He got up slowly, circled the desk to the right. Evenly, heavily, he walked up to the closet on my right, opened one half of it, and reached inside. I was not surprised to see a whole row of whips of every kind—lined up like orderly suits hanging in the closet. He took one whip and held it by its wide handle. My eyes wandered over the whip's length—all the way through the tightly woven leather, down to the lead tip. The man took one step toward me. He put the wide handle of the whip next to my nostrils.

"*Rich mal!* Smell it!"

I sucked the air through my nose.

"Harder! Smell it!" The wide handle was touching my nose. "Smell it!" I sucked the air with all my might. Like at the doctor's, breathing in hard.

"*Smell it!*"

Faster and harder, with all my might.

"*Gut. Jetzt pass auf!* Look out! You go back and do your very best, and more, and I mean your best. If I hear one more complaint against you, *one more*, you won't be smelling it anymore—remember! You'll feel it! Now get out!" His sudden scream pierced my ears.

I clicked my heels. "Danke schön. Auf Wiedersehen."

"No. I don't want to see you again. Remember."

I had left the street ages ago. Now the sidewalk looked wider and cleaner, the people friendlier, and the horns of the automobiles rang merrily. My heart was jumping out of my body. I could not get back fast enough—to tell everybody.

✠ ✠ ✠

"Well, well," said Pikalski, who greeted me from under the hood of his truck in the shop yard. "Tell the truth, I didn't think I'd see you again in one piece. How in hell did you manage?"

I told him, and he told the others in the evening. Exactly what happened. They listened and, in spite of some inevitable sarcasm and jokes, their faces acknowledged something, it seemed. From that day on I noticed the difference—I was treated more like an equal, like one of them. Almost. Including Wojciechowski. And the same evening, too, Vacek added, pensively, his usual sarcasm absent:

"The screaming from the other room, you said—I don't know. Don't know for sure but they say the Krauts play a recording in the other room, sometimes, even if no one's there, just to condition you when you first come in. On the gramophone."

Though I tossed many times in my sleep as if pulled by forces in many directions, it didn't quite hit me until the next day. The realization of what might have happened behind the leather-quilted door. I was shaking all of the next day and beyond … And at least I told them—after all, my roommates were the only family I had.

Chapter Nineteen
Surviving American Air Raids

IT WAS SUNDAY AFTERNOON, and we were sitting on our bunks. Pikalski had organized some crude vodka, and there were hot potatoes to go around.

"There's only one good thing about the Germans," said the old man. "They're cleaning our house for us."

"Which house?" I surprised myself by asking.

"Cleaning out the Jews in our society, the gypsies, and all the leeches. Got to give it to them: quick solution and efficient—up the chimney, man, I hear. The only way."

"I kind of miss the gypsies," said Vacek. "Who's gonna tell the fortunes from now on?"

"Oh, I just loved to have my fortune told by them," offered Marysia, smiling and squirming next to Vacek. "Right, dear?" and she snuggled up to Vacek.

"And get gypped out of your money in the process, for recreation," finished Vacek.

"Well," countered Marysia uncertainly, not daring to contradict, "if you are careful …"

"Don't matter," replied the old man. "Point is, Pani Marysia, society should not allow any element in its midst to prey on it—the unproductive elements which ..."

"Some Jews were productive," Marysia dared. "I remember in Poznań we had a tailor; he worked from morning till night, always bent over, morning till night, damn good with the needle ..."

"Makes no difference," said Wojciechowski. "Sooner or later he'd cheat you, he couldn't help it, it's his nature, a curse thrown by our Savior when he said ..."

"Let me get this straight—wait a minute," interrupted Vacek. "I'm no lover of Jews, crap ... er ... excuse me, my dear." Marysia feigned a slight blush to maintain her dignity. "Christmas Eve this week, I shouldn't, with ladies present ... but like I said, I'm no lover of Jews, still ... you can't, in the twentieth century, get rid of an entire race ... it *is* the twentieth—am I right?"

Marysia wasn't sure if Vacek meant it as a joke. "Of course, dear, it is."

"Oh, shut up, I know it is, it was just ... a phrase."

"The point is ..." interjected Pikalski, who'd had a few gulps of vodka in the interim. His speech, though animated, was halting. "Today it's the Jews and the Gypsies ... then it's us."

"You *can't* have Jews in any society," the old man joined in eagerly. "You take, for instance, two stores, right? Belonging to a Jew and a Christian. The Jew will work long hours, *and* Sundays, if you let him. He won't drink; he won't do sports. His kids go to *heder*, studying, studying, no fun, just so they can get ahead of us; he'll cut prices, sell for less, and—first thing you know: he's richer than the rest of us. Next thing you know—he's controlling the economy."

He spread his arms in a gesture of having arrived at the point of perfect lucidity. "There, you see! That's it, in a nutshell! ... Any Jews in your village?" the old man turned to me.

"Yeah," I answered, "we had one. Always smelling of onions and garlic, couldn't even speak good Polish." I was conscious of Wojciechowski watching me, my heart in my throat.

"Right, you see? Now, among them, they speak a foreign language in our midst—Yiddish. Which nobody understands. I used to understand some of it, to know what they were saying. Had lots of friends, Jews. But I learned how to deal with them, ho, ho!"

I had been boiling a few potatoes from the meager food rations. Wojciechowski was just taking off my pot, as had happened before, setting it aside while he put his pot on. I protested. The old man just snorted. "Respect for my age."

At this moment Pikalski lurched, grabbing a huge kitchen knife lying nearby. He pressed the sharp blade against the old man's belly, making a visible indentation in the latter's shirt.

"Look out, you old fart, one more time you bother this kid and I'll stick this blade all the way through your fucking guts. Got it?" With one motion he jerked on the old man's pot, slamming it onto the shelf nearby. "Go ahead, kid, make your potatoes."

Wojciechowski turned pale, speechless.

Victor attempted to restore a convivial mood.

"Speak of Jews: we had Jews, too, in our village. A couple were the best you could find. You had money or not, they let you buy on ... what you call, Mr. Kazik ... er?"

"On credit, you mean?"

"*Tochno*, right! I wouldn't let anybody hurt them."

"Yeah, till the next time they cheated you," parried the old man.

"They wouldn't cheat me. I trusted them better, er ... if not most others." He meant "than." "Against the law in Soviet Union to hate others because of race or religion."

Pikalski leaned back on his bunk. He was nursing his vodka.

"You're a good man, Victor, but you're full of shit. The Soviet heaven: no persecutions, listen to that!"

"*Na vierno*—really, Pan Staszek, everybody make any religion he wants in Soviet Union, or make atheist, like me. I believe only in beautiful women, good vodka, and the devil, ha, ha!"

"The same thing—a beautiful woman and the devil, don't you know?"

Pert Marysia gave Pikalski a feigned offended look. "Are you calling me a devil?"

Pikalski smirked, as always, with the male superiority of a gentleman.

"Hmm ... begging your pardon, there is a devil in every woman."

"Devil, hell," blurted out Vacek who'd had a few, too. "Christmas is around the corner, hey, Victor, how about a carol?"

"Opium for the masses, Pan Vacek," said Victor.

"How about a walk?" asked Sikorski.

"Yeah, let's go for a walk like back home with *Diadia Mroz,*" exclaimed Victor, referring to Grandfather Frost.

Moments later we were outside, mushy sleet underfoot. I was the last one to leave. The conversation about Jews had left me half-paralyzed—as in my dreams, which occurred frequently, when I knew I had to flee but could not move a muscle.

✠ ✠ ✠

The next night we were shaken from our sleep by sirens: one whining sound, then another, until a whole disjointed cacophony of sirens assaulted the ears, each at a different pitch.

"Fire," concluded the old man, just waking up.

"Fire, shit!" yelled Victor. "Airplanes … coming. Yes, gentlemen, Soviet airplanes!" He jumped in the air. We scrambled outside. While the powerful German anti-aircraft lights crisscrossed the sky, we were herded into an air-raid shelter in an adjacent shop annex by the German air wardens who materialized from nowhere.

After that, the air-raid sirens sounded almost every night. Soon I received a letter from my priest. He wrote cautiously, obviously not to run afoul of German censorship:

"There may come a time, perhaps soon, when our lives would be caught in renewed turbulence. The crucial line is no longer hundreds of kilometers away. While, of course, we hope that it will not get worse—for we wish for our protectors, the Reich, to remain here—it is possible that I may not be able to write to you. In any case, please remember your prayers and, in particular, the three Acts: of Love, of Faith and of Hope.

"Even in an emergency, it will suffice—a matter of seconds—to say: 'I trust in you, Christ. Thy will be done.' If the sacrament of confession is not available to you, it is sufficient to confess your sins followed by an act of contrition.

"I am sending you another package. Your beautiful crucifix is standing on my desk. I think of you daily ..."

This time the package arrived: a large loaf of bread which, when touched, separated into two halves: inside the carved-out space was a fat sausage. I shared it with the others.

✠ ✠ ✠

Two days before New Year's, a large van backed up to the gate of the shop. The largest cylinder lathe—Toussaint's prize possession—was loaded on. It was to be shipped to some place near Berlin—"Falkensee," Pikalski had overheard.

"He's moving his shop there," he stated. "Soon as he's moved all his machinery, we are to follow."

A few days after New Year 1945 we were huddling in the shelter an hour before midnight. Suddenly a whistle was heard; it grew louder and louder—rising to an almost unbearable pitch. Then it stopped. The pause was terrifying, as if the sound had drained all force from it. Then we heard the deafening thunder of the bomb. Minutes later, as we hoped to recover from a series of explosions that blasted our ears, I wondered if we had been buried. Someone managed to scramble out, someone ran, someone shouted: "They got the shop!"

"Nobody leaves!" yelled Meister Gruber.

Later, when an all-clear had been sounded, I followed the others. The shop had gotten two direct hits, right through the roof. "Our artillery," boasted Victor proudly.

We worked through the night and into morning, attempting to clear some of the ugly rubble. Later, helped by the German workers, we labored more; Wandt, Gruber, and Toussaint tried to estimate which of the machinery could be salvaged for shipment. It would take all week to carry all the debris and bricks away and resume operations, whenever possible—the roof being the first problem.

Three days later when, in total darkness, we walked, groggy from being up at the air-raid shelter at night, to start work at six, a steady, distant rumble shook the earth. When the gray morning light came up, the rumble grew suddenly. Nobody had to tell us to run for the shelter, even though the sirens hadn't sounded yet. It was January 12,

1945, and the Russian offensive had blasted through the Prussian front, amidst the punishing cold winter.

The next three days were spent in the shelter. There was hardly any heat and even less food. On the second day a direct hit took care of the shop's roof, and the place was allowed to burn down. Gruber at first ran around emitting agonized commands: "Get that pail! Haul more water!" But there wasn't much anybody could do. In the end he had to be persuaded that it was no use, and, by exposing themselves, they just might get killed.

On the sixteenth, the artillery noise subsided, and Gruber got us all together.

"Be ready in two hours. Take with you what you will, but only what you can carry. And stay out front. We're moving out."

"Where to, Herr Meister?" asked Sikorski.

"To Allenstein, *Ostpreussen*. Then we'll see."

✠ ✠ ✠

Earlier, he had placed us in some barracks outside of town. Two days later, we were put on a train to Königsberg by the camp overseers. When we arrived there, it was no longer a city. There was only a short wait at the train station before we boarded—a real passenger train with compartments! When we reached Allenstein, Gruber gave us papers— official orders to move to "Falkensee bei Berlin." Then he left himself, never to be seen again.

Blocks, dozens of them, into the hundreds—as far as the eye could focus—were charred skeletons. This was no longer rubble wreaked by explosions from bombs—"phosphorus bombs," someone said. Americans or British. They had burned everything. What remained were just the steel columns and charred bricks; a testimony to human genius in construction and an equal genius in destruction. A burning smell still permeated the foul air. It seemed like some weird futuristic picture that must have cost millions to produce.

"Oh, Mother of God," muttered Sikorski. "Upon Christ's wounds. Must have happened weeks ago. All this time we didn't know about it."

Pikalski, gasping under the weight of two suitcases and a pack with bedding strapped to his back, just shook his head. He didn't grin this time.

For the first time I saw proof of a superior might visiting havoc upon the invincible Germany of Hitler. I wanted to shriek, sing, and praise God and share it with Father Falkowski, or write a poem ... except for the days that were yet to come ... but then I thought of all the people who must have gotten burned there ... oh, hell, served them right—for my parents, my classmates, my teachers, my friends, for the Jews, for all the bestialities ...

"Just to see the bastards lose the war, just to survive to see the first day of victory and die happy—that's all I want," uttered Sikorski.

"Yes, to see the sons of bitches beaten and destroyed, that's all I want, too," I echoed.

We looked around for our group. Victor and Wojciechowski were gone. Perhaps, at Allenstein, they had gotten in with another group; no one knew. Just Pikalski, Sikorski, Vacek, and me. And Kobylak. And lots of strange new faces: Poles, Ukrainians, Lithuanians, Byelorussians. Soon we were joined by prisoners of war: French, Belgians, and Italians from the Badoglio Army, taken prisoner by the Germans. There was no more food or water. And nowhere to get them.

We were marched past charred columns reminiscent of crosses at the cemetery—out into snow-bedecked plains. No one knew where we were going; no one dared to ask the guards. Someone said we were being taken into the fields ... to be executed? Someone said: "The Krauts will not let us survive—to triumph in their defeat."

Then I saw the beginning of the long column disappear up ahead. We were getting closer to a point where the column was disappearing. Soon we, too, came upon an opening in the snow, descending into an endless tunnel dug beneath the ground. An air shelter, a hideout for the troops? Candles were lit in the pitch darkness broken up only by the crisscrossing of the guards' flashlights. This was it until further notice, we were told. "No one leaves except to take care of our business, in groups and under guard." A few boxes and crates were strewn about. There was no water. Everyone found a niche and wrapped himself in whatever rags there were, hoping for sleep. I wedged myself between Pikalski and Sikorski to steal some body heat.

My body began to fall and fall through space. It felt so heavy, yet I was falling and falling ... weightlessly.

Whew! *Whew! Whew!* Whew! *Whew!* ... It must be Russian planes. Well, good! Let them get the bastards; let them bomb the hell out of them ... but how come there are no explosions ... "How is this night different from other nights?" Who said that? *How is this night different from ... Whew! Whew! ... Whew, Whew! ... Ma nishtana halaila hazeh* (Why is this night different.../from a Passover prayer). Almighty! Who said that?

Sikorski was sitting up, several voices whispering. I was waking ... My God, did I talk in my sleep? *In Hebrew?* God, I must never ...

"Katyushas," I heard.

"Katyushas?"

"Guns mounted on tanks or artillery," said Sikorski.

"Yeah. Must be right over our heads. The front must be close to us."

The artillery bombardment continued unabated until light showed its sparks through cracks in the tunnel. When it ceased, the guards took us out in groups to relieve ourselves in the ditches: women, then men.

The air was quiet and gray except for a few single flakes of snow aimlessly adrift. Straight ahead of the tunnel entrance, some roofs and charred building columns were breaking through the blanket of snow. On the other side of the bunker there was just snow, and more snow, mountains of it—until somewhere far away, at a point not at all too clear, it merged with the dirty sky. Some black specks could also be spotted against the wavy horizon.

"What's that?" I wondered.

Pikalski took a lazy look. "Bugs or something," as he squatted down over a ditch, gasping with relief.

Sikorski handed us a roll of rough gray toilet paper.

"You're too much," mused Pikalski, "of all things he remembers ..."

"*Schneller, schneller, beeilt euch.*" (Faster, faster, hurry up.) The German guard hurried us, his feet stomping the ground, his rifle slung over his shoulder, the muzzle pointed skyward.

"Bugs? You crazy? In winter?" erupted Sikorski.

"I don't give a shit; bugs or Soviet locusts swarming at us."

"Locusts? In an atheistic land?" It was Vacek's wry humor. "Tell them, Victor."

"You and your fancy expressions," kidded Pikalski.

"Hey, no kidding, look at them, they move," exclaimed Sikorski.

The little black specks on the distant snow began to move toward us. Soon they became a whole swarm. The specks soon became little sticks which resembled human arms, waving. The German took out his field glasses.

"Our troops," he declared.

In a minute I was able to recognize clearly human forms moving toward us. Most of them were wearing white coveralls over their uniforms; but some, lacking them, had overcoats on. They carried rifles, some long bats with round, large, pear-shaped heads.

"Look, grenade launchers," observed Sikorski.

"There he goes again, the little marshal," mused Pikalski, waving his arms in and out, for warmth, and stomping his feet. "Now, how in the fuck would you know that, Kazik?"

"I know. Seen enough pictures in the papers."

"You don't say," grinned Pikalski. "You know something? I think he's right."

They came closer, and I was able to see some faces. They looked like elves emerging from a deep, frozen forest. Some even wore white face masks. Their faces were either blackened or dirty, unkempt. So these were the German frontline troops. A couple of them began shouting in our direction, waving their arms. Our guard got the point.

"Schneller, schneller, get back in, quick!" he shouted to the latrine detail.

We obeyed. Despite the biting cold, I wished we could have stayed outside longer to see the troops from close in. I wished I could see something in the faces of these frontline troops ...

"They're pulling back, that's why they don't want us there. I bet you anything," said Vacek.

"Pulling back?"

"Withdrawing, you dope, what else? The Russians are coming," opined Vacek. "Get ready, we'll have fun. Anybody want to join the Communist Party? Now's the time. Step right up, men. Get your applications here."

"Oh, shut up, Vacek, that's not so funny any more."

The German guards didn't look funny. But inside, again, they were quiet. A half hour later, as if by magic, two loaves of bread appeared, and some water. They were carefully distributed among us in the shelter.

When night came, the Katyushas started again. Right over us, and low. A whole cacophony let loose. Some of us who ventured toward the bunker's entrance discovered that all but one of the guards were gone. The news spread like lightning. The guard told us that the Soviet tanks had broken through German lines into the center of the city.

"Let's go into town," concluded Pikalski.

"What's your hurry?" cautioned Sikorski. "We've survived this far. If the Russians are here, they'll find us; another day or two. Right?"

"Well, another day or two, I'll be too weak to scrounge up some food." Pikalski wasn't grinning anymore, his face set grimly like he was looking fate in the face.

"Well," said Kazik, "you're right, I guess, but you don't want to cross a stray bullet."

"I am going," concluded Pikalski. "You with me, Joe? Anybody?"

Sikorski's Adam's apple moved a couple of times before he answered, "Me, too," although he was trembling, white in the face.

"I'm with you," I said.

Another group was getting ready, too, for a foray into town, to search for food. It was decided that they would leave twenty minutes apart. The lone guard threatened to shoot at first but finally relented when Vacek told him: "What if the Russians are here already? We might put in a word for you."

We struggled through the mushy snow that reached in spots to our knees. The sky was cloudless, blue, and encouraging. The yellow sun had a bleached look, as if it had just traded places with the moon but for the daylight. Trudging was exhausting. We were all weakened from hunger. City houses were silhouetted in the dry air ahead.

When we first reached a broad street with apartment houses, there wasn't a soul in sight. A single-engine airplane whirled low above rooftops, unchallenged, letting out cascades of staccato warbles that ricocheted against the buildings, chipping off bits of plaster that came down and rose up in the dust around us.

"Duck, quick!" yelled Vacek. "Get in!" We ran through the gate of a house.

"Machine guns, from the planes," said Pikalski. And, when the salvos subsided, he added: "Let's go. It's our best chance to look for food in stores. The Germans must be gone."

We pushed on, carefully, tight along the walls of buildings. The light plane turned back. We could just about see the pilot's face. Bullets sprayed around us as we flattened ourselves against the stucco surfaces.

When the plane's whirling faded away, Pikalski said: "Fuck them. I'm going." We followed. We passed several intersections. At each of them, on all corners, red placards stared us in the faces with their fat, fresh, black lettering:

WER PLÜNDERT, WIRD ERSCHOSSEN

Just like in the Warsaw Ghetto, I thought. "Plunderers Will Be Shot." Just then we came upon a large square enclosed by buildings. Right in the center of it stood the still-smoldering skeleton of a tank with a red star on its side. Above it, halfway through the open hatch, a blackened figure in ragged bits of uniform was doubled over the hatch's rim, face down. Then we saw another.

"This one almost made it," said Vacek. I followed his eyes. Several paces away, another smoldering body lay, face down, half leaning on one elbow. Fire had eaten through one leg and consumed it. The remaining flesh ranged in hues from brittle black through various shades of purple and red. The dead soldier's white buttocks were exposed. Nearby, a deck of playing cards was strewn about like an unfinished trick of a collapsed magician.

"Yeah, almost made it," echoed Sikorski.

A couple of German civilians materialized from nowhere. "There were three of them. The other one vanished," said one.

"Listen, grandpa," Vacek accosted him, "where are stores around here? A bakery?"

"Over there." He pointed to one of the side streets. "But it's all gone, the food. And be careful; don't let the *Feldgendarmerie* catch you. They mean business here; some are still around, the swine."

Three blocks up the street we heard voices. Some twenty men and women stood in a line that stopped short of a narrow doorway. Presently the door opened slightly, and a man hastily emerged, carrying a one-kilo bread loaf under his arm, hurrying away. Another man who had stood at the head of the line was admitted inside.

"You guys get in the line. I'll look around," said Pikalski.

A minute later the door opened again and the lucky owner of a bread loaf shuffled out hastily. The baker's head appeared in the doorway.

"That's all. Have no more."

This caused a commotion: several voices rose up mixing disappointment, supplication, and outrage. Several men tried to force the door open.

"You swine, we're dying of hunger. Open up! … We've been here for hours!"

"Out!" screamed the baker. "Or I'll call the gendarmes!"

"Go ahead, call them!"

"Hey, Joe, let's go! Over there!" yelled Vacek.

Pikalski was standing on the corner, motioning to us. "Over here, quick!"

We ran toward him. "In here," he urged.

Around the corner a store had been ravaged. The shelves were empty. In the center of the floor a trap door had been pulled open revealing an entrance to a storage room below.

"There's some stuff down below. Cans of marmalade. Each man grab two; one in each hand. Wait for your turn!" yelled Pikalski.

Back of the counter stood some cartons. I began to turn them upside down; I might find something, perhaps, the others had overlooked. Nothing. But here, the cash register. I pulled on the drawer. It was stuffed with ration card coupons—invaluable. A few marks. I stuffed them greedily in my pockets.

"You out of your mind?" shouted Pikalski. "What d'you need this crap for, now? Wipe your ass? It's worthless!"

It was for me a reflex action, and I kept them, anyhow. "Jump down under in the cellar, hand me some cans, and grab some for yourself," Pikalski ordered me. Kobylak and Sikorski were climbing through the hatch door. "Don't waste time." He looked down. "Over in the other corner, go get some!"

I jumped down and tried to read the labels on the pails. Those weren't marmalade cans. Perhaps over in the other corner. Nothing doing. I came back to the hatch door, some four inches overhead.

"Can't find any marmalade," I yelled into the store above. There was no answer. All was quiet, no voices. I wanted to get back up, but needed a hand up. Silence above. Frantically, I pulled up a crate, stood it on top of another, and, on the third try, managed to grab the edges of the hatch door and scrambled up. It was empty. Cautiously, I approached the door. I saw silhouettes running away. To my right, two field gendarmes, rifles slung over their backs, were approaching from the opposite side of the street. They were about one hundred paces away.

Something was freezing up inside me ... a paralyzing fear like in my dreams. Now they were several paces closer. Five more steps. If they come closer, see me, and find the store plundered? Get back in and hide in the cellar! But if they look down and find me, I am the plunderer, and they'll shoot me on the spot. So far they hadn't noticed me. Well, has it come to this? After all this, to be shot like a dog by the gendarmes? One of them had been alerted by something; he had unslung his rifle. Holding it at the ready, he moved ahead. Five more steps. What do I do? Sit it out, hide, or make a break for it? Joe, Joe, make up your mind! *Now! Now!* What if they see me? *Now! Take a chance!*

From behind the door frame, I took one quick look ahead to spot the approaching gendarmes, then a bold step into the street, turned away, and immediately lapsed into a leisurely walking pace, as if I had been strolling there all along.

One, two steps. I was still alive. No shots fired. How long does it take for a bullet to reach you? No looking back—it's a dead giveaway. Two more steps.

"*Du! Halt!*"

I took off at full speed, zigzagging my way along the sidewalk. Behind me I heard sounds like corks popping. Plaster was falling off the edge of the building ahead of me. An iron gate to my left. Three more leaps. Dash into it! Is it open? Yes! From the corner of my right eye, I caught sight of a green uniform running after me. Into the courtyard! There, it's a fence, up on it! I hurled myself on top of it, like a cat. Hands and feet, scrape it up to the top, *go!* Will I make it? … Yes! Over the fence. Something snapped in my pants. Keep running! Another backyard, another fence … Keep running! Another street. Which way the bunkers? East! There's the sun, good!

I slowed down when I hit the big snow on the outskirts. Up ahead were the bunkers. Only then did I look back. The city looked peaceful except for the faraway whirling sound of a cruising single-engine airplane. I got away. I couldn't imagine myself dead. Not now. Not yet, anyway.

Soon after I reached the bunker, the others arrived.

"Why didn't you warn me?" I demanded bitterly. "You just left me there. They would have shot me."

"Warn you?" repeated Pikalski. "We yelled to you: 'Get out of there!' Ask them."

Vacek exploded. "What'd you want us to do? Sit around and wait? Lucky we saw them first, in time to beat it."

Sikorski nodded his head, sitting on a crate. "It's true. We hollered to you; there was no time for anything."

"Which way did you go?" I asked when bitterness subsided to curiosity.

"We ran away from the gendarmes; left the cans behind except him," pointing at Pikalski.

We traded some of the marmelade for a loaf of bread, with each relishing a chunk of fresh, dark bread topped with the thick goo. It was a feast.

Chapter Twenty
Another Escape

OTHER GUARDS CAME FOR us later. It had just gotten dark. We were told to fall out of the bunker and line up outside—four abreast. After we reached the city, another detail of guards took over. They were the SS, but they looked rested and vicious.

It was obvious that the first wave of the Soviet attack on Königsberg had been repelled, and the Germans were still in control. Liberation had been so near ...

Then orders were given.

"Pick up your things and march ahead. You don't look left and you don't look right, but straight on. And pick up your feet. Anybody left behind gets shot."

Soon the column was joined by a motley crowd of sundry nationalities. The Germans had rounded up all foreigners in sight. There were two, perhaps three hundred humans, shuffling in the slush and snow, mainly men but some women, some without any belongings, others balancing bundles on their backs, some even carrying suitcases and rucksacks tied to their backs.

Just out on the open road, shots were heard from behind. Pikalski glanced back.

"They're shooting people."

A minute later, two men just ahead of us left the column, staggered a few steps to the left and lay down on a snowbank.

"Get back in!" shouted one of the guards.

One of the men lifted his arms slowly, then dropped them.

"Can't."

Three shots fired, just steps away from me. The man jerked his body up a bit and turned his head sideways. Then he lay still in the snow.

Later, the ominous sky changed colors, and a few stars punctured the dark blue.

"We're going west," someone said.

After a while the guards changed places. A tall, gaunt guard trudged next to us, and he was talkative.

"Too bad we have to do it; I don't like it but orders are orders. War is war. Nobody gets left behind."

"How long we have to go?" asked Vacek in his near-perfect German.

"Till we get there."

"And where is 'there,' if I may ask, Herr Offizier?" He was upgrading the guard.

"*Unteroffizier* [non-commissioned officer]," the guard corrected him, sounding pleased.

"*Ach,' tschuldigt* ['scuse]," Vacek jumped in. "I'm sure it won't be long. You have a fine military posture, Herr Unteroffizier, you look like a regular officer. I can't tell the difference."

The guard nodded.

"It's getting rough for some older men," probed Vacek.

"Ja, for us, too. You men carry all those packs, you'll never make it. Get rid of them and you'll get there."

"Where?" Vacek again.

"Oh … a little town, hmm … about twenty-four kilometers. We're about halfway through." Only twelve kilometers remaining. Ever so inconspicuously: "Only some two hours. Hang on, even if you must drop your belongings, but don't drop out."

Men up ahead were slipping out of the column. Perhaps they preferred to die quickly. Shots were heard. Here and there dark objects were seen lying at the roadside. At times, it was difficult to see if they were bodies or abandoned bundles, except that occasionally one of the bundles would flutter in the snow.

Minutes became hours until it seemed to get warm, at first, then hot. I felt my clothes sticking to me. Blood went to my fingers and stung the tips. No one said a word anymore. To survive meant sparing every effort, every breath. Time turned into a curse that became still, forever, it seemed.

And then, much later, some shadows started breaking through the darkness.

Fata Morgana, I thought. I remembered reading of caravans lost in the Sahara Desert, yearning for an oasis … or am I there? Now? But there's no snow in the desert, no slush … no wet snow in my shoes …

"Are we … there?" gasped Vacek.

"Yeah … almost … maybe," Pikalski's moan was a whisper.

"That's the place," said the guard. "A kilometer."

In half an hour we dragged ourselves to the front of a three-storied modern building in a small town. We had made it. We were herded up the stairs onto the second floor. The building had been a school. Some doors were still marked as classrooms.

I followed the crowd to a large room with windows drawn with black shades as precaution against air raids. The lights were on. Strewn mattresses covered most of the floor. It was hard to fathom we'd made it and were actually sheltered indoors … The next morning I heard that hot soup had been served later that night. I was angry with the others for not waking me.

The calendar on the wall showed January 13, 1945.

"It bothers me, this thirteen," Sikorski winced. "Is the date right?"

"Who the fuck cares, anyway?" replied Vacek.

"You never know," countered Sikorski. "After this long sleep indoors, anything is possible. Even survival." His smile came back, faintly.

We were just waking up. The guards had left us alone till mid-morning, and there were rumors about Ersatzkaffee to be served later. Also, that we were going to stay put here, perhaps indefinitely.

I went downstairs and looked outside through the gate. The modern stucco school building was fronted by a stone stoop. Several feet further out stood a field gendarme wearing a metal plate that hung down from his neck to the center of his chest. The guards who'd brought us here were nowhere to be seen.

"Good morning," I offered to the gendarme.

"Morning. The sun is shining."

This is a new man, I thought. Perhaps he doesn't even know who he is guarding inside.

"You are from East Prussia?" I was probing.

"Naw, from Germany—Köln."

I knew Köln ... of course, Cologne, from geography. And Walter Abendrot, the renowned conductor of choirs, who had befriended my father and later corresponded, had been the "*General Musikdirektor der Stadt Köln*"—I often saw it on his letters.

"Ach, so," I answered. "The weather is wonderful."

"*Stimmt* [correct]," said the gendarme, not at all prohibitively. He nodded and walked away slowly.

✛ ✛ ✛

"What do you think, Mr. Kazik, is going to happen?" I asked Sikorski after the coffee had been ladled out from a pail. He held a pensive pause, sipping the hot liquid.

"Nothing good that I can see."

"How d'you mean?"

"Well ... I think we're here to stay for a while. Either they'll find another place for us, or ... frankly, I think they just want to keep us together for whatever ... If they decide to get rid of us before the Russians come, they'll have a few hundred of us in one piece. The Russians are coming; it's only a matter of time. Are we going to survive till then? It's a toss-up."

"What kind?"

"The Krauts don't want us to triumph in their defeat, that's for sure. I hear they might execute all foreigners."

"And if they don't?"

"We're sitting ducks here for Russian artillery or bombs. And they don't know us from nothing."

"I don't want to be a sitting duck," I said.

"Who does? But what choice do we have but sit? Some trap. I hear the Soviets will kill anything that moves—before they ask if you're a German. The first wave of Russian troops is taking its vengeance out on anybody on German soil; that's what Victor said. How're you going to telegraph them that we're Polish? They'll shoot first, ask questions later."

"Well, if it's coming to an end, I want out of this entrapment," I decided. "I don't want to die in this building, shot by Russian artillery *or* by the Krauts."

The little man looked at me incredulously. "How're you getting out of here?"

"I'll try to get past the gendarme. This one seemed friendly. He might let me pass."

"Ha! If you can, lots of luck. Look me up in Warsaw after the war."

Sikorski still didn't believe me, I could tell.

"Only, please, don't tell the others till after I'm gone," I pleaded.

"You really mean it?"

"Yes, something tells me to go. I have to follow my instinct."

"Go ahead. I'll watch you from the window."

I knew from the Ghetto that survival meant separating from the herd. The only way was to get past the gendarme, to get out of this trap. Then to walk straight, as the most natural thing. Then, perhaps, I could ask for the road to Danzig. (Today it is called Gdansk) I had, after all, a typed "to-whom-it-may-concern" letter from the shop attesting that I was ordered to proceed—*in Marsch gesetzt*—to Falkensee bei Berlin.

The same gendarme was still pacing in front of the building. Should I ask him if I could go for a little walk? What if he'd say no? No, the best thing would be to walk out, turning right onto the road. I smiled at the gendarme; he recognized me and smiled back. I kept going. Is he going to challenge me? I walked straight on, aware that Sikorski would be looking down on me from the window. Just before I turned the corner to get out of the gendarme's sight, I looked up. Sikorski's face flashed in the window. I turned the corner and picked up my pace. I felt free.

Chapter Twenty-One
Crossing the Vistula with German Soldiers

INSTINCTIVELY, I MADE A right turn on the road. It was hard to believe, but two kilometers later, the main highway leading to Danzig came into my view. It was a sight.

The highway was teeming with fleeing Prussian civilians. Most were walking, hauling all they could manage on their backs. The lucky ones had hay wagons pulled by horses straining in the snow, the women and children stowed between bundles.

On both sides of the road, abandoned possessions to satisfy every human need studded the deep snow. There were suitcases and bundles, overturned hay wagons and all imaginable carts. Many bundles were torn open by owners frantically retrieving some items from packs too heavy to carry, or by pilferers. All within my sight.

The Polish population had similarly clogged the roads, I recalled, back in September of 1939—dying of hunger and thirst, being picked off by the swooping planes of the Luftwaffe. Now it was their turn, the invincible Germans. Well, there may be a God in heaven, after all.

All at once, in mid-afternoon, the whole procession swayed. A roar was heard from the rear.

"They're coming, they're coming!" people were shouting, and those on foot scurried toward the snowbanks on the roadsides. A military motorcycle appeared, with an officer in a sidecar hollering, "Clear the road, or you'll get run down."

He fired twice in the air. A couple of overloaded hay wagons pulled to the side. They immediately got stuck in the entrapping snow, one turning over, the horses struggling against the collars that were choking them. Seeing their plight, other men unharnessed their horses to free them to the sides, keeping the wagons themselves on the road. Then came the roar of the tanks. A long column, perhaps twenty or more. As they passed through, sending mists of powdered snow to each side, the first sideswiped a hay wagon, dragging it a few paces, then turning it entirely around. The reins, which the driver had lost, got sucked into the Panzer's tread. The near horse was pulled under the tank, his head crushed. There were agonizing screams from the occupants of the hay wagon; then the tank splattered the horse's flesh and blood all over the snow. The second tank, unswerving, ran over the wagon and its occupants. In the blood-soaked wreckage lay a human body, missing an arm. Behind me I could hear yelling and cursing, the Prussians waving their furious fists at their own Panzer troops. They were finally getting a taste of the bestiality they had visited on the Poles and Jews, the Russians, and others, through the same Hitler troops. I couldn't help thinking: *Oh, if only Sikorski and the others could have witnessed it!*

I had to keep pace with the fleeing Prussians, a couple of times scrambling atop one of the hay wagons before I was chased off. Then I felt my left foot getting wet and discovered a hole in my shoe. Only a rag, with which we used to wrap our feet, remained between my foot and the snow.

A chill of fear crept over me. At this rate, without shoes, I would not be able to get very far. I got off the road and, with a few other men of dubious nationalities, rummaged through abandoned suitcases. Someone yelled at me, and I got back onto the road. I had not found any shoes, but it was too dangerous to take more chances. Plunderers were still being shot on sight when caught by the field gendarmerie, even though it was obvious that the abandoned possessions strewn alongside had been left behind for good.

And then it was getting dark. I knew that if the long, never-ending column ever came to a halt during the night, most would not see the next morning being frozen in the night. Although my body, in motion, generated sufficient heat, I could tell by the stinging of the frost against my nostrils as I inhaled that the temperature was dropping rapidly and that few would survive on the open road. Too, the wetness in my shoe would turn into ice once the column ground to a halt.

In the descending darkness I saw three men break away from the caravan. They headed toward a roadside house. I followed them. Inside the spacious living room, past a hallway and staircase, a hefty middle-aged German barred the way. He already had ten people for the night, he said. He'd have to take us, too, the men told him. What if others tried to come in? But he looked frightened. We would keep out the others, they said. The owner reluctantly stepped aside. There were four of us.

We located some cold soup left in the kitchen, which we devoured. In the next room I found a couple of rags that looked like remnants of window drapes. I took them for wrapping my feet. The house was barely heated, but I curled up in the corner on some other rags and, in gratitude, began to say my prayers … I heard some voices through the night, but I didn't care, or make an effort …

Somebody kicked me in the morning.

"Los, Mensch! Out! Get out now!"

Then I remembered that I ought to look for shoes. I showed the owner the hole in my shoe.

"Don't have any," he shrugged me off, impatiently.

"But, if you do, sir, please help me; how else could I go on?"

"You a German?"

"Y … yes," I stuttered, "from South Prussia." I knew there were Prussians along the erstwhile Polish border who did not speak very good German. "I'm a German national—ein Volksdeutscher."

The German mellowed, but only some. "No, don't have any shoes."

On the way out, off the hallway, I looked inside a door partially ajar. Inside, several men were searching through closets, throwing the clothes down on the floor. One of the men was trying on a pair of shoes.

"What do you want?" I knew instantly he was not German.

"Same as you," I answered boldly. "I need shoes." They were a matter of survival.

"Out! Out with you!" He looked mean and strong. Then I noticed a pair of black boots, toppled over one another. They looked smaller. The man was trying on other shoes which didn't seem to fit him. If I could leap over, grab them, and run …

"All right," I said to appease him as he was bending down, gasping and trying to force a shoe over a sweaty piece of rag wrapped around his ankle. I lurched forward, grabbed the boots, and ran. In the hallway, I bumped head on into the owner. Slipping under his outstretched arm, I stormed through the main door and across the snow toward the road. Later, I sat down and tried the boots on. They were a bit too large, but I found some women's clothes, tore them up and stuffed them into the boots. They spelled imminent survival. Thus I was able to continue in the long procession toward Danzig. It had turned gray and cold. Freezing snowflakes gyrated around in an ominous dance.

Late that night a farm couple let me climb up on their hay wagon. I fell asleep.

Next morning, as I was shaking off the snow and the frozen strands of prickly hay, I heard a new military column approaching. A German officer on horseback, followed by soldiers with rifles at the ready. Then the rest came—shadows of men in rags, some still covered by military overcoats, a few dressed only in shirts. Some had fading blankets thrown over their shoulders; others shielded their bodies with sacks tied together. A few had no boots, their feet wrapped in rags. These were prisoners of war—Russians. Some stumbled. Those who fell down were set upon by the German guards and beaten with rifle butts until their fellow prisoners managed, despite the blows, to lift their comrades to their dragging feet.

The Germans yelled at everyone to let the prisoner column pass through. Some Prussians obeyed, muttering, but only one wagon budged.

"Get over to the side!"

A couple of older Prussians went up to an officer, pointing to their wagons and objecting.

"Nonsense!" yelled the officer. "Get off the road!"

"You must be cuckoo," a farmer shot back, pointing derisively to his temple. "Where do you come from telling me, an East Prussian, to get off the road?"

Other hay wagon drivers had gathered around the farmer.

"What do you think of that? A Bavarian, no less, telling us Prussians to leave our road!"

The army officer, muttering something, finally waved his arm in disgust and motioned to his troops to lead the Russian prisoners around the halted wagons. The Prussians stood there, turning and gaping at the limping dregs of human beings stumbling past. One Soviet prisoner, taking advantage of the commotion, stooped down, gathering some dirty snow in his cupped hands and stuffing it into his mouth. But one of the German guards saw it. He smashed at the man's hand, hitting him in his mouth. There was an angry murmur from the Prussians. Another Russian, a scraggly blanket wrapped around his shoulder, looked up at a woman sitting on a wagon next to me, and begged:

"*Wasser, bitte, Wasser, Brot!*" (Water, please, water, bread) His eyes rolled upward in a plea for life.

The woman fetched from her bundle a chunk of country bread, broke off a piece the size of a fist, and tossed it down toward the prisoner. He caught it while another prisoner tore at it. But, again, the guards were soon upon them, clubbing both men while yelling at the Prussians:

"Don't give them anything! It's verboten!"

"For God's sake, they're humans, too!" screamed the woman.

"He's right!" someone else yelled in the crowd. "He's a Bolshevik. Don't give him nothing!"

But as soon as the guard had passed, the woman tossed more bread to the other prisoners. She was joined by a younger woman, and together they followed up with chunks of cheese.

"Please," I said, "may I have a small piece, too?"

"This is just for them," hollered the woman. But in the end, I caught a chunk of bread.

This was when a long stream of uniformed men on horseback caught up with us, flanking the road. They had German uniforms. One of the Russians nudged his comrade: "Vlasov riders." I understood instantly. True enough, they had shoulder patches indicating their identity. Vlasov was a Soviet general, taken prisoner by the Germans, who had pledged, with his troops, his allegiance to Hitler. The Vlasov riders must have watched the treatment of the prisoners. One of the latter hollered to the riders: "*Vy Ruskie?*" There was no reply. "If you are Russian, *tovarishche*, help us, we're dying, we can't go on."

One of the mounted men yelled back, in Russian: "You're no *tovarishch* to us! *Uhadziy! (Get away)* We're no Bolsheviks! We're fighting Stalin!"

"Fuck Stalin's mother, but we are your brothers, help us, we're dying!"

There was something very Slavic, I thought, about the intensity of these desperate supplications that knocked at another's conscience.

"You're not my brother!" shouted back the Vlasov Rider, and a couple of his riders laughed.

✠ ✠ ✠

By mid-afternoon the column of men and vehicles came to a complete halt. Soon we learned that this was not just another delay occasioned by a stuck wagon up ahead. The word had spread that we had reached the vicinity of the Vistula River. Danzig lay on the other side.

"Donnerwetter," exploded a mustachioed Prussian. "Why don't they let us across? We're Germans, too; we have a right to save our families."

"Bridge is out," someone said.

I forged ahead on foot. Some twenty minutes later, the road widened and the farmers' wagons were lined up tightly on both sides as far as the eye could see.

"How far to the river?" I asked a woman who peered from under a hooded wagon, all bundled up, rocking her body to cope with the freezing air.

"Maybe a kilometer and a half."

"What're you waiting for?"

"To get across."

"How long you been here?"

"Three days and three nights."

I whistled. "When d'you expect to go?"

"We don't know. They say today or tomorrow." She started to weep. "What if the Russians catch up to us before then? We'll all die."

I was tempted to say: "Should have thought of that before you attacked Poland and Russia," but I said nothing and forged on. Beyond the river lay a sprawling valley and the Vistula. In its majestic but murky waters lay the remains of a bridge, crushed, useless. Two ferries shuttled between the shores, their stacks emitting black smoke.

Another road was spilling army vehicles and tanks onto the main road. As I came nearer, I could see in the distance clusters of military men and field gendarmerie, keeping away throngs of Prussians, while waving by military traffic. I followed the line of waiting military vehicles to the rear, walking past two tanks and a few trucks. A military ambulance, dark gray-green, splashed with mud, idled its engines, large red crosses peering at me from the white background on the sides. I stepped to the rear and gazed inside a small window in the door of the ambulance. I knocked. The door was flung open.

"*Grüß Gott!*" I said.

"How are you, Kamerad?" answered one of the soldiers. He was sitting on hay near the ambulance rear door, his hand resting in a white sling. He had on a military gray undershirt.

"Where're you going?" I inquired in my best *Plattdeutsch* Prussian.

"*Nach Danzig.* The hospital there." He exuded a relaxed expression, as if I had interrupted a jovial conversation. I thought: *Being wounded, he probably relishes being out of the deadly spin.*

"Oh, yes? Me too. I want to join my parents in Danzig. We got separated."

"Where you from?" asked the soldier.

"Insterburg."

"*Um Gottes Willen* [For God's sake]," replied the soldier. "The Russians are probably there already. Hop in, we'll give you a ride. Hey, Kurt," he hollered toward the front seat, "we pick up a little fellow, wants to join his parents in Danzig, all right?"

A head up in the front seat turned sideways.

"All right, but don't pick up no more! We're already crowded; the men have to breathe."

Minutes later, the ambulance got the right of way. By three in the afternoon we crossed the river.

Chapter Twenty-Two
American Air Raids, Again: Liberation!

Danzig. It had meant to me, since my geography lessons in school, a way station of urbanity and civilization, of bright lights, a window on the sea and the world beyond.

The soldiers, at my request, had left me at an intersection outside Danzig, for I dreaded arriving at the military hospital—guarded, no doubt. Once on foot, the open question was what to do next: food, shelter. Walking through the center of the city, I spotted a Polish man whom I had picked from the passersby by dint of his appearance and clothes.

"Don't walk around—there are many cops in civvies," he warned me. "They'll pounce on you in a second." This, despite having torn out my *P* patch (if anything, I'd say I'd lost it). "You are supposed to report to the Arbeitsamt. Only, most likely, they'll send you to the front to dig foxholes for the Germans. That's what they do with foreigners here."

I thanked him and, after much mulling it over, decided to go to the train station. After all, I had a letter mandating me to proceed to Falkensee bei Berlin. Passing a bake shop at the station, I felt in my pocket the stack of ration coupons which I had stuffed there in the aborted raid on the food store previously. I had some money which I'd stuffed in with the coupons, and I bought myself some sausages and bread—not all at once, lest a handful of ration cards incur suspicion. Food! Can it ever be described?

But what next? I never wanted to work for Toussaint again—wherever that might be. But all I had with me was this letter to report to Falkensee. Otherwise, at the first encounter, my identity would be checked and, roaming about, I'd be arrested immediately—at best, to dig foxholes at the front.

My instinct told me to forge westward, hopefully to meet up with the advancing Americans or the British. But where were they? I bought a copy of *Völkischer Beobachter*, the prime German daily which reported on the status of the war and the front line, perhaps approximating reality.

At the train station, a huge map of *Grossdeutschland* was on display. In between people milling about, I stood with the unfolded newspaper, looking up the current official reports from the *Oberkommando der Wehrmacht*. Just where were the Americans? The front line I followed ran somewhere through the *Schwartzwald*. God forbid, I would not aim to head for it—too suspicious. A place, then, some fifty to a hundred kilometers from the front line—safely to the rear. Erfurt, a large city in the province of Thuringia, seemed right. The trek I resolved on ran through Berlin, then south. I went outside and circled the train terminal, accosting the first man I ran into, to ask which way was west. Then I proceeded along the railroad tracks, keeping a safe distance. Freight cars of every kind idled there. Presently I heard several voices emanating from one of the cars. The door was open and a few soldiers were sitting on the floor, their feet dangling outside. Before I could say anything, one of them addressed me:

"*Was ist los mit dir?*" (What's the matter with you?)

He was merry and, by the voices of the other soldiers, it was likely that they had been drinking. During the conversation that evolved, I answered several questions as to where from and where to. I said I was hoping to join my parents in Berlin. Soon the soldier offered: "Well, I don't know exactly when you'll get there; but if you want, hop in and get a ride with us. You see, they didn't give us our train schedule." This caused an outburst of laughter from the soldiers.

"When I am allowed, sir," I replied. "It would be an honor to ride with *our* soldiers."

The soldiers, who had been lying on the plentiful straw, then shared their food and drink with me, treating me as one of them. The next several days and nights were spent with a carload full of soldiers. I slept, my limbs intertwined with theirs.

✛ ✛ ✛

The loudspeaker blasted as we pulled into the train terminal in Lauenburg: "Everyone, without exception, is to proceed to Platform One, to have his identity checked." I had to leave the soldiers, thanking them for their company. On Platform One, a large sign with an arrow pointed to the terminal annex. The sign read: "Foreigners." In the line I soon recognized some Poles. They had gotten wind that all foreigners were being conscripted to the front to dig foxholes for the troops. When my turn came, I stood before an SS officer who commandeered me aside to join a group to be shipped out. I did as I was told, but in a minute I approached the SS officer again, telling him in the best military fashion I could muster that I simply *had* to proceed to Falkensee or I would be in a lot of trouble, since I was working for the "war effort." After a moment of hesitation, he stamped my marching letter: "SS Lauenburg." I was free to proceed.

Freight trains were leaving the station westward, and I jumped on one. Riding between cars, I ran into a young Polish fellow. But all along I wondered what would happen when I reached the vicinity of Berlin. Then a thought struck me: the Germans respect boldness and this situation called for that. I asked the Polish fellow if he had a red crayon. Miraculously, he had one. I wanted to borrow it for a minute, I pleaded. He wanted something in exchange. I hesitated and offered him a pocket knife given me a year and a half ago by Father Falkowski. With the red crayon, I boldly crossed out "Falkensee," heavily underscoring "Berlin." If anybody questioned it, I thought, I would invoke the SS officer's stamp, claiming that it was he who'd changed my destination.

It was daytime when the freight train pulled into Berlin Main Station. For a while I meandered through the streets. Lo and behold, I passed two young men who spoke Polish. During the encounter, they told me:

"Don't stay another night in Berlin. Last night the Allies bombed the living hell out of the city. Go to the Labor Office and tell them you must proceed further. Stay another night, and you'll be buried alive."

They gave me directions to the Arbeitsamt: I was to take the S-Bahn (or the U-Bahn—I don't recall anymore)—the Berlin subway—to get to the office.

It was late afternoon when I got there. After I explained to the civilian official that I had to proceed to Erfurt, claiming that the Toussaint shop had meanwhile moved there, the decrepit official was suspicious:

"Now, why would they order you to Berlin, not Erfurt?"

"Sir, it was because the SS officer, aware that meanwhile my shop had been moved to Erfurt, told me that I would have fewer problems if I first reached Berlin."

He didn't buy. Instead, he told me to report the next day for assignment in Berlin. "We have enough work right here," he snorted. "We need all hands available to clear out the rubble." When he dismissed me, I had not the slightest idea where I was going to spend the night. A few minutes later, however, I decided to cling to the only possible straw. I returned to the office, telling the official that I and even he would get into serious trouble if I failed to arrive in Erfurt—the site of my relocated shop, which was vital for the "war effort."

He relented, issuing me a free railroad pass and an official slip reading: "*Nach Erfurt in Marsch gesetzt.*"

I left on the first available passenger train before nighttime, sharing a compartment with German officers and their wives. In the middle of the night, the train ground to a halt. In the far distance, one could see huge explosions and fire and hear the roar of airplanes.

"Halle is under air raid," someone said. Halle, I deduced, was a city en route to Erfurt.

The bombardment sounded ferocious, exacerbated by the roar of diving aircraft. It lasted over two hours. The officers and their wives in the train compartment sat in stony silence, but once one of the women offered me half of her sandwich.

Early the next morning we pulled into the Erfurt terminal. Next to it I came upon some barracks. I spotted a Polish face. He disclosed that they were transient housing for Ausländer—dozens of foreign workers milling around, refugees of sorts from other parts of Germany. I soon found out that on arrival they had to report to the German Labor Office—the Arbeitsamt—within twenty-four hours and obtain, or wait for, an assignment. My continued impersonation of a German Volksdeutscher (national) was out of the question.

In the midtown office I pleaded total ignorance as to the reasons of my dispatch to Erfurt, knowing there was no way they could check on it. I was a seasoned automobile mechanic, I was told, and they'd try to place me accordingly in time; but in the meantime, the only thing available was kitchen help at the railroad terminal restaurant. Was I interested? I could hardly believe this: no one had ever asked me that in Germany.

Two old shrunken spinsters ran the *Bahnhof* restaurant. I slept in a tiny attic with a Serbian chef—a strapping, long-limbed man in his twenties who acted as if the vodka he somehow managed to procure never wore off. The food served to German travelers against their ration cards was doled out microscopically. Bread slices were counted by both sisters, and, although I worked twelve-hour shifts, I was always hungry. Relief came only when, occasionally, I would be assigned to scraping raw carrots. Despite constant supervision to insure that only the thinnest outer skin was removed, I would manage, here and there, to bite off the end of a carrot and imperceptibly chew on it.

One of the sisters was present in the kitchen at all times. Both ran it as a strict military camp, and saw to it that it was kept spotlessly clean. In the evening Yosif, the chef, two Ukrainians, and I scrubbed all pots until, glistening and dazzling the eye, until they passed the spinsters' watchful eyes.

Kitchen help was allowed exactly ten minutes for breakfast, fifteen minutes for lunch, and thirty minutes for supper at six. The work day began at six in the morning. The two sisters were everywhere; they anticipated each task, trotting by, always poised just at the right spot, just a little ahead of each task, breathing just behind the shoulder of a worker: another instruction—be careful of this, watch out for that, pour just the right amount, don't waste a drop. The slightest departure from the rigid instructions brought on reprimands—all in whispered tones. Whenever I turned, I felt the eyes of one of the sisters on me: quick, methodical, efficient, ceaseless. Three weeks of that.

I was caught twice stealing food. Once they traced an extra portion of bread pudding to me; I'd hidden it in the corner pantry for later consumption. The second time, the prevailing strict orders to the contrary, I was caught shoving an extra slice of bread into my mouth between meals.

Soon after, early in March, the younger sister called me over to the office. Her long, shapeless dress hung on her like a nun's habit. Her wizened face towered over it unflinchingly. With her sister, she said, they had decided to give me a choice. They liked me, she went on, and, to be forthright, I must be aware that help was difficult to get these days. But they had to run this place according to rules, what with the shortage of critical supplies and the effect my "misappropriations," she called them, would have on the morale of the other workers. And so … would I firmly promise to abide by the rules which, of course, they hated to enforce—or they might refer me back to the Arbeitsamt for another job. No, no, they wouldn't want to hurt me; they'd even give me good references. Well, I thought, in that case …

"Perhaps you'd better send me back."

✠ ✠ ✠

At the Labor Office I was referred to the office of one Hans Kost, a builder. There I helped filing papers away, sweeping the floor, and running sporadic errands to various construction sites. Occasionally, Kost's secretary let me help her with some simple typing. He'd been told by the Arbeitsamt that he could have me if he found me a place to stay. The foreigners' camp was overcrowded. It happened that Kost's friend employed a Pole, Franciszek Morawski. Kost arranged for me to move in with Morawski into one small room in the Trade Headquarters building in the town's central plaza. Next to our room was also the headquarters of the Hitler-Jugend.

It was an hour's walk to get to my new job, but I relished the freedom of movement and the stroke of luck that kept me from landing in the foreigners' camp where, Franek told me, discipline was fierce and beatings were frequent.

On the first Sunday, I walked around the city, even fought my way with a large crowd into the local cinema. There were minimal penalties for failing to display the *P* patch on the outer clothes, but this was no Prussia where Poles were hated, and most Poles, Franek told me, didn't even bother sewing it on.

The night after I moved in with Franek—a taciturn, spindly, and doleful man—the first air raid came. The bombs came down preceded by the wailing of sirens. We'd run down the stairs to the shelter in the basement. There, in the company of some Germans, we wrapped ourselves in blankets, awaiting further explosions. There were short intervals, each culminating in a whistle that grew in intensity, its pitch sinking progressively until it reached an unbearable register, the lowest possible I'd ever heard. Then, it'd cease suddenly, and the ominous pause that followed lasted a long, long time—two seconds, perhaps, or three. This was even more frightening; even the Germans were seen praying.

If we heard nothing within the first few seconds, the immediate danger was over, and the Germans would heave a long sigh of relief; the explosions would break out further away. But if the first mounting rumblings, rapid and growing, came within a second or two, the Germans in the shelter would assume hunched, curled-up positions, bracing themselves for an explosion near or imminent above us. There could be seconds left in one's life, maybe less.

A few times the explosions came very close, riding on shattering clapping detonations, painfully invading the ears, followed, in spurts, by a long rumble of collapsing structures. These were, Franek concluded, serious games: the American bombs.

When the all-clear was sounded in long fermatas, I would follow Franek to our room, up three flights of stairs. Chilled to the bone, we'd throw ourselves on our bunks ... sometimes the next siren would sound off minutes after the all-clear, in skin-curdling short spurts, or shortly before dawn. At times, we slept on the cold cellar floor all night—throughout the air-raids, until chased away by the air warden, a helmeted Nazi in his late age, with flesh overhanging his cheeks.

Each night averaged two, three, or more air alerts, later as many as seven or eight, each lasting a minute to an hour. When, in the morning, I reported to Kost's office, I often fell asleep in the midst of filing papers or typing. I used Sundays for sleeping.

The second week Franek brought in a friend: Antos, a hefty, robust Pole from the Krakow region. He was a restless, wisecracking, good-natured man, much devoted to Franek, for whom he'd often bring small packets of food which they shared with me.

The Germans were getting frantic, Antos was saying. The grapevine had it that they'd round up and execute all foreign workers. We discussed some alternatives of survival: "They're not going to get our hides," we maintained repeatedly.

All around us, the buildings had been hit. One could hide in them when the time came, but when? Who'd warn us? If we hid too early, would they not look for us, if we failed to show up for work? The nights were still too cold, and then the air raids ...

"Like on the battlefield," said Antos, "the shells never hit the same spot twice. The ruins are safe for hiding." But no final decision was made.

Meanwhile, the nights turned to hell. The raids were getting more frequent and lasted longer. Franek and Antos, who spent some nights with us, gloated over the punishment being visited on the German city. With most buildings at this central city plaza burning or lying in ruins, we feared the nights and a direct hit. Still, with artillery sounding off at night, we had taken our blankets to spend the night in the air raid shelter. But the air warden barred our way. "Unrestricted space in the shelter, outside of actual air raids, is accorded only to Germans," he pronounced.

On my way to work in the morning, I saw a house across the street, which had received a direct hit, crumbled like an accordion, still smoking. A dozen or so men with shovels and pickaxes stood over the smoldering ruins. They'd been up all night digging.

"People still in there?" someone in the gathering crowd asked.

"A direct hit," replied one of the crew. "We'll never get to them, not without heavy equipment."

"By God," snorted a man angrily, "why don't you get it?"

The crewman turned on him. "Mensch, you know where to get it? Go get it! If you can find a free crane in this city!"

That night and for the next three nights all of the houses around us were leveled—save ours. On April 11, it took me the better part of half an hour to climb over mountains of rock and smoking debris to get out of the house on my way to work.

The sirens wailed at ten in the morning—the first daytime raid. Kost hadn't shown up, and his secretary ran down to the cellar when the first wailing bombs started falling. I was standing at the entrance to the cellar outside, facing the courtyard alone. The sky was flawless and still. And from that heavy stillness, a few dark crosses floated up over the azure horizon. A whole flotilla of other crosses glided up behind them, sailing into my vision. More and more still were sliding behind, like a huge anthill—from a seemingly inexhaustible supply—until the whole sky was covered with little crosses like hordes of distant vultures surveying a battlefield before swooping down on it, and still others kept emerging. I thought of the Biblical locusts—at first distant and harmless, until they filled the whole sky, blocking off the sun, plunging the earth into total darkness. The armada looked strangely peaceful. And unchallenged. Not one German plane in sight. Their flak had been silenced.

So it had come to pass. Allied planes ruled the skies. Only down here, there were gnawing fears about survival, of being rounded up any time ...

I expected the armada to go into a steep dive at any moment, one by one. I didn't much care about where the bombs would fall. I wanted to see those harmless-looking bombs spill out of those planes and float down to earth ... those American flyers up there, they must be Americans ... the British could not possibly have so many planes ... what did they think about? ... They ruled the skies ... arrogantly.

The bombs never came; perhaps they had a rendezvous elsewhere. The air flotilla merely glided past, majestically, as if it were parade day and they were being guided on their floats down Main Street, in full force.

That night the sirens wailed again. I refused to go to the cellar. I was too tired to care ...

A gigantic explosion threw me out of bed. It was goddamn awful close. When I picked myself off the floor, I saw briefly the window sliced open inward, tearing right through the blackout paper. "Artillery!" A powerful fear tossed me through the door. I hurled myself down the staircase, leaping two, three steps at a time, gliding the rest of the way down to the cellar.

Franek surveyed my nightshirt and my speechless face.

"Aha! The hero! 'I don't care, leave me alone!' Look at him! Someone painted your face white?"

"Artillery," he concluded, after I had stuttered out the events of the last few minutes. "They're close. Just heard it from the Krauts—horse's mouth: the Americans have taken Gotha." No more bombs, he added. "From now on it's going to be artillery, just so they don't hit their own troops by mistake. And that will make survival even tougher, 'cause they're going to come without warning, no sirens to warn you. I don't know," he concluded gloomily, "I was having my doubts if you'd survive this. But with artillery ..." he shook his head—a conversation he had held with himself.

The explosions above were closer now, more muffled.

In the morning, when we had gone upstairs during a temporary lull in the shelling, I thought I'd wandered into the wrong room by mistake. The window was gone altogether and a brutal gash, one square meter wide, exposed the red, brittle brick, its skin torn off and reduced to dusty, crushed cement. A few loose wooden planks lay crumpled in the corner where our double bunk had stood. Franek, whose face was lined with sleepless strain, and I picked up several twisted metal fragments off the floor. He shook his head slowly: "'Leave me alone,' hmm? You stupid bastard! 'I don't care, I want to sleep! ...' Well, congratulations, mincemeat! You missed it by a pussy's hair!"

Outside, our house had been thoroughly pockmarked by shells. The whole plaza was burning. Nobody went to work anymore. We scrounged around for food but found none.

The shelling continued all through the day, as we darted in and out of the cellar—to look for food, to look out for any roundup of foreigners, to combat restlessness. In the afternoon Antos found us in the shelter. He brought some bread and margarine under his coat.

"Any hour now," he whispered. "If the sons of bitches don't get us, we'll survive." His pant leg was torn and his face blackened.

"Any news?" asked Franek, munching on bread.

"Yeah. They started out pulling all foreigners out of the shelters yesterday and lined them up, ready to go, then let them go again."

"Why?"

"Don't know. Too late, I guess."

"Yeah, looks it." Franek pulled hungrily on the cigarette which Antos had rolled from crumpled butts in his pocket. "Who knows? We might yet survive."

"Bet your ass, we will," asserted Antos.

We lived through another night, limp and falling in and out of consciousness. We were supposed to be sleeping in shifts, in case "they" came for us. Then, it might just be possible to get out through the courtyard door ... The shelling subsided in the morning and all fell into a stony sleep.

Hours later we woke up to the uneasy strumming of a mandolin. I thought it was part of a dream, but there he was: the air warden sans his SA uniform, his face flushed with alcohol, plucking the mandolin. Softly, he intoned "Lili Marlene," off-key. He was drunk and wearing civilian clothes. He rambled on between verses.

"*Es ist ganz egall*—all the same now," he was saying. He turned to Franek. "You look like a ..." he hiccupped "a decent guy. I've always thought so. Well, you know, with the war, one can't always show one's ... feelings." Hiccup. "But now ... it's different. I don't care anymore. You're all right. He, too," he added, pointing at me. "He tries too hard ... otherwise, he'll learn."

We were tense and didn't know what to expect next. The man had been threatening us only two days before: "All the foreigners brought the war on." But now? "We're all in the same boat now, Kamerad. After all, we're all people, aren't we? That's all we are—just people, right?"

Something was in the air, but we were too cautious to explore. They must know something, I thought. The air was tense. Even the few elderly Germans seemed unusually quiet.

This was when Antos burst into the cellar. The air warden squinted reprovingly. But Antos was yelling in Polish:

"Get out of here, quick! And follow me!"

"Tsssh!" Franek attempted to quiet him. "Watch yourself ... this guy here ..."

"Fuck him! They're here!"

"Who?"

"The Americans! He can't do nothing no more! They're here!"

We darted behind him, out the narrow door and up the steps into the blinding daylight; over burning bricks and collapsed beams, up the narrow street off the plaza. I was out of breath, but it didn't matter. It only mattered to keep up with Antos.

Leaping and flying, we cleared the rubble. Up ahead we ran into a whole gang of civilians milling around a wine and liquor store. Some were hastily carrying out bottles, others struggling to get in. Some military-looking men, black of face, dressed in strange khakis and carrying rifles, tried to disperse the crowd. But nobody was paying attention. Obviously, no one was afraid of these soldiers; they seemed to have regard for human life. We ran until we reached the main avenue and stopped just as suddenly. It was a sight.

The wide avenue, lined with streetcar tracks, was clogged bumper to bumper with motor vehicles. Strange-looking trucks crept by, stopping and starting, white stars painted on their sides. Small, olive-drab vehicles, roofless and sideless, their windshields collapsed on the hoods, filled in the gaps between the trucks. And soldiers, soldiers everywhere—dressed casually, their helmets askew, lackadaisical and yet cheerful; some seeming tired, walking, strutting, riding in the roofless vehicles, their legs casually swung over the hoods, chewing gum, looking both fatigued and bored, spectators in a procession ...

"Americans!" Franek screamed. He ran up to the first tall soldier and threw his arms around him. "Liberation! Thank you, thank you! We Polnisch. Polnisch!"

I had no idea how I found myself in another soldier's arms until my chin struck the soldier's rifle, hard on the metal mechanism. Only when he pulled back did I notice his black face.

"Hey, man," gasped the soldier, "what's up, daddy?—Okay, okay now."

I struggled to recall some English words from my Ghetto classes; but due to the sweeping emotion, I could only utter some fragments. Only, while a few soldiers circled around, I kept saying:

"We Polish ... Polish, thank you, thank you! Viva America, Viva Roosevelt!"

"Roosevelt is kaput—nix mehr (no more)" said a soldier.

"Oh, sorry," I stuttered. "Who is president?"

The soldier turned to another creeping by in a short vehicle. "Hey, Mack, what's the guy's name, the president?"

"I don't know," came the answer. "Something like Furman or Truman."

"Viva Furman!" we yelled joyfully.

It was April 13, 1945.

✛ ✛ ✛

"Dear, dear Father," I wrote, hoping that mail might be reaching Poland one day soon. "I am alive and the war is over. The Reich is destroyed, though it is still hard to believe. It can't all be a cruel dream. It must be true, thank God. God has triumphed, I am alive and am traveling with American Army units through Austria (really!), and these are no ordinary units, either. They call them 'counter-intelligence': we are rounding up Nazis and I am interpreting, and thus learning more English every day.

"The other day, our unit stopped by Hitler's mountain resort at Berchtesgaden. A few days. I stood at Hitler's window on the world—imagine! How my parents would have loved it!

"I have all these feelings and turbulent thoughts now, yet it's difficult for me to sort them out. I know I should be happy to witness the retribution, in many forms, being visited upon the evil people and, you'd think that, given a chance, I'd be glad to take part in it. But I find that I can't. I can't even watch the beatings being meted out to the

Germans by one of our intelligence agents, an Alsatian attached to our unit. I get revolted, or is it your teachings of love and forgiveness?

"Father, understand me please, how could one forgive the killers—for my parents and my sister, my teachers, my friends, and all the others? It's not for me to forgive them, but for the departed ones, and nobody's heard of them ... But I have a pretty good idea.

"Father, how do you reconcile Christ's love with the punishment the Germans deserve? For all the murders, humiliations, and suffering? How do I continue as a Catholic amidst all this?

"And then, the Americans are with women a great deal. I have so many occasions and temptations ... what do I do? ... How long will I last without your guidance?"

I had other problems, too difficult to formulate for the priest. One of the Americans had asked if I was Jewish. I demurred. I still could not believe that the persecution had ceased permanently. For whatever reason, the world hated us and, if it had allowed mass murder to occur, surely it was bound to happen again. Meanwhile, I had carte blanche into the Aryan world; perhaps it would be safe to keep it.

And then, the American doctor who gave me a medical exam had me strip and examined my penis and testicles. I had been shaking. I was sure the doctor was checking if I was Jewish.

I often had nightmares, and lately one in particular which recurred regularly, recalling a scene I had witnessed in a Berlin street on my way to the Labor Office. In my dream I kept seeing a man I had witnessed, the last man staggering behind a line of prisoners prodded forward by German guards. The man was coatless, at the end of January, his feet wrapped in rags, with horrible sores on his legs. As I, with other Germans, was made to stand on the sidewalk, the ragtag column struggled past. From their looks I just knew they were Jewish. The eyes of this one man actually met mine, and I saw in them a bottomless suffering, an ocean of pain—and utter condemnation. Jewish eyes, sad beyond description. I felt a cringing shame: what right did I have mixing with the Germans when other Jews were being led to extinction? ... I looked away, afraid of being recognized. I had followed the column of prisoners down the street, but the man ignored me.

I would wake up in a cold sweat, frightened and in helpless despair.

✠ ✠ ✠

"Father," I wrote, "why so much suffering? I remember you saying that Jews had brought this upon themselves, by rejecting Christ—and that it is this suffering we should wish to take upon ourselves, since he died for our sins. Father, what sins did my parents have? They were good and righteous and compassionate to others.

"Although you never put it quite this way, I feel that I have made a contract with you and, through you, with Christ. I want to dedicate myself to this. You have been and are my spiritual advisor, my friend, also like a father to me. I hope to prove with my life that I am worthy of your teachings. You said before that being Jewish and Catholic is a beautiful gift, and you wished you could be both. This is very hard for me now. But, in time, this too will become clearer to me."

Chapter Twenty-Three
In My Adopted Country

I was resting on the sofa in my studio apartment on East Seventy-first Street in Manhattan. The year was 1962, ten years after I had migrated to the United States from the refugee camp in the American zone of occupation in Germany. My sponsor, the National Catholic Bishops Conference, had guaranteed in an affidavit that I would receive gainful employment lest I become a "public burden." The initial job secured for me was a back-breaking work at a Connecticut cigar tobacco farm where I, along with some other Polish immigrants, was put up in primitive barracks, which had housed a group of Jamaican blacks. On weekends they secured Jamaican whores who offered their services in the back seat of a rickety car. Weeks later I was lucky to meet an older Polish immigrant who secured for me a job at a factory: in hot summer without much ventilation.

War in Korea ("a conflict," they called it) broke out in summer of 1950. Hoping to end the factory drudgery—but also propelled by a sense of gratitude to the country that had liberated me and felt threatened now, I volunteered for the U.S. Air Force. It would take some time to process the papers; in the meantime, the army got to me first. I was drafted and, after several weeks of basic training, I was shipped to Japan and later to the Korean battle zone (five decorations and two battle stars). Coming back stateside, eventually I was granted the GI Bill and, along with two other scholarships, landed at Yale (MFA) followed by a PhD at New York University.

That's where a wartime friend of my father's introduced me to a couple: she originating from a Polish-Jewish senator to the Sejm; he a wartime partisan hero, a young Polish Army officer with an MD degree.

As we exchanged wartime survival stories, he related to me how he had escaped from the Ghetto and roamed the countryside, coming upon a Soviet Army renegade sporting a rifle. "I had my high boots on, and he demanded that I give them to him. I refused. A struggle ensued; I had wrestled the rifle from him.—I don't have to tell you who won. You see me here."

It was that couple who introduced me to Kami, who was visiting with them from Israel. "She is from your neck of the woods," they announced to me. I felt my pulse coming to a halt as I met her in their country home: she was absolutely beautiful, dressed in tight-fitting slacks.

✠ ✠ ✠

I shivered at the thought of seeing her legs. As we relaxed in my apartment, I attempted conversation:

"To tell you the truth," I stumbled, "I should tell you … I would really like …"

"Well, go ahead. For crying out loud, you make everything so … important, profound. Come on, tell me."

I swallowed hard. "Well, it's just that I am a … leg man. I mean, I never know if a woman really turns me on until I see her legs."

She smiled. "Is that so difficult to say?"

She stood up.. Then she faced me, the skirt rolled high, one knee slightly bent, like the pin-up girls in American magazines. Her legs were longer than I had anticipated, smooth and olive-skinned, her thighs just a bit heavier than the commercial American images.

I knelt in front of her and stroked them. She held a steady gaze on me.

"Well?"

"Kari, you are beautiful."

She let her skirt drop. "That's all."

"But, please ..."

"There's always the next time. Anyway, I want to know more about you. You came over as an agricultural laborer and you ended up going to Yale? By way of the Korean War? That's some going! But, what is this theater business?"

Her English was fluent. We were alone in my modest apartment.. The sun was receding this early fall evening.

"It's not *business*, as you say. It's an art form," I parried.

"In America? Where've you been? I've been here a couple of months and, from what I see and hear, it's only money, money ..."

"There's room for serious theater."

"So ... why are you working in the telly?"

"Telly is in England; here it's television or TV."

"Have it your way. And what about the theater?"

"I'm waiting for a break."

"You're an idiot—excuse me," she added, half-playfully. "But that's not where the money is. Why didn't you study something useful like law or medicine, or business?"

"Neither law or medicine would respond to my aesthetic needs, nor, for that matter, business."

"I see, Mr. Adopted American. All America is big business. Once you make a lot of money, you're free to play with your theater."

"I don't need a lot of money. More important for me is what I do with my life—the content."

She viewed me with benign amusement. "Are you really an idealist? After what we've been through in the Second War? That's naïve, to say the least."

I became belligerent. "Why do you say that?"

"Because I know why." She stayed calm. "But tell me, what do you think is the purpose of life?"

"To pursue truth and beauty ... and to elevate humanity."

She looked at me in disbelief. "That so ... You really are something. You really think somebody gives a damn."

"Anybody," I corrected her.

"All right, anybody. Excuse me. I didn't go to Yale."

The kettle was whistling. She'd made herself at home quickly at my East Side walkup and presently poured tea for both of us.

She smiled. "I didn't mean to offend you. You take everything to heart. Come on, smile. That's better."

We sipped the tea. She grew silent. Her long blond hair flowed down her back. I had never seen a woman who looked equally gorgeous from every angle. I looked down at her perfect ankles supported by Italian shoes with thin straps.

Her azure eyes looked at me; they presently darkened with her mood.

"Are you Jewish?" she asked. She must have been told by the friends who introduced me to her.

"Me?"

"No, Greta Garbo. You're too moody and vulnerable to be Polish. And defensive. Unless you're Chopin. Which you're not."

I admitted it, for she exuded familiarity with my background and social class and seemed to understand me.

"I am Jewish." The moment I said it, I regretted it.

She clapped her hands like a little child whose wishes were fulfilled.

"I knew it, I knew it! Bravo! You *are* one of us!" Then she sighed deeply. "What do you know?" She viewed me with a mixture of seductiveness and warmth. "Well, that's a relief. Not that I've never gone out with a goy. During the war and after, in Poland, I *only* went out with goys."

She sidled up to me on the sofa and stroked my face.

"Are you all alone … I mean, your family?"

"Yes."

"Stop it now, Joey. Maybe it's my fault, bringing it out of you. But I don't want to see a sad face. You know, my mother and I survived because of our 'good looks.' But my father, a doctor, was hidden in a closet for three years. And he's practicing now in Israel. What's gone is gone. Life is for the living. Now smile!"

She walked to the window looking down on Manhattan's East Seventy-first Street and turned around, propping herself on the radiator.

"Somehow," she said, "you're getting under my skin." She looked at me steadily. "Mmm ... your whores, the ones you've been out with, what did they do *before?* ... Did they strip before you? Like this?" She stepped out of her skirt.

✠ ✠ ✠

She had a job with an eye institute as an orthoptics researcher. Kamila was her name, after Tolstoy, but everybody called her Kami. Her mother called her Kami—so as to recall her Swedish ancestors who came to Poland in the seventeenth century, in the wake of the Swedish invasion, before they got mixed up with Jews. In England, where she studied, she passed herself off as Kamila, which fared well with the Anglo-Saxons at the research institute. She'd gone to Israel with her parents after the end of World War II.. In Israel, she had served in the army, before obtaining a divorce—nearly as difficult there as in the Vatican. After a few weeks of intimacy, sex with her husband, she told me, was a contest of wills and little victories, with scarce tenderness.

Later, when we made love deliriously, and I queried her with concern; she tried to reassure me, stroking my hair.

"Don't worry. I could not come with anybody but him. That's what he told me ... But I hope it was good for you ..."

Over a drink later, she inquired: "Tell me, how was it in Yale?"

"*At* Yale."

"So be it—at Yale."

I had been lonely at Yale, I told her—what with the intensive curriculum and part-timing as a waiter, albeit with two scholarships and the GI Bill. The American students were either bookworms or rich people's kids pursuing sports, expensive fashions, and women—and, often, other men. The girls I met were either shallow—by my standards—or cold. They wanted to have "fun." And most were brought up to believe sex was sinful and dirty. All that was left were black whores who charged five to ten dollars. Even at those prices, I could afford them rarely.

Kami pounced on that subject, wanting to know exactly what they had done with me.

Still, my classmates at the University were a sympathetic bunch. Yet, on closer encounters, I felt myself apart from their pursuits: they seemed superficial and, on closer inquiries regarding my past, I would clam up. On holidays and summer recess, they would go home and I had to do odd jobs—driving an ice cream truck, washing windows, or making layouts for the *Yale Daily News*, to make ends meet for the next school year. Even though I was lonely most of the time, I managed to graduate among the top 10 percent of my class. Graduation meant survival, and I had pulled through.

I told Kami about Father Falkowski. I had looked forward to his letters. It was good to be loved thousands of miles away, and yet life centering around a little village church bore scarce relation to the sophisticated, smug, and pragmatic attitudes of the mainstream of my life here. Their pursuits of temporal values—*carpe diem*—were completely at odds with the Christian tenets espoused in the priest's letters. The Catholic world of Father Falkowski seemed light years away.

✝ ✝ ✝

"I got a job in the television," I told Kami on the phone. After a few weeks of staying with me, she had sublet an apartment from a friend on the West Side. "Why don't we take a few days off before I start, and I could show you Washington, then swirl around to Niagara Falls."

"I'd like that," she said.

In pouring rain we finally found a motel on the outskirts of Washington. We made a dash for our room and ducked inside, wet and breathless. Kami's dress was clinging to her breasts, and I cupped them. She looked at me, half mischievously. I knew I had to break through her mental barriers. If she could not climax with me, I'd never fully possess her.

"It's a foregone case," she discouraged me. "He said I could never come with another man."

"Trust me," I parried. I didn't doubt it, for there was no other way.

By three in the morning, I was covered with layers of sweat, but Kami was struggling. I had held back, trying to arouse her in any possible manner, but she was not letting go.

"There's no point," she kept saying with her put-on childish lisp, which she always used when I was in a dominant position.

Light was breaking outside when she suddenly dug her nails into my back. I'd nearly given up several times out of pure exhaustion, but the thought of failing to propitiate her drove me on. "Faster, faster," she whispered through her clenched teeth. "And harder." I bit into her lips, muffling her sounds. I dug into her desperately until I felt her distant wave approaching. She soon lapsed into uncontrollable spasms. They went on for a long, long time. She screamed, yelled, and shook; and just when I thought her fury would subside, her body would be seized anew.

"What you did to me ..." she sputtered. "I came three times!" We lunged into sleep like two bunnies hugging for dear life.

✠ ✠ ✠

We had a huge breakfast the next afternoon. Kami looked radiant— her elegant scarf flowing at her neck.

"You know what turns me on about you?" she asked. "You look like one of those Roman debauchers—full lips and nose. And at the same time, you 'send' me. I think because you have such a lost look about you. You need help ... you need a mother."

Later, munching on a piece of toast, she said: "You know, I still think you'd be good at business."

"What makes you think so?"

"You know how to ingratiate yourself with people. And you are smart."

It was a flawless summer day, warm but lightened with a fresh breeze. We were driving to Washington DC and then, via a huge loop, through Pennsylvania to Niagara Falls—a site for lovers, I explained to her.

We had made plans to find an apartment in New York following Kami's trip to Israel. She was leaving for a month to battle it out with the religious court there, seeking a final divorce.

"You know, I like so much about you," she mused, "except ..."

I knew she was going back to the "business" theme. "You know, I loathe business and the wheeling and dealing that goes with it. It wouldn't give me a purpose in life."

"Purpose? After everything we've been through during the war—purpose? The purpose of life is to make a good life for yourself and those you love."

"You mean: you," I parried.

A huge trailer truck was passing us on the three-lane highway. "Don't start." I couldn't hear the rest.

"Don't do it for me," she continued. "Do it for yourself. And will you keep your eyes on the road?"

"Kami," I said, "I love you."

"Well, I do, too. Except, I told you, you want all of me, and I've just been through a terrible marriage, and you want to put me in a cage. Isn't it enough that we are together? ... Don't bite your lips. And when I say you should get into business, I mean do it for yourself, for good life."

"Without you I can't have life."

"Oh, come on now. Don't make me responsible for your life. That puts a lot on me. And you keep talking about the pursuit of Truth and Beauty as an end in itself. You want to be a saint? And don't tell me you still believe in those Catholic fairy tales and Christ-God and Virgin Mary."

"What's wrong with Christ?" I asked.

"Do you believe he was God?"

I paused. "I'm not sure any longer whether he was God or not. In the end, it doesn't even matter. It matters that there existed a man named Yehoshua—later abbreviated as Yeshu or Yezu or Jesus—who spread love and forgiveness; that's what I believe in."

"So? You can't have love and forgiveness without all that fancy talk and genuflecting? Have it if it suits you. Who cares? But you *are* Jewish, aren't you? You're still one of us. And you, you can argue a point to your convenience, with all seeming sincerity and conviction. That's why you'd be good in business."

"Well," it was my turn, "I'm not sure if I'm Jewish. I am a Catholic, and without Catholics, I wouldn't be alive today."

"*Azoy.*" She used the Yiddish word (Oh so), mockingly. "So any decent person would have done the same thing—helping you survive—as many *have*, but no one would have taken out a contract on your life. That would be synonymous with a barter for human life—instead of just heroic life, as you have put it. 'You do like I tell you, and I'll save your life.' Anybody signed a contract with you? Even if so, it'd be invalid as you were underage. It's absurd."

'I felt an inner trepidation of maligning my character. "It's not absurd. I have taken obligations you don't understand; when I was lost, he sheltered me; when I was hungry, he fed me; when I was lonely, he consoled me. You know I told you that."

"And you have repaid him many times over: you brought him to America twice; to Israel, for a pilgrimage to the Holy Land; paid for his trips to the Vatican and to visit his aunt in Belgium. *And*, if it wasn't enough, earlier, when you worked in the factory, you got a second evening job pumping gas to send him food packages to Stalinist prison Enough with your 'obligations'!"

We slowed down approaching the majestic Delaware Bridge.

"Isn't America beautiful?" I asked.

Kami shrugged her shoulders. "Yes, it is, but so are other countries. Wait till you get to Israel. We have everything in that tiny country: you should see our Galilee mountains; Sfat, an artist colony; the sea; the desert."

We drove in silence. "What about your family?" she asked.

I answered reluctantly. I had an uncle in New York somewhere. "But what's the point? I never met him and, besides, he would never understand; he'd likely disown me."

"Crap," she said. "Your father's or mother's side?"

"My father's brother."

"Well, let me tell you something: you're going to contact him, period. This is unbelievable. Your closest relative, and you have not looked him up. You have to find him."

"I'll think about it."

"Yes, you will. I'll call him myself."

"I'm not ready for this."

She gave me a long look. "All right, I'll give you two weeks." She touched my thigh and stroked it. "I still don't know why you 'send me.' Joey, you want me?"

"You know I do."

"Even now?"

"Even now."

"You want me to do it to you?"

A shiver went through me. "How?"

"There's always a way." She unzipped my fly and soon found me. I had been conscious of driving, but could not resist her. I must have been weaving in and out of the lanes. Suddenly I became aware of a state trooper who motioned us to the side.

Kami showed a mixture of amusement and apprehension.

"Oh, my, do you think he saw us ... I mean ...?"

As the cop approached us, I led the way: "Anything wrong, officer?"

"That's what I want to ask you; is everything all right? You were swerving in and out."

"I'm sorry, officer. These were unusual circumstances."

The cop looked down at us. He grinned. "I understand. Newly married?"

"Right on."

"Only watch the road. Good luck."

"You too, sir."

☩ ☩ ☩

When we got back to New York, I found a letter from Father Falkowski.

"You wouldn't believe it, my dear Jòziaczku," he wrote, "but even within the Mother Church herself, there has been some dissension here. Oh, nothing that our church has not been through before. We have survived the Dark Ages and the Reformation and schisms, false popes, and others. I am sure we will survive this time, too, although these are very difficult times for the Church in Poland. On the one hand, the atheists and the restrictions. On the other hand, there are fresh breezes from the Vatican itself: adapting the Church to closer contacts with the faithful. I believe with the pope that, if we are going to save young souls from godless atheism, we must change the language of the liturgy.

"It surprises me to have these thoughts, for I know the arguments in favor of Latin: only a 'dead' language can preserve the true meaning of the Eternal Truth (your people have done the same with Hebrew and the Talmud). It is true that the changing mores and the vicissitudes of language should not alter the eternal Truths, but equally compelling are arguments in favor of the opposite course of action. (I am only a poor village priest, but I try to search for the truth, and I read a lot to make up for my ignorance.)

"There have been some encouraging developments at the Holy See in favor of amending the language to the vernacular, for otherwise we will lose the young people—who don't understand the liturgy: to believe that there *is* hope and salvation in this world—through good deeds, through the love of God and our neighbor. Else, 'what benefits a man's soul (if I may paraphrase) if he gain all and loses his love for his brother?' *Yes,* we are all our brothers' keepers.

"Forgive me, Jòziaczku, if I have allowed myself to go off course. I have not many close friends and I, too, get lonely and doubtful at times. You are very dear to my heart and I miss you so …

"Anyway, because I have followed the pope's word, bringing to bear the Word of the Lord in the Polish vernacular, I have run afoul lately of my superiors in the Church. It appears that a conflict with them is imminent. But—God's will shall prevail.

"I pray and hope that you'll keep your faith and faith in God's grace and his love for you …"

✝ ✝ ✝

"So?" Kami said, with a belligerent question mark, after I had shown her the letter. "He happens to be a good and sensitive man, but who says you have to buy all his goods?"

"Wait a minute," I retorted; "you think I should meet my uncle—my family whom I've never met. This priest *is* my family."

Next week Kami moved in with me. With my new income (a job in television, with an assignment to the United Nations), I took care of our basic upkeep, but Kami often bought things for the house herself and a beautiful, slim watch for my thirty-fifth birthday,

☩ ☩ ☩

One evening, as we ate supper together, Kami, who by now had become an expert at reading my face, asked what was the matter. I responded that a colleague of mine had reprimanded me for doing my job too quickly and too efficiently. "We have a union," he said, "and you're going to spoil it for the rest of us."

"He's right," she said. "What for do you want to work so hard?"

"Why should I not strive to do my job the best I can?"

Her eyes lit up with fury.

"That so? All this time here and you haven't learnt yet. The first thing in America, you have to get along with people—which means: smile, and pretend you agree with everybody. Here they call it 'a team player.' Look at me: a few months on the job and everybody likes me and looks up to me. America believes in 'teamwork,' which means that most of the time you have to be a hypocrite. But you, *no*, you have to go impress everyone with how much you know. For that you have to go to Yale?"

"What's wrong with that?"

"Plenty. And on top of this, you are a refugee Jew and you're trying to hide it. The two don't mix. Pick one identity, like me, and stick to it. At least then some will not like it—screw them—and others will admire. At least, if you were a rich American who doesn't give a damn and had a good education ..."

In anger, she was more beautiful than ever.

"I don't care, anyway," I said. "I don't even know that I care to live."

"Well, what do you care about?"

"You. I only want to live for you and be with you. Without you ..."

"Yes?" It was said belligerently. "That so? That's quite a responsibility, you know, to be the sole reason for your living. And I'm not sure I can handle that."

I was choking. She approached me, stroking my face. "Come on, Joey, don't be sad. I love you, you're so vulnerable—Oh, God, my pancakes are burning." She'd been making potato pancakes for us. "Okay, you taste these; you never had better pancakes in your life. Even my mother says so."

"One more thing," she added between bites, "you're afraid to get out into the real world; forget about this theater—a bunch of homo weirdos—you're going to have to make a stand. You think you'd be—how you say—pinned against the wall, to make a choice between Judaism and Christianity. You know something? Nobody gives a shit. Anyway ... we'll have to—how do you say?—'get this over with'—your American expression. I am going to look up your uncle, one way or another."

"He'll probably throw the Bible at me," I said.

"So let him. Speaking of the Bible—it's a chisel of the worst kind. You ever read it ... I mean from beginning to end? We had to, in Israel, in gimnasium. Everybody screwed everybody. Wife, brother-in-law—ha! A real circus. And like the Talmudists: challenge them against the wall, and they'll find a way to twist everything in their favor. And *you* want to be an idealist? They'll sell you down the river and laugh at you. The world wants idealists like you so they can draw circles around you. You'll be miserable and, *maybe*, after you're gone, just *maybe*, they'll put up a monument for you. Shove the honors and make your money. You've got to chisel, too. Just like our ancestors."

"You mean, including my parents and yours?"

"Well, between you and me, we are of a different ilk, we know better, it's, unfortunately, our upbringing, ethics and all that, but that's our nice cover. Live and get all you can out of it. Screw the rest of them! ... and, speaking of screwing," she approached me with a prankish childish grin, and stroked me lightly between my legs, "are you getting it, Joey? Let's have a real beautiful fuck right now ... just you and me ..."

Chapter Twenty-Four
Falling in Love

IT WAS THE SUNDAY before Christmas. Snow covering the streets was turning into wet slush. Kami and I, wrapped in our winter coats, walked to Rockefeller Center in Manhattan. We had made sure to be early. The meeting had been set for three o'clock, and the round antique clock at the jeweler's showed 2:45.

We had passed the sunken plaza in front of the imposing Center. Fashionable skaters crossed the small ice rink in snobbish strokes, tourists staring down at them.

"Hope they're on time," said Kami, shivering in the afternoon cold. "At least we scheduled the meeting inside."

We entered the lobby through the revolving door.

Kami had finally located my father's brother the week before on Saturday. First, we had looked in the telephone directory for Fajwiszys, then for the name's possible mutations: Fajwisz, then Feivell, and even Feibush.

Kami had called all of them in all boroughs asking if they had had a brother in Poland with the first name Israel. None did. That left only one of them: Feivish in Brooklyn.

When she called there, a woman's voice answered. In response to the inquiry, the woman had at once become cagey.

"Who wants to know?" she demanded.

But Kami was too streetwise. If she had reached the right party, she thought, the old lady might get a heart attack, if confronted with her nephew's miraculous return from the dead seventeen years after the war.

Instead, she said quietly: "I am from Israel, and it is possible that one of your relatives might still be alive. But, to make sure I have the right party, let me ask you: did your husband have a brother, Professor Israel Fajwiszys?"

This time the woman spurted words breathlessly.

"Yes, yes, my husband had a brother in Łódź, Lord have mercy on us. And who are you?"

"A friend from a kibbutz in Israel. Trust me, we're in social service, and I'll call you in two days, just as soon as I have confirmation."

Two days later, Kami called again.

"I found out," she said, "that your husband's nephew, Joseph, is alive, and you can meet him in New York."

The old lady was stuttering with excitement.

"Oh, my God! Sam, listen, are you listening? Your nephew, Joseph, son of Israel, is alive! In New York! Oy, Goteniu!"

"Excuse me," tried Kami.

"No, no, excuse *me*. I was talking to my husband. Oh, my God, his real nephew, and we don't have children, real nephew! Please, don't mind me, it's the excitement, we haven't slept for two nights … Oy, Goteniu!" And she began to weep.

✠ ✠ ✠

By now it was 3:30 in Rockefeller Center, and they still had not appeared. I paced back and forth. Kami, usually talkative, left me alone. Any minute now, I would be meeting my father's brother, a figure from a world long buried; a younger brother who'd left Poland in the early 1920s, before I was born. Perhaps that was why I was empty of feeling.

"Suppose we try the other entrance—on Sixth Avenue?" asked Kami.

"Is this the main entrance?" I asked. "Then this is where we made the date, and this is where we stay. Maybe they're delayed. We don't move."

An elderly couple in dark overcoats emerged presently from the revolving door, half-running, breathless, shuffling nervously. The man appeared shorter than the woman, albeit at close range he appeared of the same height. The woman was stout, her lined, sagging face wrapped in a babushka. The man wore a gray hat lined with a brown band. Under it, his yellowish face was dominated by thin-rimmed glasses.

They saw Kami and me.

"Are you …?" the lady gasped. I nodded. "Oh, my God!" she exclaimed, clasping her cheeks in both hands.

The man with the wizened face rushed toward me, throwing his arms around me, but only for a second. Then, just as quickly, he withdrew and rushed to the lobby's corner, away from everyone. Facing the corner, he leaned on his hands upon the two naked walls. His bent back shook as he wept.

His wife rushed toward me placing an awkward, wet kiss on my cheek. Then words cascaded out of her.

"It's all his fault, please excuse us. I was telling him all the time *this* was Rockefeller Center; but no, he was stubborn like always. He is a wonderful, good man—don't misunderstand me, but stubborn, he was saying Radio City on Sixth Avenue, that's where the main entrance is. You must've been waiting a long time, well, thank God! … Oh, my goodness, he's crying. Sam, stop it already! This poor boy has to see it!"

Kami took the lady's arm, tenderly.

"Please, let him … that's all right."

I felt awkward but calm. My feelings were frozen. But I slowly approached the sobbing little man in the corner, and touched his elbow lightly.

"That's all right. Please … that's all right."

He turned around slowly. Took his eyeglasses off and wiped his eyes.

"Excuse … Sheyne," he turned to his wife. "My brother's son. *Gib a kik*—take a look, what a beautiful face, still a child. His face … I would know my brother's face in a crowd … any time."

Then he turned away again, sobbing uncontrollably.

His wife turned to Kami. "You must forgive him: all this time, those years during the Holocaust, he stayed up nights for months. Couldn't sleep. What he suffered, you have no idea. He loved his older brother so much; we would not be alive without your father. He'd helped Sam emigrate; that was before he met me. We sent money to the Warsaw Ghetto, but then it'd come back. It couldn't be delivered." She wiped her eyes. "All right, enough now. Sam, let's go sit some place, the poor boy must be hungry and thirsty."

Uncle Sam led us to a Times Square cafeteria. As we sat down, he informed us: "The food here is very good. And the prices are very low," he added, with a bargain hunter's air.

Soon he became more serious. But, as he talked, he was halting in his excitement: now and then, he'd garble his words, and Sheyne ("Call me Shirley," she said) would say: "Sam, speak clearly, the poor boy can't understand you; he hasn't lived with you all his life, like me."

In a sense, I couldn't help feeling a letdown: their accents, even after decades in America, were those of poor immigrants. I'd hoped my uncle would turn out to be a man of position and means: a strong, calm man. But the little man had the expression of a dejected rabbit, too introverted to listen to others. He would hear without listening. Indeed, when he got excited, his facial expressions telegraphed all his feelings in advance; by the time the words arrived, they were superfluous.

My "relatives" were everything I had been trying to get away from, to forget. Yet, I promised to visit them the following Friday for supper.

Chapter Twenty-Five
Coping with New Family

Kami did not go with me. She had to meet some Israeli friends, she said.

Theirs was a walkup above their store in Brooklyn, set back from the street, under a large horizontal sign proclaiming "Work Clothes for Father and Son."

"Come in, come in, *Yingele*," my dear child, my aunt welcomed me. "Take your jacket off and your shoes, too, if you like. I'll serve supper right away."

It was a spacious and neat apartment, but it reeked of antiquity. The sofa and chairs were old and uncomfortable, covered with plastic slipcovers. "This is so they shouldn't get dirty. Your uncle and I, we work all day in the store, and I can't attend to the house the way I'd like," she explained.

But she served excellent food: gefilte fish in carrot sauce with real homemade mushroom soup, chicken, *tzimmes*, stewed prune compote, cookies, tea and sweet *hamentasch*.

Throughout the meal, my uncle said a few prayers, but without expecting me to participate. However, I'd put on the yarmulke at his suggestion. I felt strange about it, but did not want to offend them.

✠ ✠ ✠

The food was served simply, and as we progressed, I began to feel around me the atmosphere of my early childhood, and commented on it.

"You like my food?" Aunt Shirley glowed. "God bless you, you should live so long. I am very, very happy. At least you don't criticize it like my husband," she added resolutely, winking an eye at me, but also appearing whimsical toward her husband. It was obvious that the two loved each other. (I'd come to recognize the ability of people to kid each other as a sign of underlying affection; this was something my family had lacked.)

"Well, ma'am," I began, trying to find the right words.

"What, *ma'am*?" she protested. "I'm a *ma'am*? Madams are only found in … you should excuse the expression, in …"

"Sheyne, stop it! He's a young boy!" interjected my uncle.

"That's all right. *I'll* say it. He's served in the army: he's a big boy now." She turned to me confidentially, continuing, unimpeded: "Like in a bordello. All right, I said it. You don't like it, Sam, get yourself another cook and bottle washer. And, by the way, *Mamele*, I hope I don't impinge on your feelings, but please call me Tante Sheyne, or in English: Aunt Shirley. Capisce?"

"All right," I replied, kissing her hand. The lady blushed. She turned to her husband. "Is it all right, Sam, for me to kiss a young man?" And she placed a kiss on my forehead. "I'll only do it once lest I violate my proper bounds," she kidded. "How is my English?"

"Fantastic," I answered.

"Thank you. Now let's go to the living room and have some chocolate and seltzer, shall we?"

We sat down in the uncomfortable living room chairs. Aunt Shirley brought out an old cardboard box and emptied it upside down. Old photos were spread before me. Most were mounted on very thick paper, in sepia; I immediately recognized them as stemming from old Czarist times. I'd seen their likes in the photo album of my childhood. Suddenly I spotted several photos of my immediate family.

"You should know," interjected Uncle Sam, "that I owe my life to your father. Now, after the war—"

"You mean, the First World War, Sam," his wife corrected him. "The poor child, he doesn't even know which war you mean."

"Yes, the First War, when I, by accident, met your father in Lemberg—Lwów, in Polish; he was already an accomplished conductor, and I was nothing, fourteen years younger, just searching for my future. Your father it was who pulled the proper strings and money to help me emigrate to Palestine. I then went to England a few years later, then to America when I met your aunt on the boat going over. Without your father, I would …" His eyes got misty and he wiped them.

He composed himself and propped himself in the chair.

"We are very proud of you, my boy: you survived and have done everything on your own, gone to Yale, and now you're working at the United Nations—which is, what the prophets said in the Bible, 'the peak of the mountain.' What I want to know, after all that you've been through, are you still Jewish?"

"You mean … sir?" I'd had a foreboding all along that it'd come to that.

"Uncle Sam," whispered the aunt.

"Yes, Uncle Sam, you mean … Jewish, by religion?"

"Religion, or in any way, what's the difference? Jewish is Jewish; you are your father's son, no?"

"I am. Except, you see … I became a Catholic, and as far as my father—"

"What kind of a Catholic are you? A convert, by necessity?"

"No, I am a Catholic because I've come to believe."

"You believe in Jesus Christ as God?" He raised his voice.

"As the Son of God."

"And you go to church and pray … still?" His disbelief was scolding.

"Sometimes I do, but that's not important."

"What is? You had converted out of necessity, and now you can convert back."

"No, I converted once, when I saw the Truth, but I don't switch twice."

Uncle Sam shifted in his chair, then got up. Without his usual, small, nervous steps, he walked slowly to the window.

"You are what you are. Every one of us is. You mean to tell me you are Christian, you joined their club while, for centuries, for generations, they have slaughtered us, and they murdered your parents and your sister ..." His voice trailed off but he found it again. "They have always used every pretext to kill us, and all in the name of Christ. And now you have joined them."

"And it was in the name of Christ, too, that a village priest risked his life to save mine, and so did other Poles and Catholics who did the same, and what's wrong with a religion in the name of which, and in the love of one's neighbor, people do that?"

"That was an exception, not the rule. The rest of them have persecuted us for ages. The blood of innocent Jews could fill the Red Sea."

"I don't care about the rule and the exception," I parried. "Tell me, Uncle Sam, how many Jewish people *you* know who would have risked their lives to save a total stranger, a Christian?"

"But, how can you equivoc—"

"Just a minute, Uncle Sam, let me finish. What if the situation were reversed, if Christians were persecuted, how many Jews do *you* know who would put their lives on the line to save a Christian boy? A total stranger? There's your rule and the exception. And all in the name of one who proclaimed love and forgiveness!"

"Love and forgiveness?" My uncle was foaming. "That what you call it? The Inquisition, the pogroms and killings? And who murdered six million of our brothers and sisters? Wasn't it the Christians?"

"Besides, Uncle Sam, where were you during the war? By what right do you point an accusing finger? What if America were taken over by gangsters, would *you* risk your life to save total strangers?"

"What if, what if ... who risked his life to fight against the *numerus clausus* at Polish universities before the war—when Jewish students had to sit on separate benches and were beaten up, tell me?"

"That's not the same as killings. Tell me, Uncle Sam, just what did you do during World War Two to prevent our slaughter?"

"We didn't know until it was too late ..."

"Bull! Because it was convenient not to know! When we were starving and dying in the Ghetto, what did you do?"

"I tried to send money—"

"Money! It didn't even get through except once. "

"And do you know what it was like over here? America entered the war, we were a minority ... we could only petition Roosevelt ..."

"So, decent Christians were a minority, too."

My uncle waved his hand impatiently.

"Don't dismiss me, Uncle Sam. I've been waiting for this a long time. Just what did *you* do as we were being led to the gas chambers? Did you lie prostrate in front of the White House protesting day and night? Answer me!"

Uncle Sam lowered his voice.

"I only want to know one thing: are you Jewish? Your father, God bless his soul, had given you a good education, taught you what was right and what was wrong. You are Jewish; you can't change that!"

"My father! My father didn't even wink when they separated me from him at the gate to the trains!"

"What would you have him do? From what you told us, SS were all around, with guns. I'm sure he loved you, that he'd try ..."

"Sure, Uncle Sam, just like you!"

In the silence that set in, Aunt Shirley was clearing the dishes, her face drawn tightly.

"Uncle Sam, if you talk about emulating my father, he always taught me to strive for perfection, to search for the truth ... he would be proud ..."

"Abomination! Don't take your father's name in vain. God, if he only knew ..." his voice trailed off, choked with emotion.

Aunt Shirley came back into the room.

"So now, why are you both standing? Not enough chairs for you? Sit down, Sam; what is this, a marketplace? It's my home, and here people sit in a decent manner, not stand shouting at each other."

"All right, Uncle Sam, I've been through enough, and I don't need this kind of reception. If you really care to have a nephew, you'd support me in trying to find my own truth, back me up in what would give me a sense of being true to myself, instead of preaching to me about things you don't know except by reading and generalizing, any more than others have put you in a box and generalize because you are Jewish."

"Generalizing? You join the killers of my people and talk to me about fancy words. Mr. Joe College! Tell you what: either you are a Jew, or you're nothing to me! That's it!"

He stalked out of the room. I approached his wife.

"Aunt Shirley, it's time for me to go."

"Shush. Stay. You don't know my husband; he's the kindest man I know. Stay. He got excited."

"No," I countered, "I'm sorry. He's struck at everything I hold dear."

Her eyes grew sad. "I lost everything I ever had, and I've been alone. The only thing left to me is my dignity and what's inside. This no one can take away from me. But he wants to take that away from me. That's all I have. And if I lose that, I'll have nothing left anymore."

She sat on the sofa and drew me to her. "Please, Mamele, listen to me." She took my hand. "He's a broken old man, you'll never know. You were in the midst of it, fighting for your life, but he could do nothing, and it's been killing him for years. Understand that, please. Do this for him. Go and tell him you want to go with him to the synagogue."

"I can't. I died a long time ago. I am someone else now. I can't turn on those who saved my life out of love for their God. I can't."

✠ ✠ ✠

Going down the stairs I felt like the loneliest man on earth.

Chapter Twenty-Six:
Conflicts: Searching for Identity

"**Y**OU SCREWED UP THE works, goddamn it!" Kami was yelling at me. "I went through all the trouble for you to come back into the fold of Abraham. Damn you, why couldn't you be nice to your uncle? Your own father's brother!"

"It's all over," I kept repeating dejectedly, stretched out on the sofa, staring at the ceiling. "I'll never see him again."

"And for what?" She was bent over me. "What did you try to prove? He's an old man, damn it. All right, so he didn't have the education. But he's a decent man. You expect him to be a liberal philosopher at his age? Answer me! Don't turn away, answer me!"

"He won't let me be. If he had any feelings for me ..."

"It's your own fault!"

First it was my uncle, then the woman I love. Both rejecting me.

"Yes, your fault. You want everybody to love you, to feel sorry for you ..."

"Sorry, for me?"

"Yes, the worst part is you don't even realize it yourself. You antagonize people. You do it to me, to everybody." She smiled as if to soften the impact. "For once, can't you see?" She sidled up, taking my hand. I withdrew it. "Joey, I want you to face reality, to face yourself.

At this rate, I swear, they'll fire you at work, after you insist all the time to tell everybody your version of 'truth.'"

"What do you mean?" An icy tremor came over me; she was pushing me away with her "values."

"Yes, you can't tell people the truth. Who do you think you are? *Moyshe Rabeynu?* Moses, our teacher? Telling everybody this bullshit about striving for perfection … integrity—your version?"

"My father taught me: you should be true to yourself; after all, the ancient Greeks … and if you are, other people will respect you for it, even if they disagree with you."

Kami looked at me with utter disbelief.

"I don't believe it. Where've you been all these years? In ancient Greece? You come to this country as a war refugee, carrying with you all kinds of goodies in your rucksack. And keeping mum about it. You are drafted and go to the war in Korea. Two years. But—you haven't learnt a fucking thing about real life. Get a tape recorder; listen to yourself!"

"It's enough if I listen to you."

"First your father; he was a musician. If he was good, he could spew forth fairy tales about idealism; then, the priest who has not prepared you for the real life: only clichés from a never-never land. This works among the rich ones, the elitist circles—they can afford it. But, outside their high-faluting social talk, they'll cut your dick off. That's why they're rich. You want to be judged by the honesty of your feelings? Here they judge you by your ability to be a hypocrite. That's what they call 'teamwork.' I've been here a short time, and I know …"

"Yes, I know, you told me that before."

"Don't be so flippy—I mean, arrogant. So I told you … so what? You don't know how to get along with people. You want it your way, all the way—like with me. Nobody gives a shit if the truth is on your side. What if it's on somebody else's side? You and you only have the patent on truth? That's what each religion claims, and look at history: they kill each other in the name of their god—to this day. And now you're going to cry, God!"

"No, I won't. But, my God, they don't let me be. I've been split right down the middle. And I don't know how to be true to myself anymore."

"Joey, please try to see reality. I beg you."

She took my head in my arms and placed it in her bosom.

"My love, my love," I was saying, kissing her hands, her face, her thighs. "Just love me. I'll get out of this somehow. I have to find out who I am."

"Yes, if only you wouldn't be so rigid. You alienate people. You do it to your uncle, in traffic disputes, even me."

"To you?"

"To me. I don't know what to do with you anymore."

She was taking off her clothes, getting ready for bed.

"Where've you been tonight?" I asked.

"Where? Please, Joe, don't choke me. I've been ... What's the difference? Are you hungry? You want me to make you some eggs? Come on, the way you like them, okay?"

"There is a big difference. You know where I've been. So why don't you tell me ...?"

"All right, all right! Where've I been! I met with some Israeli friends of mine. Is that enough? Satisfied? You think I'm going to sit here, darn your socks, and wait for you to come to terms with your split identity?" She spread her arms in a mocking gesture. "To find yourself ... seventeen years after the war? To find your 'true self'?"

"Of all people, the woman I love?"

"Love? Is that the only thing in the world? So ... in the name of your love, I'm supposed to put up with your eternal search for beauty and truth?"

"Some of the greatest people in the world did that. If you cared ..."

"Yes, and I am supposed to marry Socrates."

"I am not Socrates, but if I were ..."

"If you were, I wouldn't put up with it. I don't give a shit what glory would follow me after I die. I want to live, to be secure, not to live from hand to mouth, not waiting till you find yourself and share your torments with you! I have my own torments from the war."

"So that's what it is ..." I heard myself say.

"That's what it is. You should know."

"And you're seeing others?"

"What others? Who says *others*? I'm only telling you: as the first step, go back to your uncle and make peace with yourself and the war. The war is over a long time ago. You are a Jew, period. So face up to it—and make money!"

She walked over to me, grinning, as if to lessen the impact.

"Come on, Joey, turn off the light. I love it when you put your face between my legs and ... do it like you always do ... no one does it like you ..."

✝ ✝ ✝

Aunt Shirley was traipsing busily around me. "No, Mamele, don't even mention it again. Who should be angry? Who's angry? On the contrary, as they say, we are totally delighted. You are our blood and our flesh. Please, Mamele, have another potato latke. They are good and fresh; I made them before you came."

Then Aunt Shirley lowered her voice.

"He'll be right back; he's in the bathroom. Don't tell him I told you, but he was saying all last week he admires you for everything, even for acting with integrity, as you see it ... quiet now, he's coming."

"Brought something for you," Uncle Sam was saying as he joined us at the table. "Here it is, in Hebrew, the story, how you say ... the mythology ..."

"Anthology, Sam," offered Aunt Shirley.

"Hmm? The mythology of the greatest heroes in Jewish history: their dignity, their devotion to the faith, how they struggled, how they survived and remained Jews. And also about Masada, the place of martyrs your father wrote the famous song about. I want you should read it, and be inspired by it."

"I ... don't read Hebrew well anymore, Uncle Sam."

"He will, Sam, he will; he was telling me," Shirley was winking at me, "before you came back, he said he wants to read Hebrew again."

"Well, that's good," he said, adjusting his glasses. "You think you're a Jew again?"

"Now, wait, Uncle Sam," I retorted; "you don't expect me, in a week ... after all, here you talk about integrity ... What is integrity, Uncle Sam? Isn't it to be true to yourself? So you should ..."

"Let me put it this way. You're an educated man; you went to the best college. So you can't be a little objective? You heard a lot from the Catholic side. So, now, why don't you try to hear the other side, too?"

"Like what?"

"Like, please, Joseph, I'd like you to meet with a rabbi. What've you got to lose?

I was taken aback. "Well ... I suppose it's only fair. Only I don't know a rabbi."

"I know a prominent one. The president of the New York Board of Rabbis, a PhD. Not only that. A former U.S. Marine chaplain and an officer. One of the advisors to President Roosevelt ... Please, I'm not asking anything else from you; just see him."

☩ ☩ ☩

Before calling on the rabbi, I had resolved to seek an audience with the bishop. Bishop Fulton J. Sheen, a princely looking man in his prime years, with prematurely grayish hair, had, in barely a few years, become a television star. His weekly network show was watched by millions. He'd converted a number of prominent Americans to Catholicism, including Claire Booth Luce, the wife of the founder of *Time* magazine and an ambassador to Rome. He'd become a confidant of the rich and illustrious.

His private office was away from the archdiocese on Madison Avenue, in a Murray Hill brownstone. The address given to me by a whispering secretary on the telephone was couched in discreet terms: "It's the bishop's private office. But, please, for obvious reasons, please don't give it out to anybody else; the bishop is so much in demand."

I'd carefully picked my clothes for the day, making sure that, while everything matched, the net effect would be that of restraint and subdued good taste. I made sure that I arrived at the bishop's residence a half hour prior to the appointed time.

An elderly, well-composed but somewhat stern lady opened the door. "Yes?"

"I was asked by His Excellency to be here at five-thirty."

I was left standing in the small vestibule that reminded me of the private brownstone homes in London I'd read about in Dickens's novels. The furnishings were conservative: a balustrade polished in dark varnished brown, angled upward invitingly at the rear of the vestibule.

Presently, the bishop emerged from a side door. He was dressed in a long soutane, the discreet purple buttons lined up the full length of his garb all the way to the floor.

"Welcome, welcome," he smiled.

At that very moment, a luminescent, slim woman traipsed down the steep stairway. She looked like a model.

The bishop seemed slightly embarrassed.

"I'll see you tomorrow," she said, but I had the feeling that, but for my presence, she wanted to say more.

"My secretary. Would you believe it? Until recently, one of the most successful models in the country. She'd given it all up. Searching for the faith. Now she's working for me, raising money for the Office of the Propagation of the Faith."

A portly priest emerged from behind the closed door, accompanied by a civilian. Both shook hands with the bishop warmly on their way out.

The bishop led me into a tiny room, right off the vestibule, virtually unfurnished, save for a small table and a chair. Its walls lined with quietly patterned wallpaper, it seemed like a small storage room, not for occupancy.

"I'm pleased that you came. May the Lord be with you. It wasn't possible to go into much detail; but, at the first meeting in my office, when you sought help, you impressed me with your fervor in delving into faith. You should be both happy and privileged; I am sought after much, as you may know, but I choose individuals with seemingly great depth.

"By the way, you saw this priest on the way out? All the way from Australia, coming to see me. Serving God in a virtually desert territory. Hundreds of miles. Nobody there except a handful of faithful and some aborigines. Even water has to be transported from far away."

"Why is he here, Your Excellency?"

"He's begging for volunteer priests to come there."

"And isn't anyone willing?"

The bishop spread his arms. "What can we do? It's difficult."

"Forgive me, Your Excellency, you mean that in this whole country there isn't anyone to volunteer to go where life is hard, in the service of the Faith?"

"I'm afraid it isn't always possible to tap the highest motivations in people." He seemed slightly annoyed. "Anyway, please sit down and be comfortable; someone will be with you in a little while."

"Thank you, Your Excellency."

He walked away, his long robes behind him emitting a barely audible rustling sound.

I felt suddenly alone. I'd been awed meeting a prince of the Church, but at the same time I couldn't quite understand what was happening. After all, the bishop had "chosen" me to be the recipient of his attention. I had looked forward with trembling anticipation to a series of in-depth exchanges with a prince of the Church, to be able to entrust to him my doubts, my inner battles, and—above all—to reach out for the affirmation of the faith, to a purpose in life, to justify my conversion and the alienation from my people. Would that the endless suffering, the black abyss of my aloneness, be dispelled by this great man, this prince, who would restore my faith to me, and show me the way.

I looked at my watch. Fifteen minutes had elapsed and no one came in. I became aware of a tape recorder on the coffee table.

Fifteen more minutes. I hesitatingly opened the door leading to the vestibule and entered the hallway. I felt strange and unsure of myself. As if I'd invaded the private sanctuary of a temple. After some hesitation, I tried a small door and knocked. Once, twice. The tidy Irish lady emerged.

"Yes?"

"Excuse me, ma'am, but I've been waiting in the other room. The bishop asked me to wait there."

"Well, you should stay there; someone will be with you soon."

"Oh, yes, thank you."

Back at the tiny cubicle, fifteen minutes went by. I returned and knocked at the door again. This time a starched, middle-aged, lean lady came into view.

"You are Mr. ..."

I stated my name.

"Oh, yes, why haven't you gotten started?"

"Started ... on what?"

"The tape recorder. The next person is arriving shortly."

"The next person?"

"Didn't anybody show you?"

"No."

"Oh. I'm sorry. Well, you *should* have been shown." She led me to the tape recorder. "Here it is. Every time you come in ... you're here for the thirteen-week series, aren't you?"

"I beg your pardon?" I asked.

"The series. Please, there's little time left and, since you haven't started on time, I'm afraid we have to skip today's session, but I'll show it to you so that you'll know the next time." She focused her attention on the few gadgets of the tape recorder. "Here's what you do. Every time you come here, on Tuesdays, the recorder will be ready for you. Come in, and all you have to do is press down on this button here, sit back and listen."

"Listen to what?"

"The bishop's condensed lectures on the Restoration of Faith. You've been enlisted in the thirteen-week course on faith. So each week, this is what you do, you understand? And please, be on time."

"Excuse me, ma'am, does that mean that the bishop will not be with me when I come here?"

She looked at me with a reprimand.

"The bishop, sir, is a very busy man. He would like to attend to you but, you understand, it isn't possible. But, anyway, you'll be given a thirteen-week session and, at the end, the bishop will have an interview with you. Now, you have ten minutes left before the next person comes in; if you want to try the tape, go ahead."

I felt cheated. But, as she left the room, I pressed on the button and, at first, heard a lot of applause. The bishop's voice came on, and I heard him refer to members of the "flock" who, through no particular fault of theirs, at one point in their lives had given up on their faith, becoming "alienated" from their Lord, Jesus Christ, the Supreme Source and Fountain of all Grace and Salvation. He then went on to analyze the Ten Commandments.

There was a knock on the door. The expressionless latter lady appeared at the door.

"I'm afraid you'll have to leave. The next appointment is here. Come back next week at the same time. Make sure you know how to press this button here. The bishop wants to help as many of the faithful as possible."

✠ ✠ ✠

Still, I went back for three more weeks. Each time I'd turn on the tape recorder, I'd listen to the bishop's voice, but my mind wandered. I had the feeling of being let down. In the fourth week, the day before my appointed session, I called and offered an excuse. I never went back again. Nor did I hear from the bishop's office.

✠ ✠ ✠

The following Thursday at seven in the evening, I approached the rabbi's study, as it was called, located in a spacious brownstone building in the upper Sixties. I had never met a rabbi in my life; among my childhood peers in Poland, the orthodox rabbis were usually the subject of much derision and many ironic anecdotes. Also, rabbis were supposed to display medieval garb—long black habits, beards and sidelocks—an ancient appearance from another epoch, topped by an antiquated demeanor. Now, for the first time, I was going to meet a modern, educated, American rabbi.

I was doing it only to please my uncle, but simultaneously, I was consumed by anxiety. With the exception of Kami, my uncle, and my aunt, I had never admitted my background to anyone.

New York was heading for the spring. The trees on the East Side were yielding fresh buds. I rang the bell and was let in by an energetic lady in her mid-fifties.

"You are Mr. … sorry, I can't pronounce it," she stated with a courteous smile.

I felt aggravation rising. I pronounced it carefully. "But, if you'll make an effort to pronounce it, I promise to pronounce yours."

She turned in dismay while leading me to the waiting room. "Oh, mine is simple: Mrs. Greenberg."

"How do you do, Mrs. Greenberg."

"How d'you do. Your name, you must be ..." she caught herself. "Please have a seat. The rabbi will be with you shortly."

I felt perspiration under my shirt. I wasn't going to take anything from these people. Where were they, after all, when we were being slaughtered all over Europe? And what did they do to prevent it? Nothing, I was sure.

I had agreed to meet the rabbi, but I would make it short and sweet. Anyway, what could the rabbi offer me that I didn't know? Except that I had seen the true Light and the promise of Salvation, and the rabbi would still dabble in the old serpentine rationalizing based on the superiority of the Jews.

I looked around. The waiting room was quiet. The décor was subdued, the walls lined with striped wallpaper; the small mahogany side tables supported conservatively shaped small lamps I had seen in the Madison Avenue shops.

"The rabbi will see you now," announced Mrs. Greenberg.

The rabbi rose from behind a massive desk and briskly came around to greet me. His face was rugged and clean-shaven, topped by a crew cut. He had neither sidelocks nor a long habit but, instead, wore a quiet, dark suit, white shirt, and a striped tie.

"Welcome," he said warmly but firmly. "I am Rabbi Golovensky. Come on in and sit down, and make yourself comfortable. Go ahead and loosen your tie; there's a warm evening outside."

The phone buzzed. The rabbi spoke to someone on the other end. I looked around discreetly. The walls were covered with diplomas and World War II mementos. There was a doctor of philosophy degree from Columbia. The rabbi, in a navy uniform, with President Franklin D. Roosevelt; the rabbi with admirals and U.S. Marine generals.

The rabbi hung up. "Well, young man, I know what brings you here. Your uncle told me a few things about you on the phone. A very lovely man." He had dark and penetrating eyes and a warm curiosity about him. "Tell me. I think I understand a lot. You converted during the war, of course, because you had to ..."

"If I may, Dr. Golovensky …" I wasn't going to recognize this man's religious claim.

"Yes, go ahead."

"I don't know what you've been told, but I know why I am here. I promised my uncle that I would see you and I kept that promise. Other than that, as long as I am here, I intend to tell you only the truth."

The rabbi looked at me steadily. His attitude became one of restrained attention. "I'll appreciate that, you can be sure."

I swallowed. "First of all, if I may correct you: I didn't convert because I 'had to.' Rather, I converted because I'd come to believe."

"Hmm … you came to believe in the Christian religion, in Christ; I understand. But you were only, how old?"

"Fourteen, fifteen."

"And at that age … tell me," he said abruptly, "do you still believe in Christ as God?"

"I do."

"I see. Well … that's fine if that makes you happy; if it makes you a good human being. I have no objection to that. I know, in my work, many fine Christians, as long as they don't attempt—as a way of justifying their religion—to espouse hatred and even wanton killing."

"Now," I retorted, "why would they do that? Surely you know that the fundamental teachings of Christ are those of love and forgiveness."

"Oh, yes, I know that, Joseph. I'm sure, as well as you. I know what Christ taught, but I also know what heinous crimes have been perpetrated in his name over the centuries. You know that, too."

"I wouldn't be here today, Rabbi, if it were not for Catholics—and one priest in particular—and he was not alone. Hundreds of priests and nuns were killed in concentration camps or executed outright for harboring Jews. They implemented their love for Christ and fellow humans at the risk of their lives."

"Which, I am sure, made them fine and noble human beings; but for that you don't have to be a Christian."

"Again, if I may, how many Jews do you know who would have risked their lives for the sake of saving simple strangers, non-Jews?" I knew I was on the offensive.

"There've been many of them throughout history."

I shrugged my shoulders. "What does that prove? It doesn't negate anything."

The rabbi shifted his position.

"Tell me something, Joseph. If your devotion to Christ and to his religion makes you happy, why don't you just go on that way? Then you should have no problems."

"Well," now I shifted in my chair, "I suppose I have my doubts, but they have nothing to do with Christ, only with the man-made laws and interpretations. I feel somewhat ... alienated."

There was a pause. "Why, Joe?"

Something was choking me.

"I don't know. Lately ... I just realize, I'm not sure where I belong. Probably, nowhere."

"Of course you do. Every man belongs somewhere: to his fold, to his family, to his people. So do you."

"But, you see, I can't reconcile it. The Jewish people would ostracize me, I'm sure, if I proclaimed myself a Catholic. And the latter, if they found out about my Jewish background, they would reject me, too. So would you ... Deep down, I think I'm a traitor."

"Personally," replied the rabbi, "I don't care whether you go to church or to a synagogue. I only care about you as a Jew, a human being who was born a Jew." His dark eyes were flashing. "You are a Jew, no matter who you pray to."

"I haven't prayed in a long time."

"I'm not talking about this. Tell me, incidentally, how do you know Christ was God? How can you be so sure?"

"I believe. A messiah was due, and he fulfilled all the prophecies, didn't he? And do you know, Rabbi, that he wasn't? What makes you so sure your god is the true one?"

"There's only one God, whatever you call him. And here they took a man and made him into a god."

By the way, Jesus himself never said: "I am God; I don't want to be a Jew anymore; I want to start a new religion," for he was a reformer WITHIN his Jewish religion. Only later St. Paul who, having escaped to Greece, and aiming to acquire a flock of followers among pagans, proclaimed that in order to follow Christ, they had to embrace Judaism first. They were all Jews and you are a Jew. One does not exclude the other."

"But he did fulfill the pronouncements in the Bible wherein the Messiah would arrive under those circumstances…"

"Wait, don't interrupt me!"

"If you want to know the truth about the Gospel, do you know that the first Gospel had been written some 70 years after the Crucifiction, and not by the bystanders of the purported exchange between Herod and Jesus, wherin, allegedly some Jews cried to Jesus: 'Your blood will fall upon us and upon our children?' Alright,"

"Up to two thousand years later? While their own Gospel states in their prayer, 'Our Father …as we forgive those who trespass against us!'Also, about the Crucifiction: what kind of God is this, as they claim, who sacrifices his own son for the 'trespasses of others?'"

"Nonsense. Do you know the historical background? Have you studied it? The Roman legions occupied the land of Israel. There was extreme hardship, restrictions, discontent—perfect breeding ground for false messiahs. Do you know how many Jews went around preaching, purporting to be messiahs at that time? Sixty, seventy maybe. Christ was only one of them. That's all. A good, virtuous man. Fine. But God? No. The rest is only an excuse for persecuting Jews—Christ's compatriots—by pagans who followed Jesus and wanted to break away from Jews. After all, all the Apostles save one were Jews. And those who proclaimed themselves to be the 'reformers' of the Judaic religion—and there was justifiable room for that—should be forever grateful to us. But look at the facts: after all, if Christians took his preachings seriously and with integrity—'love thy neighbor' and so on—would they, in the name of Jesus, a Jew, go on killing and persecuting members of his race … for two thousand years?"

"But what is wrong in trying to follow the teachings of a man who advocated love and sacrifice, as did the priest who saved my life?"

"Not a thing. But in so doing, why do Christians have to try to convert us? We don't go around trying to convert Christians. To each his own. We leave them alone; let them leave us alone. Why do they have to uproot and convert our children and steal their souls? We don't do it to them. Let each man praise God in his own way and respect the rights of others."

"But, Dr. Golovensky, the priest always told me to remain a Jew and even proudly proclaim this to the world."

"So why don't you?"

"I can't. I can't serve two masters. Trying to serve both, I'm alienated from both."

"That's just it. You've cut yourself off from your people, from your heritage. You've withered, cut yourself off from the main trunk, from the lifeline. My God, you're so valuable to us. You are the living testimonial to the persecution; you have a precious heritage: your father and his music. You have a sacred obligation to proclaim the truth—if, indeed, truth is what you long for. You owe it to all who have shaped you into what you are: your parents, your teachers, to all your school friends brutally murdered, to bear witness. You are an educated man; you have a holy obligation to tell the world what happened. The world has not heard enough. You must bear witness!"

"How do I do that?"

"That's another matter. I don't have too much time now; I have another meeting. But I would like to have you in my home, and have my wife and kids meet you. Will you do me a favor? Come to my house next week for Friday night supper. Will you come?"

"I ... suppose so."

"Good. You'll feel at home. In the meantime, do you still keep in touch with that priest in Poland?"

"I do."

"Good. If you write to him, you can tell him that you met me, and that I send him my best regards, my respects, and my good wishes."

I walked back slowly. The breeze was cool and, for some reason, automobile horns shrieked at me when I crossed the street. I felt very lonely, but at least I still had Kami.

✠ ✠ ✠

Upstairs it was dark; Kami had been out. Soon, however, she came home and kicked off her shoes in a huff.

"Oh, I walked and walked. I'm so tired. So … what happened at the rabbi's? Has he converted you into *Moyshe Rabeynu's* fold?"

I wanted to know where she'd been. She always made mountains out of insignificant things when she had something to hide.

"With Rachel, my friend from Israel. What am I going to do? Sit and brood while you're taking a few years to find yourself? Come on, tell me already, so what happened?"

I recapitulated the meeting for her. "A regular fellow," I summed up.

"That's good. Talk to him more; maybe he'll make you see the light, although I can't stand those religious men."

"This one is different," I said.

"Maybe."

"He wants me to come to Friday night supper with his family. I'm going to call and say you're coming with me."

She thought about it. "All right. I'm curious. And I'll size him up for you."

After we'd had our late tea, Kami said: "Rachel is going on a trip around the world. Be gone a few months. Will you help me fix up her apartment? She's letting me have it for free."

"What for?"

"My mother is coming to visit with me. I told you. What do you want me to do, have my mother stay with the two of us in your chicken coop? Or spend a fortune on a hotel? I'll be with you as often as I can."

"Meaning what?"

"Meaning what it says. Honestly, you're never satisfied. With you, it's give him a finger and he wants the whole hand."

"The whole hand! Am I not entitled? Don't we love each other?"

"We do, but not the way you'd want it."

"Meaning, you don't want to marry me."

"You're crazy, I swear to God. What more do you want? I am with you every day, we fuck together, I give you my understanding and patience, and I cook for you. But no, you want everything; you're never satisfied."

"What's wrong with everything?" I had a foreboding of things to come.

"Because you can't have everything."

"Why the hell not?"

"Because. Oh, come on, Joey. It'll take years for you to get everything straightened out. I'll be your friend, as I am now. But I can't give you everything. I have a crippled father, and a mother, and a brother who's not all together because of the war. And they need me. And you can't provide for all of us."

"I'll share every—"

"Not enough. Hell, you barely have enough yourself. Whatever job you have, you can get fired any time, what with you preaching about perfection and idealism. Be happy with what you have; I've never given as much to a man." She took my hand. "Come on now, Joey, cut the bullshit and make love to me. Enjoy it; nothing lasts forever in this world."

She took off my clothes and put her mouth to me where I was totally defenseless.

Chapter Twenty-Seven:
From Bishop to a Rabbi;
"Saving the Priest's Soul"

EVENINGS, WE CLEANED AND scrubbed Rachel's apartment in the West Fifties and then made love.

The following Friday evening, we went to the rabbi's house in Westchester for supper. They, and especially the rabbi, were delighted with Kami and made a lot of her beauty. Kami spoke Hebrew with their children.

It was a warm home; yet I felt myself a stranger. The traditional dishes were served to a minimum of required prayer. The *rebbitzin* was a handsome woman, stout, but possessed of a lovely face. Somehow, despite a domineering exterior, she exuded a sensitive and catering disposition that just missed being overwhelming and was, instead, pleasingly hospitable. At dessert, she said to me: "My husband, David, was telling me, you've had your share …"

"Well …" The rabbi tried to play it down out of courtesy to me, I sensed.

"He'll be all right," interjected Kami.

"But, Joseph, if you don't mind," the rebbitzin pressed on, "what do you aim to do? I mean, besides the theater?"

"I want to write."

"Well, have you done any …?"

I swallowed. "When I figure things out in my mind."

"But who's going to read it?" Kami burst in. "You'd better have something to say that hasn't been said before."

"Well, he just might," observed the rabbi diplomatically.

"Might, might not," retorted Kami. "It's in the nature of the Jew to suffer, and this is his share: wanting to suffer and write instead of making a good living. But the world doesn't care."

"A share might also be valuable," intoned the rabbi, "but this young man has been put through hell. He should know that we want him back, that he's very dear to us. Maybe I can arrange … would you like, Joe, to tell my congregation about your struggles—I'd like to arrange for that."

I exchanged a look with Kami. "After all, what do you expect," she said later. "He's an American. They do not know from sensitivity; they come across like woodchoppers. Oh, yes, go for public confession, like those preachers on TV, and you'll attain salvation."

"I don't think I could do that, Rabbi," I answered.

"Why not? It should do you a lot of good. Better than going to a psychiatrist. You need a catharsis, to purge yourself of the horrors of the past. And the best way is to talk about it—the Ghetto, the systematic dehumanization—the world should know about it. In the process, you'll find your way."

"You want me to talk about *everything*, Rabbi? My conversion, too?" I asked.

"Well," the rabbi seemed uncomfortable, "you don't have to go into all that."

"Why not, Rabbi, if it's the truth?"

"Excuse me," interposed Kami. In front of people she was always on her best behavior. "Don't you know that people don't care to hear the truth?"

"What then?" I asked.

"People want to hear … what they want to hear."

"It's not really that," said the rabbi. "The point is that, if not for your terrible odyssey, there would not have been the conversion and the religious and identity crisis you're afflicted with now."

"Rabbi," I said, "I offered to speak only the truth, as I feel it, right?"

"Right."

"The truth is, I despise the multitudes, and I am ashamed of being Jewish. I've seen the populace, and they're a selfish, cowardly bunch. Back in the Ghetto, who do you think advocated resistance? Young kids, idealistic young people—that's who. The multitudes were vehement against it, and some, I'm sure, had denounced us before going to their deaths like sheep."

Kami could not contain herself.

"Every major revolution, you idiot ... er ... excuse me, Rabbi ... in the history of the world, was started by young idealistic people. The rest of humanity is always against change, but later they take credit for it and declare national holidays."

The voice of the rabbi came back with unusual forcefulness.

"I listened to you; now you listen to me. You have a view of history but, unfortunately, yielded only by your own personal struggles, as a teenager. Thus you only carry with you a worm's-eye view. Thus, I regret that your view of history is slanted: please, forgive me, but your thoughts and feelings are marred by an amalgam of anti-Semitic propaganda and your understandable rage. As a result, you hate your own people. Hitler made you do that, and then your noble priest reinforced it—however unwittingly—with a theological justification for the persecution of Jews. Oh, yes, he saved your life out of his idealism, but in the same breath he'd inculcated *Selbsthasse*—self-hatred—in you.

"I wasn't there, but I've read virtually every descripton and witness account that has come out. So ... they locked the Jews up in the ghettos, crowding them ferociously, hauling them from all over Europe into an area fit for one-tenth of the population, nullified their means of livelihood, robbed them of their possessions and starved them, denied them sanitary conditions. Then they brought their own photographers taking pictures of the filth and the starving children in the streets, while proclaiming to the movie audiences in their newsreels: 'Is it any wonder that these are despicable people? Look at this vermin—who'd want them?'"

"But, Rabbi, most were against resistance …"

"Well, the uprising came, too late, and you were out of there by then. You've been harboring rage and anger, understandably. But instead of taking it out on the Germans, you're taking it out on your own people. You talk about the absence of resistance among starved and terrorized men, women, and children? Let me tell you about resistance. For example: how did you resist?"

"I beg your pardon, Rabbi?"

"Don't interrupt me now—"

"I have to. I was a member of a resistance group which later led the uprising. I risked my life every day: meetings, distributing leaflets, aiming and wishing for the uprising which was denied me. My own organization did not extend a hand to me in need."

"From what you told me … But let me get back to the concept of resistance. You ended up, Gott sei Dank [Thank God], by escaping through a car opening large enough only for you, a kid, to sneak through. But what if you were grown up? How would you have fought the SS with their dogs who surrounded the train and rode with you to your death? This, on top of all the lies fed by the Nazis about going to the 'eastern labor camps'—which the Jews were clinging to because there was nothing else to cling to. You saw your fellow Jews under extremities to which few people in the history of the world have ever been subjected. About resistance now: the Germans held thousands and thousands of prisoners of war, and did they resist by force? How many uprisings occurred in the POW camps? To my knowledge, none. And, consider: these were young, fit men, trained to fight. *And* they hadn't been starved; they were receiving Red Cross food packages. The Russians turned cannibals, they *ate* each other; others denounced each other for a loaf of bread. Armed uprisings? None. The SS and an overwhelming armed might rendered any physical resistance impossible. And what would you expect a starving, incarcerated people, with women and children, to do? So much for resistance.

"And now comes along a young, idealistic Catholic priest. Sure, his human motives were right; but he, too, had been infected by virulent anti-Semitism, the Church's standard flag, and voila! He wants to steal our souls, so he can rise to a good stead with his bishop—to 'win' souls. He wanted to help you—fine. People, throughout history, have helped each other; strangers, out of sheer human kindness. But, for that, you have to steal their souls? Do we go after their souls?"

The rebbitzin was doodling on the tablecloth with her fork, all in disciplined containment.

"And then," continued the rabbi, drawing another breath, "they seduce you with a few symbols: Christ on the cross, and the Virgin Mary—both Jews—adding to it their traditional hatred of Jews; after all, everyone needs a scapegoat, an escape valve for his inadequacies, for his frustrations, a diversion for one's discontent—and he indoctrinated you to hate your own people. But first, he stole your soul; and the result: you hate yourself and your own people. That's how it's done."

He got up in a huff and left the room, after excusing himself.

"Well," said the rebbitzin in a conciliatory tone, "my husband is right; you see, you must understand ..."

"Of course, he's right," intoned Kami. The silence was oppressive. But the rabbi came right back into the room.

"Forgive me. My feelings run deep about these things. Joseph, come back any time, like to your own home. Any time. And don't worry," he added, "you don't have to convert back, either. To us, you are just a human being who struggled valiantly, one extremely worthy of knowing."

Despite the apparent official air, I felt encouraged.

☩ ☩ ☩

The next morning, shortly after eight, the phone rang. I had jumped out of the shower, getting ready to go to work. It was Aunt Shirley.

"Hope you don't mind, Mamele, did I wake you? Hope I didn't. Excuse me, but you see, your uncle didn't sleep all night." She lowered her voice. "He's out now but can come back any time; he's out getting the paper. He wants to know, *Gotyniu*, you should not mind, how did the visit go with the rabbi? Do me a favor, for your old aunt, would you? Call him in half an hour and tell him. You know we have no children; he loves you so much you can't imagine. You should live so long as he wishes you. Will you do that?"

I said I was getting underway but I'd call him from the UN. There was a special session of the Security Council, my TV network was broadcasting it, and I was coordinating the program.

"What I want to know," asked my uncle later, when I called him, "did the rabbi answer all your questions?"

"I didn't have any questions, Uncle Sam."

"What do you mean, you didn't have any questions? For what purpose did you go there?"

"I went," I was spacing my words for emphasis, anger rising within me, "first, because you'd asked me to, and then, because he turned out to be a warm human being whom I decided to get to know. What's wrong with becoming friendly with a man like that?"

"A man 'like that,' as you call him," his voice rising, "is much too busy, plenty busy; he did me a favor to meet you for the purpose of answering your religious questions; it should be a great honor for you to be invited by a man like that. Don't abuse it."

"Abuse it?"

"Yes. So what did you decide? Are you Jewish or a Catholic?"

"Uncle Sam, don't expect me to be a grasshopper. I told you many times, I am a Catholic. I cannot change the fact of my birth, but I made my choice. You wanted me to meet with the rabbi—I did. But you expect instant response. I don't have any."

✠ ✠ ✠

Kami's mother had arrived and had been staying with her in Rachel's apartment on West Fifty-fifth Street. They had me to dinner; but then days went by, and my only contact with Kami was on the telephone. She was saying she was busy with her mother, had to take her shopping and to visit a number of friends. I felt deserted. Three days later she dropped in hastily at six in the evening.

"We only have a half hour, let's make love quickly," she said.

"Half an hour? And then what?"

"Come on, don't waste time; *then*, I have to see some friends with my mother."

"And what about me?" I pressed.

"What about you?"

"Why don't you ask me to go along?"

"What are you, a little boy? You have to tag along everywhere?"

"Why not? Didn't I always take you with me? Are you ashamed of me?"

"You idiot, you don't understand anything. Thick skull. We're not married. Under what pretext do I tag you along? Meet my boyfriend?"

"And why not?"

"Because."

"What do you mean, because? I want an explanation, *now!*"

"All right, if you want to know, because we have no future, that's why."

"Just when did you decide that?"

"Well, if you want to know, my mother's been asking me: 'Are you going to marry this man? And if not, it is not fair to him.'"

"And you're not going to marry me?"

"No."

"Then whom?"

"Nobody. We have no future, don't you see that? You have to 'find yourself,' and I can't wait. I have responsibilities, and I want different things in life."

"Such as what? *Money?*"

"It's not only money, though that's part of it. But I want to *live!* And next to you, I'm dying while you wallow in the past; you indulge in your guilt and your *verkakte* (shity) religious problems. For me, that's a luxury I can't afford." She moved closer to me.

"But why do you still want to make love to me?"

"There's no reason we can't make love and be friends."

"The hell with friends! If you fuck, don't you feel anything for me? Don't you love me?"

"I do, Joey, you 'send' me, you really do. I don't know why, but you do. Maybe because we're from the same backyard. But I can't live alongside you all the time, as you want."

"In that case, you'd better leave now, 'cause there'll be no more of that."

She assumed a precocious baby-talk posture, as she'd always do whenever she got passionate.

"Joey, don't you want to fuck me no more?"

"No." And I wished I hadn't said it.

"You mean that?"

"I do."

Her lips narrowed into a thin line. She clenched them.

"All right. I'll remember that."

"Hope you do." But inside, my whole world was collapsing.

She stormed out of the house, and I cried for hours.

✠ ✠ ✠

I didn't want to face the next day. Every detail in the apartment reminded me of Kami, every little item that she'd left, and her clothes. The idea of eating alone, of living without her, was excruciating. I couldn't think of going to work. In a shaky voice, I called my office feigning intestinal disturbances. Later, I dragged myself out of the stupor and went downstairs to buy some bread. A letter was in the mailbox. The handwriting was my uncle's, twisted and irregular, running downhill to the right, strenuous to read.

Dear Nephew,

I have given this matter before me very much thought and struggle with my conscience, but I must be true to my G-d, the Lord of all Jewish people. If not, I would be a traitor myself. I have now waited patiently for a few months. I hoped that my nephew would come and become my son as I loved you like my own son whom G-d has denied me. I suffer plenty, not sleeping nights, but hoping and praying as G-d is my witness. I hoped you'd come to me and say—I am a Jew. I tried everything and even called the Rabbi.

Now I am sorry to say—I cannot wait any longer, that you are a traitor to my people, that you prefer to be with the enemy of my people, and I cannot have a traitor in my house any longer. This I want you to know, even if I love you and

Tante Sheyne loves you, too. But this you want and this you should have.

Your Uncle,
Sam

It was as if life, time, and air had been frozen. I sat motionless for a long time until, when I tried to move, one of my legs was so badly cramped, it had lost all sensation. It felt like having been dropped into a huge void and flying through it, yet knowing there was no bottom, nothing to hold on to, and no way to stop. Something, too, began to gnaw and press out from within: an unbearable inner pain that wanted to break out. I wanted to scream out but found no strength.

I headed for St. Patrick's Cathedral on Fifth Avenue. No human being could help me anymore. Perhaps God would.

The doormen on Fifth Avenue looked cold and frowning. In their uniforms, they looked like policemen. They would make sure I wouldn't reach out to anybody. Below Fifty-ninth Street, all the storekeepers had bolted down their stores.

The massive stone cathedral stood aloof and forbidding. Someone had locked its portals before I reached them. They didn't want me there. I aimed for the side entrance on Fiftieth Street next to the Saks department store. It was locked—a cemetery, ancient, eternal, deserted by the living. I stood on the sidewalk and prayed silently.

"Dear Jesus, my dearest Infant Christ. I'm calling you. Do you hear me? You've heard me before. Remember the icy colds of winter in 1942 in Poland? I cried out to you then and you heard me. You helped me then and, through your servant, Father Stanisław, you made it possible for me to come to you.

"We entered into a covenant, a contract, and I was supposed to live up to it. Well, you know that I've failed miserably. I haven't prayed much, and I haven't lived up to the chastity and the daily discipline that was expected of me. I tried! Lord, God, I tried. But I couldn't. All I've wanted was to have someone love me. Is that asking too much? What is wrong with wanting to be loved, if only a little? It was you who proclaimed love as the highest pursuit of mankind. Please reveal yourself to me like you have done to others. You can if you want to. I need faith, and only you can give it to me. For I have no faith left in me. And if I don't, I am helpless to cope with life.

"Do you want me to live, God, and maybe, just maybe to bear witness to everything that happened … the mass murders, the evil in men? I beg, give me, show me a sign; tell me what to do! If everything that happens in this world is by your grand design, how do I fit into it? Enormous, mighty forces have brought me to the crossroads, and I can't solve them all by myself. God, Jesus, Christ, I need a purpose, I need strength. I need to know who I am. Everyone needs a purpose to live by. Show me that purpose; show me where I belong, for without it, how could I go on? I am rejected. I have no one to turn to. Will you gather me up to your fold, will you accept me again … show me the way? I beseech you!"

A young couple went by slowly, holding hands. They looked at me curiously and whispered to one another. A policeman walked his beat, twirling his nightstick, eyeing me suspiciously.

There was no answer. Slowly I turned back home. When I climbed the stairs, I lacked the strength to take my shirt off. I gulped down some vodka and sank into oblivion.

✛ ✛ ✛

I dreamed that I had been surrounded by a platoon of SS men in a Polish village. There was no way out; I was caught. Presently they threw me into an American jeep and drove on toward a forest alongside a dirt road. The windshield was down. In my desperation, I turned to the SS officer and screamed out: "But you can't kill me. I'm an American citizen!"

He ignored me. The jeep stopped, and the SS men dragged me out to face another officer—a woman: it was Ruth, the Hashomer leader.

"Take off your clothes!" she commanded. "Let's see if you're a Jew."

The men stripped me. She whipped me with a heavy belt, over and over, and I felt a numbing pleasure with each stroke and awoke with an erection.

"My God, what's happening to me?"

✠ ✠ ✠

The next day was Monday, and I finally had to go to work, or I'd be fired. I spent the next few days burying myself in translations and production details, plunging into great depressions in evenings, hoping for a call from Kami. I'd sit in my easy chair, in motionless stupor, drinking vodka until I could feel no sensations anymore.

✠ ✠ ✠

A dreary Saturday came. I spent most of the day staying in bed, with no energy or purpose left. Outside, a gray drizzle soaked the air as if the day longed for night. I chain-smoked, getting up only to force the rotting windows open. Smoke hung in the room in blue layers.

I was filled with rage and despair. Eventually, at my desk, I took pen and paper and, after much rubbing of my face, I began to write.

Dear Father Stanisław!

Let this be a confession of sorts—the first real one in eighteen years.

When I was fifteen and you were teaching me God's commandments (to ease my apprehension), you said: "remember that all of the commandments can be summed up in this one: thou shalt love our God with all your being and all your might, and all your strength, and thy neighbor as thyself." Now, at age thirty-three, I find that I have lived my life with rage, bitterness, and even hate, instead. The Germans hated me and all of my people; I hated them but, also, I have come to loathe my own people. Now I find that my own uncle has deserted me. And I am bitter toward him—and even you, Father.

How, in the name of God, has this happened? You taught me to love, and, through you—God, people. Not myself, though. You know something? You taught me to hate myself.

Because of you, I became a Catholic. But I have found it impossible to live up to. I have tried to love on terms that you have taught me, but it hasn't worked for me. In the end, I have no friends because you have alienated me from my own people and from myself, while you rest comfortably in your faith.

With the religious Christians, I will always be a stranger, someone they will distrust, someone who'd always have to *prove* his acquired faith (conversion for convenience's sake). I will always be on display and, if I don't practice faith in the most devout manner, they'll say, "See? We told you—once a Jew, always a Jew." (You also once expressed to me your doubt to that effect: that if peace came, *ever*, I might revert back to Judaism. I promised you that I would not "betray" Christ's faith.)

And to the Jews, I will always be a traitor; after all, thousands if not millions of Jews were tortured and killed because they would not convert. That leaves no room for friends.

You taught me to pursue the truth—your truth, Father, and it has only brought me pain and total alienation. You have split me in two; I feel that I have been cursed (not blessed) by carrying within me two traditions and beliefs— hostile to one another, despising each other. And I've had a continuous struggle trying—ever more, as the years go by—to serve two masters.

Thus, I cannot rejoin the Jews. And I have not been to Mass in three years.

So now you know everything. Are you going to reject me, too?

✝ ✝ ✝

I folded the letter and did not read it lest I weaken and change something. Then I drank myself into listless stupor, as sleep came.

✝ ✝ ✝

The buzzer was long and persistent. I yanked myself out of bed and looked at my watch. It was ten-thirty; I was not due at work until noon. The mailman stood at the door, puffing heavily.

"Registered. Sign here, please."

I tore the letter from Poland open.

My Dear and Beloved Jòziaczku,

I know that you have enough of your own problems and that is why I ask for your forgiveness in taking up your time with my own sorrows. Well, they have taken my parish away from me. No, not a transfer; this is a virtual banishment and a spiritual death verdict. In a way, this is worse than the Communist prison where, as you know, I spent two years sleeping on a stone floor, under the Stalinist regime. But they hadn't taken my faith from me. In fact, now I am not allowed to say Mass in my own church.

This is the way it happened; in fact, it started a few months ago, but then I didn't write to you about it. Somehow, I had hoped that my petition, first to my bishop and then to the primate of Poland, would fall upon attentive ears and charitable hearts. Too, as I know the Church bureaucracy, I doubt that my letters have reached my ultimate superiors; the lowly underlings have probably vitiated them.

A few prominent persons, including the celebrated author, Paweł Jasienica (you remember: I helped save his life after the liberation), tried to intervene on my behalf with the chancery of the primate, Cardinal Wyszyński. It was flooded with letters of indignation as to my suspension, but, so far, to no avail.

I have been left without any means of livelihood. All this, because I had attempted to follow the Vatican's guidelines to change the vernacular of our liturgy into our native language—from Latin to Polish—the language of the people. I had welcomed the Vatican's new stand, as for some time it was becoming apparent that we were losing our youth to the Communist ideology. This has been happening, in a large part, due to the Latin vernacular which the people in church could not understand and could not be fortified in their belief in a tongue they could understand, versus the godless teachings being indoctrinated in schools.

Coincidentally, a priest, jealous of my following among people, had tried to weed me out with untrue denouncements.

I have been accused of "liturgical errors." The bishop (an old, feeble man; the chancery is run for all purposes by his assistants who have not been fond of me because of my outspokenness about many things here including compromises they made with the Communists in our schools) signed a pronouncement forbidding me to say Mass *in my own church!* Many of my parishioners wrote angry letters voicing their disapproval, after they saw me praying in the back of the church. In a reaction, the Church has further charged me with "causing scandal and outrage."

The worst are my inner tortures. After twenty years of ministering to my flock and to our Lord, I am now condemnded to die a slow spiritual death.

My Dearest Jòziaczku! You are my last resort and hope. Can you do something? Anything to save my spiritual life? Maybe through the appeal to the press? Intervention with the primate? He might answer you—if you write from America. You can, of course, mention our friendship and our travails during the war. Express indignation that a faithful servant is being dealt with so cruelly. Perhaps you might even write to the Holy See. I think that a letter from you might get through to the cardinal, as other appeals have not.

Once again, I ask your forgiveness for the trouble I am causing you. I pray for you and pray that my inner tortures will mean something to you.

☩ ☩ ☩

I had to think about how I would help him—what contacts I could use effectively. I knew I would do all in my power to help the man who'd loved me; but, at the same time, I felt some inner relief; some cleansing that rose to the surface; some mixed feelings that I could not understand, shame and guilt about the relief they brought to me; a painful relief that my friend was in trouble and that I might help to save him from spiritual oblivion. It seemed that now it was my turn. I destroyed the letter I had written to the priest. Instead, I sat down and wrote slowly and deliberately:

Most Reverend Father Primate!
Your Eminence!

I turn to you with a humble appeal and an urgent plea for your generosity to return my beloved spiritual father, the Reverend Stanisław Falkowski of the Łomża Diocese, to the graces of our Mother Church ... Father Falkowski gave me his love and shelter when, as a fourteen-year-old, a starved and hunted youngster, an escapee from the death train to Treblinka, I had no place to turn, and no way to hide ...

Father Stanisław, in the name of one who never turned away the persecuted poor and the despairing, took care of me, protected and hid me at constant risk to his life. Later, and to the end of the war, he sent me bread packages to my labor site in East Prussia, instilling faith and hope in me, thus keeping up my spirits. He became my father.

Throughout the postwar years when I was in America, he never asked anything for himself, but for his flock and for the children in his parish, and for the tubercular. But, lo and behold, he was incarcerated by the Communists for two years, for preaching the word of God as opposed to the Stalinist ideology.

And now he has been condemned *by his own Church* only, as I understand, for preaching the word of the Lord to his flock in a vernacular that they could understand and follow, as stipulated by the Holy See. And for this, he has been banished.

I appeal to Your Eminence, who himself has suffered much under the Nazis and later, and who knows suffering, to show Christ's mercy to his faithful servant, Father Falkowski, who merely asks to continue serving his Lord and his neighbor.

Even if it turned out that he had committed some infractions, surely he has shown humility and faith in your justice. For our Lord, too, has never turned away anyone who showed penitence, and who desired to serve him. That is all Father Stanisław asks. That is all I deign to ask of Your Eminence.

I addressed the letter carefully to the primate of Poland—before correcting a few phrases—and retyped the letter carefully on a sheet of official stationery bearing the heading: "United Nations, New York."

✢ ✢ ✢

A week later the phone rang. Her low-pitched "hello," the most familiar hello on earth, seemed inevitable, a dissolver of time.

"I don't believe it," I said. "I knew it was you."

She chuckled. "So what's new?"

I told her about the priest. I also told her about the letter from my uncle.

"Well, I could see it coming," was her repartee. "It's all your fault. He's an old man and how can you expect him to understand what you are? I told you to cater to him: he wants you to be a Jew—you're a Jew. Big deal. You have any other relatives, you idiot? Now you messed it all up."

I didn't answer. This, from a woman I loved.

"And the next thing, you're going to cry. I know it. I don't have to be there to know. And you want to marry me. How could I? What have you got to offer me? 'Blood, sweat and tears'? You're not Churchill and the war is over. Be happy you're alive. What are you trying to prove? That you're Mr. Indestructible? I have my own problems; it's bad enough I have to live with them every day myself."

"At least you have your father and mother, and a brother."

"That's what you think. We—none of us is normal anymore after Hitler. Every one of us carries rucksacks with little 'souvenirs' on his back. I can barely survive day to day. Come on, Joey, you want me to come and visit with you?"

"Yes. The place is a mess. I ... haven't been able to do much lately." I told her about my recent dream, standing before a Mengele-type Nazi during the separation.

"Dear Lord, you're getting yourself into some shape. You survived the war, and where is your strength ... in your ass?"

"In my prick." I didn't mean to be vulgar; it just came out.

She giggled with delight. "That you don't have to tell me; that I can attest to."

"I'm in this condition, and you're laughing at me."

"Come on, now. I'm not laughing. I just want you to get stronger."

"Then come over."

"All right," she said. "I will."

✠ ✠ ✠

She brought me a gift--my favorite collection of Brecht's plays. We made love. By now, I knew how to reach her perfectly. I licked her everywhere, and she heaved as if her breath was torn from her, shuddering in her ecstasy.

Afterward, we lay still, at peace. In a while, I put the kettle on for tea. We looked at each other across the little table.

"Come back. Live with me," I said.

"I can't."

"You love another man?"

"No! I can't live with you because you'll carry on, I know, onanizing with this goddamn Warsaw Ghetto, and this Catholic crap, and your Christian 'loyalties,' and your Jewish verkakte guilt, and the Catholic conscience. And I just can't stand it; don't you *understand? I can't!* I have to live. I want to *live!* Me, I don't give a shit what the Church or the rabbi think of me, or what I leave behind for posterity. Screw posterity. Now, don't! ... You taught me those words, so don't stop me now ..."

She shifted to a deliberate, mocking tone that meant to humor and to soothe. But it was always after the damage was done.

"I'm not stopping you ... God, I'm not! ..." I stumbled.

"Don't."

"When … will I see you?"

"I don't know." She coaxed herself into a deliberate drollness. "Maybe next week. But … don't hold me to it."

"In …" I tried to get my voice back. "Next week? In the midst of all this? God, can't you see? This is the biggest battle of my life."

"Yes, my Napoleon," she jested.

"It is, and, goddamn it, don't laugh! In the midst of it, how am I going to survive without you? I love you."

"Don't," she said. "I mean, love me … I don't want you to stop. I want you to love me. But I can't live with you any longer; you wake up some nights in cold sweat after your horrible nightmares I can't! I need someone who fills me with peace, not like us, who carries huge rucksacks laden with war-time souvenirs"

"If you love me, stand by me. I promise you, I'll be different. I know how to be firm and pursue things. You look how I survived; doesn't it tell you something? You want my body; what about the rest of me? Please! If this isn't the ultimate …"

"Go on, I'm listening. Just don't use those fancy words, or you'll lose me." She was trying to humor me, I knew.

"All right. Fuck it …"

"You see," she jumped in, "and who taught me all those dirty words?"

"Okay, you win."

"You know I don't. It's you, *you*, who win all the time. Because you want to have it your way—always. You want me, so you can bounce your pity and self-indigence against me."

"Indulgence."

"Indulgence, fuck. Excuse me, Mr. Yale University. I didn't go to Vassar, my father didn't come here on the Mayflower, he was hidden in a closet for two and a half years. And you give me this crap about conscience. Conscience is, you know for whom? For the ones who can afford it—said by George Bernard Shaw. You don't need it and I don't need it. We've had enough conscience to last our progenies for generations. We now, finally, deserve to live! And you still jerk off your conscience. What good is it going to bring you? Damn it, tell me what is the purpose of your life, and I'll tell you why I can't live with you. *Now!*"

She, like everybody, had always wanted everything from me, *her way*. First my father—I had to be the best, no exceptions—then Father Falkowski—everything from me, my loyalty, my identity and submission—and then my uncle, and the rabbi.

"Don't you see," I was screaming at her, "everybody wants me to be like themselves, nobody gives me a chance to be myself ..."

"What *is* yourself?" she posed calmly.

I could not answer.

"I know what you want to be," she stated. "You want to be Moses, Christ, Marx, Freud—all in a tidy Jewish package: always inquiring, always searching for the Truth and Beauty—*your way*. And I can't live like that. I'd go insane. But you carry on, and mark my words: sooner or later, they'll all reject you. Nobody wants a Don Quixote next to him; only in fairy tales.

"Like you told the rabbi all about your inner struggles. You think they care about them? Only if you're a 'good Jew'—be like them, act like them. Same with the Catholics. And you not only stew in your juice—you want to write about it, when you have *untied the knots* in your soul. And who'll want to read it?"

"What if all the artists thought so?" I asked.

"Some comparison. But, all right, take yourself, as long as you insist on the comparison. People like you wrench themselves dry with fighting the windmills inside, only to go down in history ... *maybe*, if they're lucky. But their lives are miserable. Because they *care too much*. And I don't want to care too much: for the world, for people, or it'll kill me. And take your priest, for example. He knows what to do with his idealism, and it makes only trouble for him. At least he doesn't whine to share this with others—on a 'share this with me' basis."

"Just keep the priest out of this."

"Well, let's stick with you, then. You have no idea what to do with your idealism. You just keep on harping about truth; for that you got the wrong world, or you got off at the wrong station. Everybody tells you, you can't get off here, but you insist. And me, I got to keep going, or I'll perish. I want to live without constant squirming; I wanted it with you, so you're okay, and I'm okay. Is that asking too much? *Is it?* For a living person, after what we've been through?"

For the first time since I'd known her, tears started streaking down her face; but she was too strong to pay attention to them. I approached her gently.

"Don't," she said and she pushed me away. "I'll call you sometime. You have to go on alone now, without me."

At the door she smiled, kindly this time. "Adieu," she whispered, as if she was blowing me a kiss.

Three years later I learned that she'd married a rich Italian whom she had met at that party she attended with her mother but without me.

✠ ✠ ✠

The mail brought me a letter. I opened it, staring at the scarlet raised letters on the stationery.

> In response to your letter of …, I kindly inform that the matter has been looked into, and that Father Stanisław Falkowski has been restored to his parish.
>
> Thanking you for your brotherly greetings and your good words of our common cause in Christ, we send you our heartfelt blessings.
>
> In brotherly love,
> Stanisław Cardinal Wyszyński
> Primate of Poland

A few days later, a letter arrived from Father Falkowski. In it, amidst words of ultimate gratitude, he wrote:

> "…You have saved my spiritual life."

So it has come to that: A life for a life.

✠ ✠ ✠

The tall, old massive trees in Central Park closed in on me and on the cool path I followed into nowhere. The blue gas lights had flickered off before the yellow sun blinked in. A few surprised squirrels stood, poised silently, watching me.

✠ ✠ ✠

So Father Stanisław had been saved. A wave of warmth flooded me. I had repaid my debt, perhaps even my contract, as Kami would say, though not in the way others would want me to. And what next? I was free now myself, maybe, though what that meant for me exactly, I was not sure. The struggle to live on with myself might be only just beginning: who am I? Where do I belong? How to reconcile my two identities? Will I continue to hide or come out with it? And what if there follows another Holocaust? Will I continue to live clandestinely?

Meanwhile, whom do I identify with, where do I belong?

More on that later, perhaps.

✠ ✠ ✠

Afterword

My friends in the know have questioned my expanded use of the original dialogue (quoting it "verbatim") while praising my "photographic memory." Much as I agree with them as to the latter, and while I haven't drawn the dialogue from a recorder, I am satisfied that the dialogue reflects my best and honest recollections.

22446907R00189

Made in the USA
Lexington, KY
28 April 2013